the Tale of the Truth

an interconnected world

by

Marianne Hallberg

www.lightspira.com

Published by LightSpira, Sweden
www.lightspira.com

ISBN 978-91-86613-09-9
First edition, 2012

Author: Marianne Hallberg
www.thetaleofthetruth.com

Editing:	Bo Hallberg
English translation:	Paul Brook
Fact review:	Benny Johansson
Cover photo:	Marianne Hallberg
Book design:	Recito / Förlagsservice.se

The Swedish original *Sagan om Sanningen* was published in 2009 by *TÄNK OM*.

the Tale of the Truth

an interconnected world

When the Gods had created the world and humanity
they asked themselves where they would place the truth.
They did not want it to be too easy for us to find.
The proposals were numerous,
from the highest mountain peak to the farthest star,
until the wisest God said:
We will hide truth within man.
They will search the entire universe, before they realize
that truth has been within them all the time.

Oriental legend

Contents

Foreword by Lars-Eric Uneståhl

It was with great curiosity and high expectations that I began reading Marianne's book. Knowing Marianne since many years back I knew that she used to take every opportunity– through courses and books – to learn about every area connected to "a good life".

Yet the book has surprised me in a very unique and positive way. You seldom find a book so full of information and from such diverse areas, but which still manages to hold on to a central theme: Providing hope of – and practical tools for – a better life. The book reflects Antonovsky's criteria for a good and healthy life: comprehensibility, manageability and meaningfulness.

Marianne has succeeded to explain the most complex facts in a simple and understandable way, which is especially important for readers with little knowledge about this field.

Marianne knows that feelings of meaningfulness is important for high Life quality and wellbeing and consequently she shows how the book's principles can be used to increase the perception of meaning in life. There is an emphasize on the difference between knowledge and competence and on the development of Life Skills by the transfer of knowledge to Competence through Practice and Training. Usability and Manageability is therefore included as an key component in which both learning by doing and applications practices are connected to - and synchronized with- the training and action model.

The big emphasis on life as a "do-it-yourself" (DIY) project, together with quantum physics' hypothesis that we "create our own reality" gives this book a strong and optimistic core message, which is especially important in our time. It also gives the reader access to the principles and methods needed to create and maintain a good life.

Lars-Eric Uneståhl, Ph.D.
President, Scandinavian International University, Sweden

Author's foreword

"What do you do when the road you are travelling suddenly comes to an end?" I heard a man say on the radio. He was the victim of a mid-life crisis.

Yes, what do you do? Many years ago this happened to me as well and the confusion was total, both within me and those around me. It was 1980, before words like "burned out" and similar expressions became common. What made it even more difficult was that I could not find any plausible explanation. Everything in my life was going well – family, friends, studies and our financial situation. But even though, life suddenly felt like a black hole, I was in a constant state of anxiety and cried every day for over a year.

I was already studying psychology and gradually my search became my life's work – to better understand how I, and the world at large, actually worked. What was it all really about? After hundreds of books, courses and above all *exercises,* I realized that I was beginning to have my suspicions. I received requests for courses and in 1992 I started my business *TÄNK OM* (in English both "*rethink*" and "*what if*"), and to this day I conduct courses in personal development. Because development was what it was all about. I had come to a point in my life when it was time to take a real developmental leap. This did not mean that there had been something wrong with my life up to that point, just that I had grown out of my own ideas and needed to find a new approach to life. I needed to quite simply expand my consciousness. I had ended up in an existential crisis where my world view had cracked and – as I understood later on, that crack was inevitable.

The origin of this book, and also to my own aspirations for development, is that during my entire life I have had a magic feeling inside, and a sense of having seen "something else", something which was hard to put my finger on, but which sometimes made it difficult for me to take the everyday realities seriously. A feeling that there is a reality more real than the one we see around us. A feeling that everything really is so laughably simple, yet impossible to express, something so elusive and intangible that it cannot be captured because then it would dissolve. I have had the feeling that we are living in a paradise, but that we do not have the ability to see it. I used to joke that when we die and stand in front of Saint Peter to ask if we may come into paradise, he would lift an eyebrow in surprise and say: Well, that is where you have just come from. You had everything you needed, but were not interested. So why now?

What is it that is so obvious, yet so difficult to see?

Humbly, with the knowledge of the futility of trying to capture "the truth", I begin.

Much of what I want to convey lies beyond the intellect and is thus difficult to describe in words. The task might well seem impossible, but no less attractive. My ambition is to write in an easily understandable way, so that those who have not been involved with these questions previously will be able to understand and dedicate themselves to self-study; while at the same time, those who have already advanced in their development may get a welcome reminder.

Thank you to my guides and contributors

I often say that I stand firmly on "four feet" of knowledge through:

The Indian philosopher Krishnamurti, the first person I encountered who was able to open my mind to a more unbiased way of thinking.

The Austrian psychiatrist and author Victor Frankl, who, with his books on logotherapy, helped me understand more about our fears, neuroses and the importance of being able to feel the meaning in life.

The Italian psychologist Roberto Assagioli, student to Freud, who went his own way and created psychosynthesis, from where I learned a great deal about our feelings, emotions, love and the explanation of "the higher Self" and

Lars-Eric Uneståhl, Ph. D., Founder and President of Scandinavian International University (SIU), for the mental training, the insight into the power of thought and for his ability to bring everything to a plateau that works for our everyday life; through "do-it-yourself" structures, CDs and exercises. At SIU I received the greater part of my education and continue to receive replenishment.

I would also like to thank the countless number of contributors. People I have gratefully learned from – many of whom will be mentioned in the course of this book. Course participants who have led me to reflect further and everything that I have "downloaded" during my meditations.

A big thank you also goes to my faithful proofreaders for their valuable comments and to Benny Johansson, Ph. D., who generously donated his time to ensure the factual accuracy of the book.

I would like to add that I have been writing for many years, for my own personal growth, without thinking that it would be read by someone else, and therefore I have not always documented the source of the information. So, if any quotations should appear without proper references, I hope that the person in question will feel honored and appreciate having shared some knowledge. People who devote themselves to life-promoting questions usually think that it is more important to contribute to a raising of consciousness, than to groom the ego's feathers. In all the cases where I know the source, it is indicated.

We pick up knowledge all the time from each other and personally I see this more as adding pieces to the jigsaw puzzle – or as a relay, where we take the baton part of the way, contribute with our own perspective and then pass it on.

Introduction

The Tale of the Truth is a book about consciousness development, self-discovery and finding the path to self-realization. It is intended as a guide to help us expand our self-awareness and get in touch with our higher Self, our inner source of insight, and in so doing, deeply transform our way of seeing life.

Self-realization in this context has nothing to do with ego-realization[1] but is more about diminishing the ego. To succeed in this we need self-motivation, a great deal of patience, time for reflection, exercise, stillness and silence, so that we can begin listening to our inner self. It is said that we have all the answers within us, but we need to develop our sensitivity to see this – and the consequences are often a change of lifestyle, based on inner maturity.

This book can also be seen as an "alternative" recipe for success. A way to reach inner success by finding freedom, peace and joy within us, without having to take a detour via external success and material status.

External success is no guarantee of inner well-being, while inner peace and harmony give us a sense of freedom and reduced attachment to the material rewards of the outside world. However, it is important to point out that there is no conflict between inner and outer success. On the contrary, the more we get to know ourselves, the more easily we can see what needs to be done.

In the planning of this book, I have chosen to start with society at large, the times of upheaval and transition in which we find ourselves, along with observations of the new physics – as far as I am able to understand them – to personal development; what we ourselves can do in order to make contact with that center of unity which

1 For a definition of the ego, see Chapter 3.

exists inside us all and which – once we have come into contact with it – changes our lives forever.

In this state of being, we can see that we are part of everything, experience the whole universe inside us and there the circle ends for me. In this experience, everything is perfect and complete, and there is nothing left to add. This is perhaps the biggest paradox of life; that the more I go into myself, the further out into the universe I come and the more I experience a presence and a connection to everything. There I meet eternity and infinity.

A recurrent theme in this book is also what I am going to term a "separate or fragmented" state of consciousness versus a "connected or coherent" state which influences our whole interpretation of existence.

It is an advantage if you can read this book at times when you are relaxed and in harmony, in order to more easily come into contact with your own inner wisdom.

Even though this book is ultimately about the oneness of all things, I have chosen to structure and treat different areas under their own headings, so you, the reader, if you so wish, can choose topics which feel important at that moment, or start where you are in your own development. I also believe that we need to see through the parts to be able to discern the underlying wholeness. The intention with this structure is also to make it easy for readers to go back and reread certain areas.

Chapter 1 – Transition

You have certainly heard the word paradigm shift[1] – maybe too many times – but even so, I have chosen to use this word to label what is going on around us right now.

A paradigm shift is not a small change, but a fundamental "change of pattern", a completely new way of understanding the world and reality. A revolution in "rethinking" where we have to leave much of our present understanding of reality behind us in order to start sensing the outline of the new world order. Much of this has been brought about by modern physics, which with its discoveries, has radically changed most of what we – at least in the West – have believed in. Much is also dependent on the information flow that reaches us from Eastern teachings; which contain a message similar to that of quantum physics. More about that in the next chapter.

What we, in the Western world, have studied by examining the external world has in the East been studied through introspection, with both approaches yielding results that are astoundingly similar. The new physics has provided revelations about the universe that are quite close to what Eastern philosophers have been teaching for thousands of years. I believe that this will mean a fundamental change in our way of viewing life – both individually and collectively.

---

1 Paradigms succeed each other regularly, when new approaches and scientific findings clash so strongly with old "truths", that the earlier model of reality is no longer considered valid. A paradigm shift therefore is a natural evolutionary process where new knowledge emerges, old knowledge is discarded, and we gain new perspectives. Today it is commonly regarded that we are leaving behind the scientific paradigm, which prevailed for about 300 years, and transitioning to the holistic paradigm and its completely different world view. But even the holistic paradigm is grounded on scientific discovery and can be seen as a synthesis of modern physics and Eastern ideas.

The land of happiness

At the moment we live in a society where it might seem that "everything is getting worse". We are flooded daily by alarming reports about such things as dramatic job losses, increasing sick leave, corporate greed, widespread despair and violence. Schools are not given the resources they need. It is claimed students can no longer read or write well. We have no time to laugh. People want to retire early, dream of taking a year off or retiring to some exotic spot. Much of the global economy is perceived to be built on "air".

The four most profitable "industries" in the world today are internet poker (with much criminality involved), drugs, sex and the weapons industry.

Material prosperity was supposed to give us freedom, security and happiness. Instead, we have become trapped in economic growth. We have sold out our time so that we are not able to manage anything properly. We have to produce more and more to keep the whole process going, and we must *consume* ever increasing amounts. If we stop consuming, everything will come to a halt, and the whole system will collapse. After 9-11, the American people were urged to show solidarity and set out for their local shopping centers to "shop" their way out of an economic downturn. At some point, people are going to wake up and wonder if the most important thing is to "shop" our way out of every crisis, and thereby "save the world". There must be a higher meaning in life than to cure societal ills with a trip to the mall. One day someone will utter the timely words – like the child in "the Emperor's new clothes" – and the smoke screen will disappear. What on earth are we doing?

We humans have apparently put ourselves in the precarious situation of consuming the world's resources about 30 percent faster than they can be renewed. I am talking about the resources that with careful use, are endless. Fish that constantly reproduce, trees that renew themselves through eternity. The system is perfect, if it were not for mankind.

How many problems would there be if there were no humans on earth?

Ponder that for a while!

We, who call ourselves the crown of creation, who regard ourselves the most highly developed on earth, do not have the ability to understand the laws of nature. People much wiser than I say that our time is beginning to run out. The planet itself will probably make it (it has millions of years to renew), but something else will replace us and evolution will continue – with mankind as a small footnote in history. That is perhaps quite all right from a higher perspective, but in this scenario mankind will have failed to reach its potential.

This may sound like a doomsday prophecy, but we still have a choice and it is important to see that things were not better in earlier times. Today, we can view the world from a global perspective and observe the repercussions of our actions. On the other hand, with the help of modern technology, we also have possibilities like never before to spread knowledge and use our resources in a common effort for a better world.

During the writing of this book, I have looked more closely at people in town and I think of the old story about "the native" who said: "it is so scary to look into the eyes of Western people because there is no one there." Smiles are easily counted, especially those that are seen in the eyes. If joy and happiness were related to material prosperity, we Swedes would have laughed ourselves to death a long time ago. But we have not done that. On the contrary, depression and burn out is on the increase. We have to understand that happiness does not correlate with material prosperity – at least not beyond our basic needs. Freedom, peace and joy are inner states of mind that we can learn to reach.

Why are people experiencing burnout right now?

Maybe you could say that the time is right. More and more people are affected by feelings of emptiness, hopelessness and depression because our lifestyle no longer feels sufficiently meaningful; and without meaning, we become worn out more quickly. We are hit by a feeling of being lost. As it is said in the East: in order for something new to be born, the old must die and in between, before the new comes forward, emptiness must enter. And the point is that there should be emptiness – in order for us to be able to set a new course. There is an enormous development potential here. It is our outdated perception of reality that represents the biggest source of stress, and we can see those who are now experiencing burnout as pioneers of the new that is emerging. I believe they are the forerunners of a society with deeper values.

You could say that it is our Western lifestyle – with its exaggerated focus on material things – that creates this inner emptiness, which is now leading us to a higher level of consciousness. But at the same time, it is our material prosperity that is giving us the opportunity to take the leap. If we were poor we would have enough of a challenge on our hands just providing ourselves with food and shelter.

A new awareness is now emerging and we have a fantastic opportunity to take a giant leap towards a society where growth primarily means *human* growth. Where technology develops in response to the needs of humanity and not primarily to keep the economy going. Where our inner growth takes on a dominant role and we are allowed to develop as humans. Where we learn to make contact with our inner strength and authenticity, understand that our inner emptiness must be filled from within and where we have a higher vision for our lives, rather than just being "human capital" in the service of economic growth.

In the middle of the technological revolution, new business ideas are starting to emerge, like hotels with a silence guarantee and holidays to places where people are not reachable. The new status symbols are said to be having access to clean water, clean air and to "own" your time.

Something is obviously happening, and if it is our outdated view of the world that is the problem, let us look more closely at it and see what now is likely to come forth.

Chapter 2 – The new physics

Quantum physics – what has that got to do with consciousness development and self-realization? Well, maybe more than we think. I believe that modern physics together with some other knowledge can help us out of the dilemma that the Western world finds itself in, and which causes much unnecessary pain.

When I was a child growing up in the little town of Söderhamn, I lived in a world that was material in the sense that it was "made up of solid matter". The stones, trees, stars, people – everything I saw was the "material" world. What I was able to perceive with my five senses – sight, hearing, touch, smell, and taste – that for me was *the World.* It was solid, secure, and followed certain rules. It gave me a world view which described an objective reality that I could observe. Little did I realize then that my reality was not the whole truth, just an *interpretation* of reality. That my world looked the way it did because I found myself born into the Newtonian world view.

Now a new world view is emerging, based on, among other things, the findings of quantum physics. This does not mean that reality *itself* has changed, just that we now have the benefit of understanding a little more of the reality that has been there all the time.

What caught my interest in this area was not that I am especially scientifically oriented, but that these models of explanation are more in line with my experiences of reality; and that my experiences through these discoveries get a more plausible explanation. It helps me make life more understandable, opens fantastic possibilities and gives me infinitely more happiness.

Do not let yourself be put off by the belief that this is too hard to grasp. The less we know about the old physics, the better it seems. A professor in theoretical physics said that quantum physics is hard for everyone to understand, but almost impossible to understand for someone educated in classical physics. Then it is not enough to just think differently, we must disassemble all the old ideas. So it might be easier for us if we have no preconceived ideas. This knowledge is already available and affects us, even if we are not familiar with the subject as such.

My intention with this book is to also show connections between the new physics, consciousness and Eastern philosophy where, for thousands of years, it has been asserted that everything in the universe is connected and, in the end, only vibrations. Furthermore, I intend to show how we can make use of quantum physics' wave- and particle concept (connected – separate) as a model for understanding existence. We will explore this concept further throughout the book.

The scientific world view

The world view that we have lived with for the last 300 years – built on the teachings of Newton, Descartes and others – describes the universe as a lifeless, mechanistic place, where everything works according to principles of cause and effect and is based on matter. This is the origin of what has come to be known as the "paradigm of science" and our rational, logical way of thinking.

I found a good description of this perception of reality in an article[1] where they refer to Amit Goswani, Ph. D., former Professor at the Institute of Theoretical Science, University of Oregon, USA, and his book *The Self-Aware Universe: How Consciousness Creates the Material World*. The article says:

"The scientific world view is based mainly on five principles, five pillars:

The world is *objective*, i.e. unaffected by our consciousness.

The world is ruled by *casual determinism* – i.e. predetermination according to the law of cause and effect.

Everything has a *local* character, i.e. exists at a given location.

Reality is *material* in its character, nothing else.

---

1 The Swedish magazine Sökaren (No 5, 1996).

All mental phenomena are explained as *by-products* of physical processes. What we call consciousness is a property of the brain."[2]

The emerging world view

If I were to try to write a similar summarizing description of the world view that is now emerging (as I understand it, drawing on books, articles and other writings by David Bohm[3], Amit Goswani, Ervin Laszlo, Danah Zohar and others) it would look something like this:

We live in a *conscious universe*, a living organism/body with an intelligence, where matter makes up only a small part.

The *foundation* of the universe is instead a *non-material* energy called the *quantum field/quantum vacuum*. This field is the generating source of everything.

This is also the source of the particles that matter is composed of. In this view, there is *no absolute matter,* just an absolute matter-generating energy field, and matter can be seen as a condensation of the vacuum energy.

There is no objective reality. Our *consciousness creates reality.*

There is no *causality* and *no locality* on the sub-atomic level (the constituent parts of an atom).

---

2 Author's translation.

3 David Bohm was Professor of theoretical physics at the University of London, and the author of several books. He also worked with Einstein.

Amit Goswami is, apart from what is said above, a researcher and author of several books on quantum physics and consciousness, including the textbook *Quantum Mechanics*. He is also one of the authors of *What the Bleep Do We (K)now?!*

Ervin Laszlo, Ph. D., is the author of a large number of books, including *You Can Change The World*, founder of General Evolution Research Group and Club of Budapest, editor of the journal *World Futures*, and twice nominated for the Nobel Peace Prize.

Danah Zohar is a physician and philosopher at the University of Oxford, Oxford Academy et cetera, the author of several books, including *The Quantum Self*, and an internationally renowned lecturer in leadership.

Everything is energy

In simple terms, we could say that everything is energy – basically one and the same energy which has the ability to manifest itself in an infinite number of forms. A thought, a table, humans, are all manifestations of the same energy but with a different density and speed of vibration. A table would therefore be a denser form of energy than a thought and is perceived by us as solid matter. But examined more closely it seems that all matter – including us – is mostly space and whirling energy (up to 99.99999 percent). The void is not empty but is considered to be made up of highly concentrated energy.

All matter seems to have the same chemical building blocks. It is only the form that differs. Celestial bodies and stars are held together by the same consciousness as our cells. We humans are made of the same stuff as the stars.

Everything is also said to have both a wave- and a particle aspect – *simultaneously* – in other words everything is coherent and fragmented at the same time and it is an illusion that we are as separated from each other as we think. We can compare this to the waves in the sea. We can see every separate wave, but at the same time, they are inseparable from the sea (and constantly changing). The quantum field/vacuum – the foundation of everything – is seen as a "sea of infinite possibilities".

David Bohm used radio waves as an example of this. All programs are on the air and available for us, but only become a reality (manifest) when we turn the radio on and tune in to the station. The same applies when we get an idea. It splashes about in the quantum sea as a possibility – together with all the other possibilities – until we decide on one thought. The quantum wave then "collapses", gets an identity, is born, and takes on a form. Matter – the reality we can see and touch – is thought to be a "stimulation of the vacuum".

In a radio program,[4] Danah Zohar talked about our consciousness as part of the original source and that through "the waves of the quantum structures" we are connected to the whole universe and all of its history.

4 Radio Sweden: *Det gäller livet* (1992).

The quantum field contains everything that is, everything that was and everything that can be. The quantum field cannot manifest by itself, it merely *is*, but *we* humans can act as "tools" and transform the energy waves of possibility into particles of reality.

The dilemma of the human race seems to be that we are unable to observe the wave- and the particle aspect simultaneously; we can only see one or the other view of reality at any one time (Heisenberg´s Uncertainty Principle). When asking a particle question in a study, you will get a particle answer, and vice versa.

An objective reality does not exist. The mere fact that we observe something means that its properties changes. Furthermore, everything we meet is interpreted through our limited senses and experiences, and therefore we get a very subjective picture of reality.

On the subatomic level, there is apparently no cause and effect, it is thought to be not applicable to talk about cause and effect at levels beyond time and space. If anything, it seems that everything happens at the same time and everywhere simultaneously. Everything affects everything else in all eternity, but it is impossible to tell exactly which of the many possibilities will manifest, take "form".

We can also see quantum physics as a gateway to Eastern thinking. You could say that we in the West have devoted ourselves to developing the particle aspect, with our enthusiasm to analyze, structure and separate, while in the East they have been more inclined to the wave-aspect of existence – the overall view. Maybe now the time is right to bring these two approaches together.

We can state in summary:

If there is no objective reality, but we interpret everything through our senses, and if every thought, choice and decision affects not only us but everything else in one big interconnected web, it opens fantastic possibilities to change our world – both our own and the world at large.

Chapter 3 – Levels of identity

The new physics opens the path for the understanding that we live in two worlds at the same time – a visible/material world and an invisible/non-material world, and that each one is equally real. In the visible, material world – where we are used to existing – everything is separated and the world is divided in bits and pieces, objects and events. In the invisible energy world, everything becomes increasingly more connected the closer to the source we come. This understanding has consequences for our everyday perception of reality. And also for our "sense of self".

We humans can only learn what our senses can take in, and our senses are adapted to our current understanding of reality. To be able to understand more of reality, we need to widen our consciousness and be more "multisensory". We need to open ourselves to insights beyond the intellect.

Within personal development, we often talk about different identity- or maturity levels that we humans – and even society – have the opportunity to reach. These levels – usually divided into three or four steps – are often related to age, and named for example, the young adult, the middle-aged and the wise man but it is an individual choice whether we take these steps. We could quite possibly be 80 years old and still be at level 1.

Here, I would like to call:
Level 1 – the ego (the unconscious "I")
Level 2 – the personal self (the conscious self) and
Level 3 – the transpersonal Self (our higher Self)

We will discuss these levels in more detail later, but here are some short, introductory descriptions of the different levels.

Level 1 – The ego (the unconscious "I")

This is the level of identity in which most people in our society still find themselves, and the perception of reality that is characterized by the scientific paradigm. A description could go like this:

We see the world from the physical aspect (the material world), and identify ourselves mainly with our bodies. My "I" is my body and I understand the world through my five senses. Because I so strongly identify myself with my body, looks and attractiveness become very important, which can easily lead to an over-emphasized bodily fixation.

We see ourselves as "separated" from each other and compare ourselves to each other, we have a strong need for confirmation from the world around us and therefore need to prove ourselves – often by over-performing and by pursuing power and material status – to be able to show the outside world who we are, to be able to show that we are "somebody". We value ourselves by what we *do*, not by who we are.

We are unaware of how our thoughts and feelings affect our lives, we think in terms of "right or wrong", and easily blame the outer world for what is happening to us. In this way, we create a victim mentality, which allows us to believe that things are the way they are and that we feel the way we do because of society, work, or our partner.

We often divide people into winners and losers. Does that sound self-absorbed? Well, at least ego-absorbed! To live at level 1 is to live in a state of unfulfillment, where we are separated from our center and our real needs, and instead look for security and happiness outside ourselves.

The scientific world's strong identification with form has given us a fear of the transience of form and this interpretation of reality has contributed to a society built on fear. Fear of not living up, not managing, not fitting in, not being clever enough, being rejected or abandoned, not *having* enough and so on.

Level 1 is a description of a consumer society, and a world that is mainly material in its nature.

Level 2 – The personal self (the conscious self)

The understanding that we live in an intelligent, conscious universe means that more and more of us are becoming interested in exploring the invisible world. We understand that there is no objective reality, that our understanding of what happens affects our existence and that we are co-creators of our reality. We begin to turn inwards for guidance, dare to trust our intuition and are more prepared to take responsibility for our thoughts and feelings. Individualism increases, but also tolerance (egoism is built on fear). We search for our purpose in life and in this way become less dependent on the opinions of others. We each have our own path to follow and we can grow together, side by side, without competing.

At level 2, we still see ourselves as separate from each other, but we have a stronger connection to our center/core. We place a larger part of our identity in Being, and life is no longer so much about success or failure, but more about experiences that provide confidence and insight. There is a reason why things happen. "What can I learn from this?"

Through contact with Being we increase our capacity to live in the present which gives us a greater sense of inner peace. This stage also brings with it a feeling of gratitude to life, and an increased willingness to give, and to serve others.

Level 2 is characterized by curiosity and wonder. "There is something more!"

Level 3 – The transpersonal Self (our higher Self)

Level 3 means that we increasingly leave behind our personal view of life and see the world from a universal perspective. A connected, boundless state where we experience ourselves as part of everything, part of the whole. Where our identity is in Being, and where we can clearly see that we are more than our thoughts, more than our feelings, more than our bodies and intellect. A state from where we can observe what happens without the need to identify with it, without being disturbed or engulfed by it. Where we can begin to say "yes" to life the way it is and trust the life process itself.

We develop the capacity to maintain contact with our center, even during our day to day business, which allows us to be present in the moment, and gives us peace, awareness and joy. We can shift between the internal and external world, and realize that reality as we normally see it, is partly an illusion and we no longer need to cling so firmly to "the form". We understand that we are energy beings, and that energy never dies, only transforms.

We see ourselves as co-creators in our lives and follow our life's path. We have learned to move by ourselves between different states of consciousness and can fill ourselves with the energy we need (through meditation, breathing exercises and similar).

Here we have freed ourselves from the *bonds* to the physical world. This does not mean that we enjoy the mundane pleasures any less, on the contrary; but we become less dependent upon it. Unnatural binding or control (fear) has been replaced by nearness (love). When we are in contact with our transpersonal Self, we cannot experience fear or loneliness (which comes from thoughts of separation and a detached state of mind).

Rivalry has lost its importance and can now be seen as more of game (for "fun"), no longer connected to the valuing of ourselves as humans. We realize that in the end, nothing can be won or lost.

The third level of reality perception is characterized by deep peace, joy and mild euphoria.

We do, of course, shift between these levels, we slip back into old habits and alternate back and forth between old and new values, even with regular practice. At the beginning of the previous chapter, I wrote that I grew "into" the Newtonian world view – which in this context we can also call level 1.

Crisis as opportunity

Personal growth often starts from a feeling of dissatisfaction. We have come to a point where life suddenly seems meaningless and empty. What previously gave life substance, now feels indifferent. We find it difficult to recognize ourselves and understand nothing. The former security has vanished. We question ourselves and our opinions. Life is often seen as frightening and unreal and it is easy to think there is something "wrong" with us. It is not so easy to see that my experiences are due to my growing out of my previous interpretation of reality, and that I now am on the way to a new level. But with patience, we have the opportunity of reaching a deeper rooting in ourselves.

So what can we do to more easily take a leap in our development – regardless of whether we are stuck in a crisis or would just like to know more about how we ourselves and life works? In the next chapter, we will look into how we develop our "self" from birth.

The circle portrays our development of a self

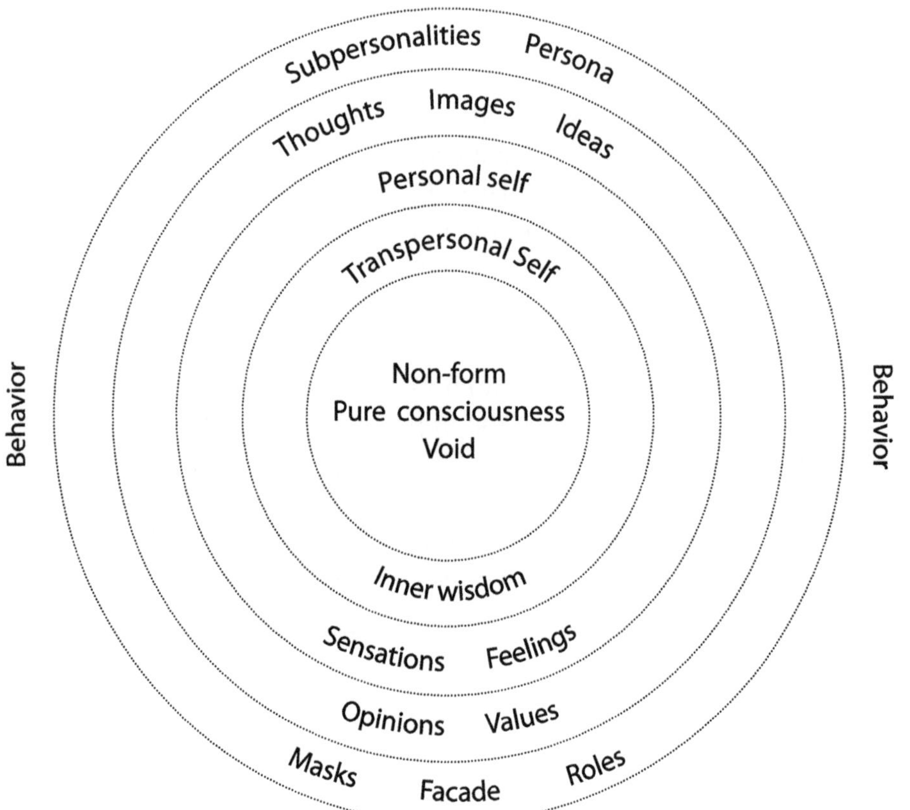

Chapter 4 – The development of a self

We can see life as a circle, where we come out of non-form, are born into the dualistic world and in the end return to non-form.

The circle diagram on the opposite page is *a model of explanation*, and does not claim to be the "truth" or all-encompassing. Like all models of explanation it addresses our intellect, but the inner rings cannot be reached or understood through the intellect. The dotted lines are just there to enhance readability. We will look at each area more deeply later in the book.

You can read the circle from the middle outward, roughly according to the following:

Apart from certain genetic pre-programming, we are born into the world as a blank page regarding our life on earth. Out of non-form we come into being, and are eventually born into this world. Our consciousness is pure, we have no preconceived ideas about how to interpret life. But we are well prepared. It is said that we are equipped with around 100 billion neurons (brain cells), most of which are unconnected. This makes us extremely flexible to different cultures and living conditions. The only neurons which are connected are those essential to life – for breathing, heart function and so on. We have access to a universal intelligence – a sort of inner wisdom. Anyone who has looked a newborn baby in the eyes would probably acknowledge the wisdom that is conveyed to us. From the beginning we have physical sensations such as, comfort and discomfort, thirst and hunger, warmth and coldness. We have the inherent ability to cry when our needs have to be met.

Gradually we develop a language and can begin to label our feelings. We begin to develop a personal "self" with thoughts, inner pictures and ideas. We adopt opinions that develop into values.

During our early years we are subjected to all kinds of strains and develop various defenses, and what we call sub-personalities, in order to deal with what happens to us. All in all, this constitutes our approach to life and is shown in our behavior and actions. We are the sum of our experiences, but are often fairly unaware of how our inner selves function.

It is around this point – when something is not working quite the way we want it to – we feel that the time has come to start our inner journey and explore our inner being. Often my course participants say that "I suppose everything is more or less fine, but I would like to feel happier than I do, because even though I have most of what I want, there is still something missing. I don't feel that real joy in life."

Here begins the journey back into the circle, to build a *conscious* self. We practice being aware of our thoughts, examine our ideas to see if they give us joy and help us grow, or if they cause problems or even unhappiness. We explore our sub-personalities in order to see their real needs. We learn to manage our emotions, to be able to enter into and come out of different states of mind by our own efforts. We learn different meditation techniques to more easily overcome the gap between the personal self and the transpersonal Self, and to eventually be able to reconnect with the pure consciousness, the essence. To get in touch with that part of me that is beyond worry, anxiety and depression. To be able to find the point within me where everything is experienced as total completeness, and to allow that part of me to be reflected in the other aspects of my personality. This gives a deeper meaning to life, and colors our thoughts and feelings by bringing the wholeness perspective into the parts, and thus harmonizing our person.

I would like to emphasize here the importance of developing a strong personal self, before we search for the transpersonal Self. The latter emerges as we mature.

The first ring we will look at is our thoughts and ideas.

Chapter 5 – The power of thought

Whether we are aware of it or not, we are always directed by internal images, thoughts, beliefs and feelings. These depend on our knowledge, our experiences as well as the understanding of existence (our "interpretation program") that we have developed throughout life.

Do I interpret life in a safe and harmonious way, or have my experiences led me to interpret most things through anxiety and fear? Often, we regard our interpretation program as a *truth*.

In order to create the "inner climate" for which I search, and to be able to raise myself to a higher level of consciousness, it is imperative that I know how I use my thought processes. Do I have thoughts that support me, that make me happy and satisfied, or do I have thoughts and beliefs that make me feel irritated, angry/unhappy or perhaps even worthless?

Heaven or hell

Studying our thoughts can start off as quite a depressing task. Usually it is the negative – the things I do not want – that first appear. One consolation may be that all this negativity has been within me all the time and drained my energy. The only difference is that now I can see it and also realize that I am fully capable of creating heaven or hell – through my way of thinking and my beliefs. If I want to develop and enhance my well-being, it is necessary that I can manage my thoughts consciously. Our habitual thinking is said to make up approximately 95 percent of the thoughts we have, while our conscious thinking only about 5 percent. So, expect some internal resistance in the beginning and accept that this will be a long process.

To succeed I need to develop a good inner observer, so I can start to study what is going on within. Without this ability of self-observation, I cannot develop in a conscious way. Here, we have every reason to spend *a great deal of energy.* Having a good observer is essential in order to see through our thought patterns and also for us to dare to approach our painful feelings. By having the inner observer with us we can free ourselves from old stereotypes and painful emotions without being affected negatively by them, or giving them energy to grow. More on this later.

Most exercises in this book assume that you have developed an inner observer – you can read more on how to do this on the next page. Allow yourself to go on a real expedition to explore your inner self – you will be surprised!

Beware of false positivism

Observing ourselves requires total honesty and that we *acknowledge* what is within us whether we find it good or bad. We must first see it and be aware of it in order for it to transform. It is about being *authentic,* seeing which of my thoughts, feelings and actions are real and come from my deeper self. Remember that we are on the hunt for the core within us.

Therefore we have no further use for that defect of positive thinking, where we pretend that everything is so fantastic, even if we really do not think so. This only creates inner confusion and takes us further away from our authenticity. Even if some studies have shown that merely *playing* a positive role raises, for example, our immune system, better still would be to work with a long-term perspective and really get to know ourselves and receive the genuine peace and joy that exists within us. However, we need to train ourselves to pay attention to what is truly positive and learn to focus on the beauty of life. *Attention is energy and we give energy to what we focus on.* Therefore, it is fatal to focus on our problems, since by doing so we give them the energy to grow.

Your inner observer

This exercise aims to develop an inner witness that collects information about what goes on inside you without any judgment, so that you can over time observe yourself from two perspectives – be the one observing what happens and simultaneously the one being observed – and then continue to develop this ability until it happens automatically, without you thinking about it.

The observer has an unbiased view, because s/he is not involved. The observer takes an interest in your well-being in general and does not become involved in individual problems, and can, from this vantage point, more easily see solutions.

Becoming aware of what you think and feel is to realize that you have a choice. It gives perspective to what is happening and ensures that you do not become engulfed in your problems, emotions, depression or the like. Observation in itself creates change.

This process will be easier if you can approach it with a sense of humor and a playful attitude!

Start by, a couple of times a day, "freezing" your current situation and note the following: What am I doing? What am I thinking? What am I feeling? Write it down! It will help you become aware of the thoughts you have and the emotions you experience during the day. Our intellect tells us what we think and our body tells us what we feel.

Practice the inner observer until you can, in any situation effortlessly move outside yourself for a moment and without judgment, observe what you are doing, what you are thinking and what you are feeling. You can then experience what is happening inside you (associate) and simultaneously see it from outside (dissociate).

Gradually you can also start to notice your energy level. When does it go up? When does it go down? Which situations or persons help to increase your energy, which make you lose your energy?

Remember that the inner observer only witnesses – with warmth and presence. If you notice that your observer judges or evaluates, you have received a visit from your inner critic, in other words, a so-called subpersonality (Chapter 9).

Thoughts are energy

Thoughts are energy. Creative energy. Energy in motion. Every thought I think has a consequence, even on an emotional level.

Practice noticing for a while how it feels in your body after a period of positive and then negative thinking. Sense the vibrations different thoughts give rise to. They will take you to a higher or lower energy level.

Our senses give us a very limited perception of life and it is important that I am aware of what I focus on, because that is what – taken together – will form my life. Remember that we are caught by the thought and the image which contains the strongest emotion – both positive and negative. It is the *feeling* which gives our thought its power.

The word "not"

Our brain understands and works with images and I am sure that you have heard about the danger of using the word "not". If I were to say to you: Do not think of a blue elephant – of course, an image of a blue elephant would be the first thing to appear in your mind. It is not possible for our brain to create an image of "not", so it creates an image of something that is concrete or substantial, something it is able to make a picture of. By using the word "not" we often create an image of the non-intended, of what we do not want to happen.

Safe thinking

A focused thought is often likened to a sunbeam through a magnifying glass. Its power is enormous. Unfortunately, our capacity for concentration is often poorly trained, making our thoughts scattered and very hard to manage. We dwell on certain issues, even when we do not want to and are unable to stop the thought processes. There is a constant chatter within us, which we are mostly unaware of – or are under the impression that chatter is inevitable.

We therefore need to develop *safe thinking*, the ability to create internal images that support what we want to achieve, that express our *conscious aim, our intention.* This requires regular and systematic training (Chapter 21) and can most easily be accomplished during deep relaxation. We need to anchor our wishful images deep inside us in order to be beyond the reach of doubts and fears. To be successful, we need to take advantage of states of consciousness other than our ordinary, "everyday consciousness".

States of consciousness

Our perception of reality differs depending on our current state of mind. Common terms for these levels of consciousness are beta, alpha, theta and delta. The figure shows the different states of consciousness (brain-wave-states) and how the brain impulses per second change depending on our state of mind.

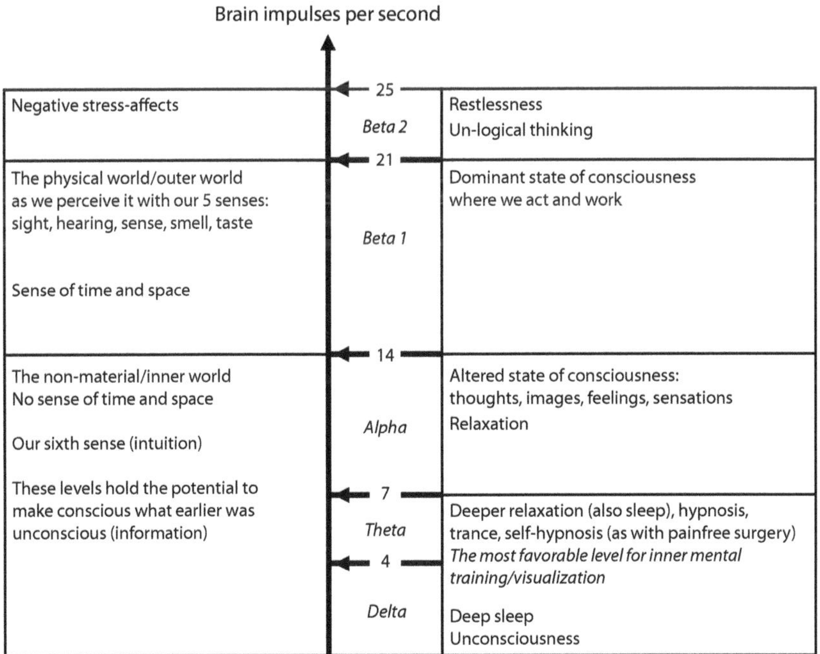

The beta level is nowadays often divided into beta 1 and beta 2. Beta 1 represents our ordinary "everyday consciousness", where we perceive the (outside) world through our five senses, where we are active and where we have a good sense of time and space. Here, we mostly use the left hemisphere, and we are in the "intellect". This is commonly known as our dominant state of mind. It is also the scientific way of describing reality.

Beta 2 describes a state in which we are strongly affected by stress resulting in restlessness and a lack of concentration.

On the alpha level, we have let go of the outside world and become more aware of the inner reality, in the form of thoughts, images and feelings. We lose our sense of time and space, and gain greater access to our intuition and our feelings. We can intentionally put ourselves in this condition through relaxation exercises and meditation, but we can also end up here spontaneously when we become engrossed in something; such as a hobby we love, painting a picture or even just daydreaming. Then we wake up amazed (to the beta-level) and realize that, wow, three hours have already passed in what feels like only minutes! In this state, the activity has increased in the right hemisphere of our brain.

On the theta level we have come even further into the inner world. Here we may have fallen asleep, but this is also the state used in hypnosis, self-hypnosis, pain-free surgery and the like, and a state which we can achieve during relaxation and meditation. According to research, this is the most powerful state for self-empowerment/goal-visualization, such as creating a strong image of perfect health. Here we perceive reality in another way and duality[1] ceases. Since there is no duality at this level, there is no doubt; and the image we want can take hold in our consciousness more deeply than is possible in our ordinary, everyday consciousness. This means that we can feel an absolute certainty about, for example, a complete recovery. At this level, we also have access to a deeper understanding of how our reality is constructed. We can gain insights and understand contexts which are difficult to explain on the beta level.

---

1 Duality: the division of reality that we use in our everyday life where we divide life in good or bad, black or white, spirit or matter, we or you et cetera.

In the fourth stage – the delta level – we are asleep or unconscious. Trained yogis are said to be able to be awake even here and it is thought that small children are able to reach the delta level. However, here we no longer perceive the world as we are used to seeing it. All forms have ceased, and what we perceive is a world of energy.

Even if we are most accustomed to the beta level, all of the levels are equally real and we can learn to use them to our benefit. Creativity, innovative thinking, creative problem solving and more happens at the alpha/theta level and therefore beyond the intellect. By using the intellect, we can only solve problems "within the system". By learning to move from one state of consciousness to another, we can enhance our creativity, improve our goal-visualization capability and get closer to our core.

Left and right brain hemispheres

The concept of the left and right halves of the brain was coined by the neuro-biologist and neuro-psychologist Roger Sperry who was awarded the Nobel Prize for this model of explanation. It was later complemented by the holographic model (Chapter 11), but we can still learn a lot from the left/right model – see figure *Left and right hemispheres*.

The left hemisphere can be said to represent our ordinary, "everyday consciousness" – the beta level – where we think and act rationally and where we have a linear mindset. We pick up our knowledge from outside and this side of the brain is given priority in our Western society and schools. Reading, writing, arithmetic and verbal expression are all abilities considered to be located in our left-brain, as well as the ability to analyze and structure. Even our concept of time can be found here. This is our IQ, or the intellect's intelligence.

The right brain represents our associative/intuitive thinking, for instance our ability to recognize patterns, faces and learn skills such as riding a bicycle and swimming. It also represents our body language and our feelings – the emotional intelligence, or EQ. Through this hemisphere we come into contact with our ability to experience

Left and right hemispheres

Linear/rational thinking	Associative/intuitive thinking
Outer framework	Inner framework
Details	Wholeness
Logic	Intuition
Structure	Synthesis
Analysis	Imagination
Language	Body-language
Criticism	Feelings/Emotions
Tactics	Creativity
Linear thinking	Ability to live in the moment
Reality-testing	Unbiased thinking
Control through will	Control through inner image
Time	Timelessness

timelessness and here we get our knowledge from within. It is also the gateway to what we call our subconscious mind and by exploring ourselves, we can allow more and more of our unconsciousness to become conscious. The right hemisphere also opens the path to our spiritual intelligence, often referred to as SQ or VQ (virtual intelligence) and to a more unbiased visionary thinking.

The intellect's dilemma

You could say that the left hemisphere *describes* reality, while the right hemisphere *experiences* reality. By using the left side we can describe happiness and joy, but to experience it we must have access to our feelings through the right side. Joy and happiness are internal states and to experience them we need not even be able to read and write. There are highly spiritually developed people who are (literally) illiterate, while many highly educated people in our culture are "emotionally" illiterate.

Here we can learn a lot from our children. Small children lead their lives from the right hemisphere. They have not yet developed an intellect and are completely unaware of concepts such as time. They have not yet been trained to perceive time, let alone seeing it as a commodity in short supply. They have a wonderful ability to be in the moment and have access to their imagination, their feelings and their natural body language.

Unfortunately, many of us lose access to our feelings throughout the course of our lives. We learn to "behave" ourselves and to displace uncomfortable feelings. This can make us emotionally handicapped, and at worst, become a so-called "brain-pede" – a walking brain on feet – totally unaware of what is going on in the body.

Knowing this, we can ourselves ensure we create a better balance between the left and right brain. If we know that we have a job where we mainly use our left hemisphere, such as in the IT industry, "number crunching" or various technologies, we can develop a hobby where we activate the right brain; such as playing an instrument, watercolor painting, dancing, singing, spending time in the nature, chopping wood, activities that put us in tune with our body. There is research which says that the very *imbalance* between the hemispheres can be a contributing factor to different kinds of mental illness, depression and burnout. The left hemisphere is considered to be overstimulated, while the right hardly receives any stimulation at all.

In the left column, you can also read the word *reality checking*, our assessment of whether what we see and hear seems reasonable, and corresponds with our past experiences. As you read this, your reality checker is active in determining whether what I write seems credible, whether I know what I am talking about. This helps us to deal with life, but our reality checker can also be an obstacle when we want to change ourselves.

If I want to program a new image of myself, for instance that I am a good speaker, and I do this in my everyday consciousness (beta level), my reality checker will probably protest and say this is not true. By relaxing and putting myself in the alpha or theta state of consciousness, I can get past this. The activity in the left hemisphere is then reduced and the reality checker is out of the picture for a while. Our right hemisphere is not concerned with assessing; it just accepts the images I create. By regularly repeating this new image, during deep relaxation, it gradually becomes a part of my self-image, it feels natural, like a "fact" and replaces the old image. I have taken *visual control* (right hemisphere), rather than straining myself through willpower (left hemisphere).

Our nervous system has difficulty distinguishing between what happens in the external reality and what we only imagine in our minds, the inner reality. For our brain, both are equally true and we can take advantage of this when we want to change our beliefs. Even if something has not yet occurred in the external reality – I only imagine that it has happened – it is taken in by the brain as a real experience. According to David H. Ingvar, M.D., Ph.D., neuroscientist and former Professor at the University of Lund in Sweden, it enters our brain as "a memory of the future".[2]

For something to become a memory, our nervous system must react. Research has shown that direct experience activates the same area of the brain as that activated by recalling from memory. A neural link is established every time we learn something. The more

2 Article in the Swedish newspaper Svenska Dagbladet (December 15, 1996).

we repeat the learning, the stronger the connection, until it often becomes automatic and natural, such as driving a car.

So far we have discussed the traditional division of the brain. In recent years we have increasingly begun to talk about three kinds of thinking, three kinds of intelligence:

IQ, EQ, SQ/VQ

IQ stands for the left-brain's logical, linear thinking, such as 1 + 1 = 2. It is also called serial thinking, because the neural links in the brain are connected in series.

EQ denotes our emotional intelligence, where the neural links are connected in a network. Every time we see a pattern, for example, the neural links are strengthened. The same thing happens when we learn skills like swimming and cycling. When we fail, no link is established, but each time we succeed, the links are strengthened until it all happens automatically.

SQ refers to our spiritual intelligence, sometimes called virtual intelligence, VQ. This intelligence gives us our ability to see contexts and the overall view. Here, creative innovation and new thinking occurs, and this is the origin of flashes of genius. This intelligence has a transforming capability, which allows us to see things in a new light. When we are in contact with our SQ, we use the whole brain and also the heart, and this intelligence can be said to be above the IQ and EQ, but ideally, these three intelligences work together.

Unfortunately, IQ is often valued higher than EQ and SQ and in our present society one can reach high positions without having developed emotional and spiritual intelligence.

I once read about an American study which found that we become stupid (in the sense of lower IQ) by having children. If this is the case, it is possible that along with our small ones we develop our EQ and SQ, making us see life in a different light (not necessarily "stupid").

Maybe we do not take the same bait any more. We have to realize that there is an immense intelligence outside the intellect.

If we accept the concept of three kinds of intelligence and thinking, the figure of the hemispheres would look more like this:

SQ/VQ
Universal/Spiritual intelligence
Wholeness/Higher meaning
Synthesis/Creativity

IQ	**EQ**
Intellect's intelligence	Emotional intelligence

We move some qualities from the right hemisphere to a bridging level. This is not an additional intelligence, we just see it differently. For example, Eastern teachings have been describing our spiritual intelligence for thousands of years.

The whole brain

By making use of our brain and thinking in new ways, we can, throughout our *whole life* establish new neural links between cells and replace old ones. Recent research has shown that even brain cells can be newly formed. Challenges, trials and difficulties help us develop and should therefore be welcomed.

We also know through research that the brain works differently during meditation (at the alpha/theta level) and that the activity is then synchronized in both brain hemispheres; the brain waves merge, and the activity in the brain becomes equilateral. We have access to the entire brain.

It is worth noting that creativity can be found in the right hemisphere (or in SQ, if we want to see it that way) and great inventions and discoveries often seem to come about during relaxation (Chapter 21).

Research has also shown that activity is increased in the right hemisphere for 10-15 minutes after meditation, and during this period we are considered to be extra creative.

Our feelings govern the brain

"To motivate the cells in our brain to work requires *emotional stimulation.* That is the key to the whole brain function", according to Pehr Leissner, M.D., neurophysiologist and one of our leading experts on the human brain.

No matter how much we appreciate our intellect, we are ruled by emotions far more than we think. It is the feeling that gives the thought its power, for better or worse. We have only had our modern brain (the cerebral cortex) for about 50 000 years, while we have been guided by our feelings for millions of years. Thus, it is not our thoughts that control us – although we may experience it that way. There has already been an emotional involvement, and this is the driving force behind our thoughts.

Slaves to our fate

As long as we are slaves to unconscious thoughts and behaviors, we are also slaves to our fate. We create our private hell by attracting the same lessons repeatedly until we finally see through them and can liberate ourselves. Life seems to be so constructed that we unavoidably attract the situations we need to move forward in our growth. The sooner we can see what we have to learn, the quicker we can rise above the old patterns, and gain other experiences.

The higher we reach in our development, the stronger the forces which put our thoughts and actions in motion. What we give out returns faster back to us and we can more easily see the connection. Only then can we get the opportunity to begin evolving consciously. We can only reach real freedom within ourselves.

Conscious thinkers

We need to fundamentally change our approach to our way of thinking. To understand that thoughts are creative, and become so aware that we can observe our thoughts and eventually begin to choose thoughts that are more in line with our wishes; hence, be able to use this fantastic tool for the management of our visions and goals.

I must be prepared to take 100 percent responsibility for all of my thoughts. Who else can be responsible? I am the thinker. With the help of our inner observer, we can break the identification with our thoughts, see that we *are* not our thoughts. We *have* thoughts – they come and go – but I remain, so obviously I am *more* than my thoughts.

Try noticing the "chatter" within. How does your inner conversation sound? How do you speak to yourself? Do you harbor a critic, or supporter inside? By observing the internal dialogue we can gain a distance to it. See that we can choose to identify with it or not.

Anxious thoughts can gradually be invited in for closer viewing and be *welcomed*. It takes the wind out of the sails. If I try to ward off unwanted thoughts, "force and counterforce" arise and the unwanted thoughts tend to take over. With a good observer, we can watch our negative thoughts without being caught up in them or nourishing them. They contain valuable information about the way I interpret reality.

Awareness of my thoughts also opens the way to free myself from thinking, be able to still the thought completely and come into contact with the pure consciousness, the underlying wholeness, which is beyond thought and inner chatter. Here, I can also more easily hear my true inner voice (Chapter 16).

Alluring images of the future

Through what I think today, I create my future. If I want health, success and love, I need to sow these seeds in my mind. I cannot reach my higher good if I sow doubt, anger, guilt and dissatisfaction. If I doubt my wishes, or think that I do not deserve them, then I am going against myself, and my wishes will have difficulty taking hold.

Our thoughts and choice of words reflect our state of mind. If my intention is clear and strong, the thoughts and words will naturally form themselves in a positive and powerful way. I then get the charged feeling which starts the ball rolling. Vision and intention is crucial. This is where we should put our energy (see Chapter 21).

Before we proceed in the circle model and explore our feelings, we will digress slightly and look at the topic of stress and the importance of the breathing for our well-being. To be able to work with feelings in a rewarding way, we need to acquire a good breathing pattern.

Chapter 6 – Stress

Astrid Lindgren, the Swedish, worldfamous author of children's literature, is supposed to have said that during their old age, she and her sister began their telephone conversations by repeating the word death three times. Death, death, death, they said, so that the issue was out of the way and they could engage in topics of a more light-hearted nature.

I would like to suggest the same thing here. For us to say in one voice – stress, stress, stress; and put it on the shelf. What I want to say is that we do not really need to know much about stress in order to create peace, joy and pleasure. It is important that we are clear about what we want to *create* and focus on that. We do not want the negative stress and therefore do not need to spend our energy there. This is more than a play on words. Imagine that you listened to a two-hour lecture on stress and its harmful consequences. How would you feel in your body afterwards? Now, imagine instead listening to a two-hour description of calm, peace, harmony and joy. What vibrations would that trigger within?

First and foremost, we need to distinguish between stress and stress-reactions. It is our *reactions* to stress which cause the problems. Not stress per se. What is stressful for me, is perhaps stimulation for you; and we can be just as stressed by having too little to do as by having too much.

It is also important to distinguish between external and internal stress factors. Even if we have good balance in the outer world, we can "stress ourselves sick" through destructive thoughts, various "musts", low self confidence and so on. Here I will focus on the internal stress factors.

Pleasure and pain

We often talk about positive and negative stress. I think this is slightly deceiving. It is a rare luxury to be so aware, that we realize when positive stress turns into a negative effect. Here I will only use the word stress to describe the *undesirable* effect on the body. The good stress, I would (rather) call stimulation or pleasure. Pleasure and pain, or comfort and discomfort, is a good way of explaining what it is all about.

Stress, in the sense of stimulation is of course healthy. It is the *very spark of life*, the stimulus, what makes us alive. The urge to perform, to express myself and give of myself and my talents. In this sense, we are made for stress.

Stimulation and pleasure go together with satisfaction and joy. I manage what I am doing – even if it is a challenge. I feel that I am evolving and growing. The negative stress – discomfort – gives a "loser feeling": I cannot do it, I cannot make it, I do not have the energy, I cannot cope. A feeling of insufficiency, which is devastating if it goes on too long. According to a survey I saw a while ago 70 percent of Swedes between 28 and 40 years of age, said they felt insufficient both at work and at home. This is obviously not good for our health. Stress impairs our immune system, among other things.

Listen to your body

Our body gives us signals all the time and we need to learn to listen to it, to recognize the breaking point between pleasure and pain, and have the courage to admit to ourselves when it is no longer fun. Maybe I just need rest and recovery, or perhaps I have reached a point where I need to move forward in my development. I have simply grown out of the things I am doing or my view of life. Unfortunately, we have learned that we should fight on and "bite the bullet", so often we struggle even more, instead of slowing down and refilling ourselves with new energy.

Here, the body can fool us by being "helpful". When we have more to do, have to accomplish more, have to manage more, the production of hormones such as adrenaline, noradrenaline and cortisol increases to help us cope. We do not notice that our body runs at higher and higher revs. *We cope with it*! Our body gets used to the higher levels of stress hormones and the entire system becomes overstimulated. We fail to adjust to a slower speed and become blind to the fact that everything is going too fast. In this situation it is often easier to work harder than to unwind. Our body and mind have become so restless that it is painful or impossible to sit still and do nothing. We need activities at all times.

I have been in this phase and regarded myself as more effective than ever before. I was like a runaway horse and did not realize that I was about to collapse. And if we do not understand what is going on, then one day the energy will run out. We collapse, cry and can do nothing. (Or "going into the wall" as it is so dashingly called in Sweden today. There is a little bit more "action" to "going into the wall" than just collapsing.)

What we really need to know about stress is that:

my mental state determines which hormones
are secreted in my body

Mental processes govern our central nervous system. The central nervous system controls the functioning of our endocrine glands and these glands determine which hormones will be secreted in the body. So depending on what signals I send to my body, how I interpret what happens in life, different hormones are produced. My mental state – thoughts, images, feelings – decides which hormones are secreted and the message goes out to every single cell.

Ponder this for a while!

If I signal that I am getting on well, I can, I want to, I have the energy, then "happy hormones" such as endorphins, serotonin and dopamine are sent out.

If I signal to my body that I do not have the energy, I cannot make it and so on, my body responds by increasing the production of "fighting hormones" like adrenalin, noradrenalin and cortisol, in order for me to cope.

We are still so primitively equipped that the body interprets this as if we were in a fight. Our ancient fight-or-flight behavior helps me cope with what I need to do, so that I am able to go back safe and sound to the cave to rest. The problem today is that we rarely get to the cave. We often live under constant pressure and react just as strongly to 100 unanswered emails as we do to a physical threat.

We are better equipped for physical stress than for mental stress and our body reacts just as it did thousands of years ago. The neck tightens, along with the shoulders and back, jaw, abdomen and thighs, so that we can fight or run. The abdominal muscles tighten to protect the vital organs behind. All the energy goes to the muscles. Blood pressure rises, heart activity increases, breathing becomes shallower, digestion and sex drive have to wait.

It is therefore important that we live so that we can strike a balance between the sympathetic nervous system ("the stress-system") that prepares the body for action, and the parasympathetic ("the peace and quiet-system") that builds up and repairs the body.

Remember that both systems are equally good – but for different purposes. If I signal danger, the body responds by pumping out the hormones I need to run or to defend myself and reach safety. It is a survival mechanism and it is all about survival of the species.

Short-term stress we manage well. We would not have survived as a species if we had not been able to endure real pressures. It is important though to make sure that we recover. It is not enough to just train physically after a long working day – then it is still the sympathetic nervous system which is in play. We also need to get complete physical and mental *rest* for the body's own repair system to be able to operate, build up our immune system and recharge the body with new energy. As yoga teachers and authors Elisabeth Haich and Selvarajan Yesudian write in their book, *Self Healing, Yoga & Destiny*: "the best protection against any and all forms of disease is a strong and balanced mind." It is also worth pointing out that we need recovery even when we do what we love doing!

Stress and feelings

Stress reduces the contact with our feelings – and this is the point! We need a high pain tolerance during conflict and should not feel pain until we are back in a safe place and can tend our wounds. But impaired contact with our feelings also reduces the activity in the brain. It is our feelings that get our brain working and prolonged stress can cause poor memory.

Take a moment to relive some memories from your life. Why do you remember these in particular?

Yes, they affected you strongly – positively or negatively. We remember what has a strong emotion associated with it. Without the emotion, there is no *experience*. Hence, the function of my memory is linked to the degree I am in touch with my feelings, how present I am.

Strong states of stress, such as "burnout" imply an emotional collapse, where we do not have access to our emotions. When we experience emptiness and indifference, the way back is to *feel* our way out of it all. We have to train ourselves to reconnect with our feelings.

Inner security

As long as we live, we will be exposed to stress. If we want to try new things and evolve, we will experience stress. If we choose to do nothing and stagnate, this can be equally stressful.

You could say that there are healthy thoughts and feelings which increase our vitality and our happiness, and unhealthy thoughts and feelings that cause problems and concerns. As we will see later on, negative stress is often equivalent to fear and lack of self-knowledge. A sense of inadequacy, a fear of not being enough and being separated from our center and our mission.

When feeling stressed we can ask ourselves: *what am I afraid of now?* The answer tends to be: not having time, not managing, not being good enough, not capable enough and so on. We can instead work on finding our *inner* security – to feel safe in uncertainty, in change. Most things in life are out of our control. The bigger the issue, the less control we have. We do not even know if we, or our relatives, will still be here tomorrow. We do not know whether we will have a job or health in a year's time.

If we want to feel good, we must learn to enjoy being in our body. There is nowhere else to go. For as long as we live we have no alternative to being in our body. We cannot escape from it, not even by taking a trip around the world. Inner security is the only thing we can have – to live with the feeling that whatever happens I will have the resources to handle it. This gives peace of mind in the middle of an active life.

In the next chapter we will look at how the way we breathe influences our well-being. Breathing can be regarded as our main tool for dealing with stress.

Chapter 7 – Breathing

As a birthday present, one of my students received a trip to attend a course I was giving in Majorca. Her father-in-law – who was a bit skeptical about the idea – asked what she would learn there. "I will learn to breathe," she replied. "Breathe?" said her father-in-law, "we do that all the time."

Yes, we do indeed, but how? In my opinion, breathing is the single-most important factor to enhance our well-being. Through proper breathing, we can increase our energy and maintain a steady flow throughout the day. We can improve our health – circulation, the immune system and more – and also work our way through difficult emotions and thus create balance in the body. Breathing is everything for our well-being and this is sadly undervalued in the Western world, especially in health care.

The importance of good breathing is well documented. There are many excellent books on the subject for those who want to immerse themselves.

The breath is considered to be the connecting link between body and soul and is one of our primary tools for personal development. Breathing is exceptional, in that we can choose to breathe consciously, or allow our autonomous nervous system to manage it for us, in other words let breathing take care of itself.

There are various opinions about whether we should interfere with breathing or let it happen naturally. As I see it, it is more about rediscovering the natural breathing pattern we had as children. Most Westerners – especially women – have very shallow breathing. Our busy lifestyle often results in an imbalance between the sympathetic and parasympathetic nervous system. The sympathetic, activating element is "on" most of the time.

Perhaps this is to some extent an appearance issue. I was a teenager in the late 50's when fashion was highly focused on the waist. Belts were tightened to the limit which prevented every possibility of abdominal breathing. But studies have also shown that children as young as six are beginning to breathe shallowly, so we have every reason to be aware of our breathing pattern and, if necessary, restore our breathing to a more harmonious rhythm.

Conscious breathing is our primary tool for stress reduction. Through the way we breathe, we can send signals of "peace and quiet" to the brain (or raise our energy if that is what we need). Good breathing helps us to gain a range of health benefits, to free ourselves from unwanted feelings and to reach higher states of consciousness. Who could say no to such a tool?

Good breathing gives good health

Poor oxygenation is a contributory factor to the development of many diseases such as heart- and cerebral infarction. Examining breathing should therefore be of great interest in cases of fatigue, worry, anxiety and the like. For example, it is impossible to feel anxiety if we have a deep and slow breathing rhythm. Our brain is a high energy-consumer and uses up 20-25 percent of the oxygen we inhale, and anxiety is related to a lack of oxygen in the brain. Poor exhalation also results in too much carbon dioxide remaining in the body, which we usually experience as anxiety. In order to feel good and function well, we need to ensure that our brain has a proper supply of oxygen. Proper breathing also spares the heart, which then does not need to circulate as much blood to oxygenate the body.

Breathing is also the body's main "waste disposal system". About 70 percent of the waste products should be cleared out through respiration, otherwise we put an unnecessary load on the kidneys, skin et cetera.

About the therapeutic effect of good breathing, it has been said that it:

- Increases the production of endorphins
- Reduces pain sensations
- Improves oxygen intake
- Lowers the pulse (so the heart need not work so hard)
- Improves the metabolism (through increased amounts of oxygen and carbon dioxide)
- Improves blood circulation
- Lowers blood pressure
- Reduces the risk of blood clots
- Prevents the accumulation of cholesterol in the blood
- Increases our intellectual capacity (by increasing oxygen supply to the brain)
- Improves our ability to concentrate
- Increases resistance to disease (viruses and bacteria do not like oxygen)
- Reduces anxiety, aggressiveness, nervousness
- Increases our well-being
- Enhances the feeling of life, takes us to higher energy levels
- Slows aging and senility
- Prolongs life and
- You can get “high" on breathing

As we saw in the previous chapter, our bodies react when we are exposed to stress. Our breathing also changes and becomes shallower, so that we only breathe with the upper part of the lungs, the chest. When we are able to relax again, our breathing deepens and goes further down into the stomach. Inhalation activates the sympathetic nervous system and exhalation activates the parasympathetic nervous system.

Each mental change is reflected in respiration and hence in the body. Every state of mind, every feeling has its own breathing rhythm. We easily adjust our breathing rhythm to other human beings, which is deliberately used in therapy, massage and the like, to put the client in a harmonious state; but we are also affected adversely, for example by aggressive people, and it is an advantage to be aware of the importance of mastering our own breathing rhythm.

Normal breathing rate

We can usually assume that our "at rest" breathing rate is between 13 and 18 breaths per minute. With practice, we can easily reduce this to below 10 breaths. Experienced meditators usually go down to between 4 and 6 breaths per minute during meditation (something we also do during deep sleep). Of the approximately 21 000 breaths we take per day, certain breaths are considered to be more life-giving than others and we can increase that number by learning to breathe in "energy", to really understand and see that breath replenishes energy – that we can inhale vitality!

Posture

For good breathing, it is necessary that we stay as straight as possible, that we keep the chest high so that we have unobstructed "bellows", which make it easier for air to flow in and out of the body, allowing the diaphragm to move easily. The movement of the diaphragm provides a beneficial massage for our internal organs. The deeper and calmer we breathe, the more the diaphragm works.

A straight posture is even more important as we get older. It is difficult to breathe deeply if we are crooked. Breathing is one of our most important energy sources so our ability to breathe deeply is therefore essential.

In order to stay healthy, it is also important that we breathe through the nose. Hair fibers (cilia) in the nose make it harder for bacteria and viruses to enter the body. By breathing through the nose we keep the mucous membranes active so that it is not so easily blocked when we get a cold (by constantly breathing through the nose it will not have time to be blocked).

Abdominal breathing

Breathing through the abdomen gives us a good base feeling. Just below the navel there is a point known as our physical center – in qi gong and yoga called dan tien and hara respectively – which is considered to give us a firm foundation on the earth. Slow and deep breathing also improves blood circulation. It prevents us from being upset or afraid, while shallow breathing is sufficient in itself to create anxiety and aggression.

Abdominal breathing is about breathing deeply into the abdomen without inhaling too much air. It is not about overdoing it. Do not force it, just follow the body. The body knows and can take care of it, given the right conditions, but we may need to help it regain its natural breathing rhythm by consciously bringing the breath further down into the body.

If the abdominal muscles are tense, we cannot take a full breath. If you have difficulty in bringing the air down into the stomach, imagine you are taking in the smell of a beautiful flower. This usually makes it easier. When we start to practice abdominal breathing, we can also tighten the abdominal muscles slightly on exhalation to increase awareness of the diaphragm's movements.

Practice abdominal breathing lying on your back, with one or more books on your stomach to ensure that you inhale properly into the abdomen. This also forces the abdominal muscles to work and gives us an insight of the sensation in the stomach when we have good abdominal breathing.

Complete yogi breathing

In yoga, complete yogi breathing is practised. This is how you can do it:

Lie on your back on the floor or some other stable surface. Observe your breathing for a few minutes, then exhale. Breathe in through the nose, first into the abdomen and let your stomach expand – like a balloon – then into the chest and further up by slowly raising the collar bone. Now the abdomen has already started to draw in, and you begin the exhalation by first emptying the stomach, then contracting the chest and finally lowering the collar bone, while letting the air out through the nose.[1] *Then let your breathing continue naturally for a while, before taking the next full breath.*

The most important thing is to draw the air deep into the stomach, the chest then usually expands by itself, but be sure to breathe up to the collar bone and exhale properly.

Personally, I find that abdominal breathing gives me serenity, breathing into the midriff provides power, and high up in the chest, I find joy – the extra heightening of the chest generates feelings of joy and happiness.

Prolonged exhalation

When we extend the exhalation, we activate the parasympathetic nervous system (the peace and quiet-system), we remove carbon dioxide more effectively, reduce the number of breaths, burn less oxygen and calm the heart rhythm.

Asthma patients, who have shallow breathing, often exhale insufficiently in fear of running out of air. The preventative practice of prolonged exhalation can help to better manage future asthma attacks.

A good breathing rhythm with prolonged exhalation is achieved, by counting to 5 during inhalation, counting to 8 on exhalation and

1 There is also a variant of this method, where you empty the air from above, in other words, first the collar bone, then the chest and stomach.

then resting for a count of 3, before taking the next breath. This is considered to be the optimal breathing rhythm according to the principles of the golden ratio, also named the divine section (Chapter 20), and the rhythm the body voluntarily chooses during deep sleep. Here the functions in the body are at their optimum.

Lie on your back on a flat surface or sit upright. Start focusing on your breathing. Exhale and on the inhalation, count to 5, on exhalation to 8 and then rest while counting to 3. Start over again, or if you are a beginner, let your breathing take care of itself for a moment between the exercises.

The prolonged exhalation increases our resistance to disease. Personally I have often got rid of an oncoming cold by devoting some time for extended breathing exercises – though with a substantial extension and a natural break (which can be quite long) after exhalation. Prolonged exhalation can also reduce breathlessness during physical exercise and is good for feelings of bloatedness, if we have eaten too much.

Spine-flex breathing

This is a technique of wave-like movements that quickly takes us back into the body and to our center if we are stressed, and also directly increases our sense of awareness. It involves arching the spine inwards while we draw breath into the abdomen and up into the chest, while lifting our head. On exhalation we slouch the spine. In this way, the spine is properly flexed – a switch between arching and slouching – which keeps it mobile and is said to keep us healthy into old age.

If we practice spine-flex breathing when lying down, we can – on the exhalation – push the back down against the surface to mark the bend even more. With practice we can perform this whole-body-breathing anywhere, the movements can be made very slight and imperceptible. It works just as well. Even this method is seen as breathing naturally – as children we have this light bending of the spine when we breathe.

To breathe <u>with</u> our feelings

The first step in being able to deal with our feelings is to notice them. Through breathing exercises, we become more observant of how our emotions and our state of mind change from one moment to the next, and when feeling restless, we can start to directly breathe deeper into the body. When we shut ourselves off from our feelings, we also block our energy.

Since ancient times, we have had a tendency to hold our breath during strong emotions. The same behavior is seen in animals that become rigid and motionless so as not to be seen. But this also means that we easily keep hold of our emotions rather than release and really "feel them through".

The cells in our body contain memories. By breathing *with* our feelings, we can get an emotional experience and understanding of what has happened, or is happening to us, rather than merely an intellectual view of it all.

We can use deep abdominal breathing as well as breathing into the physical place of the emotion to dissolve upsetting emotions and gradually let them go.

When you engage in premeditated exercises to release yourself from painful emotions, set aside a specific time for this. 10-15 minutes, or a maximum of 20 minutes at a time. Then you put it all aside and center yourself in the present. The intention is to not stay in the undesirable state, but only work with it for a while.

Sit or lie comfortably and begin to relax. Observe your breathing and focus your attention on the abdomen – the area just below the navel, our physical center – and breathe deep abdominal breathing for a short while.

Then recall an emotion that you would like to be able to manage in a better way. It may be a memory that still hurts, or a fear. Feel the emotion and be sure to continue to breathe into your stomach all the time. If you feel where in the body the sensation occurs, you can breathe to that place. Breathe deeply and slowly and imagine that you are breathing through the place of the emotion.

If you can, strengthen the feeling as you consciously breathe with it. Try to stay with the feeling for a moment while breathing either to the stomach or to the place of the emotion.

Gradually, you can feel that the emotion becomes weaker, that its energy is being dissolved. When you are done or the time has passed, let go of your emotion. Say to yourself: Cut! Now, it's enough for today.

Now evoke instead a situation or feeling that makes you calm and harmonious, and begin to breathe it in. A wonderful memory for example, and sense the positive feeling spreading through your body.

End the exercise by bending and stretching. Take a few deep breaths and start coming back to the room and the present moment. Each time you do this exercise, you dissolve the painful emotion more and more.

Conscious breathing

One single negative thought or feeling is in itself sufficient to create an imbalance in the body. By using conscious breathing, we can get it to collaborate with us – rather than the opposite. We can deliberately take deeper and slower breaths. Since we can govern the breath ourselves, we can consciously teach ourselves good breathing, find its natural rhythm and be able to live with an enhanced vitality. To truly integrate a healthy breathing pattern, we need to practice breathing while lying, sitting, standing and walking.

We can start our day with a few deep breaths to center ourselves and become present in the moment; and during the day take short breaks to ensure that we have a good posture and relaxed breathing. A loss of energy during the day often means that we are breathing shallowly. Make a habit of stretching yourself, breathing deeply, maybe getting up to open the window and taking a few deep breaths. If we wish, we can connect these breaks with certain tasks to further remind us: for instance, before each phone call or a similar activity which I know I do a couple of times a day.

Through breathing, we can reach higher levels of consciousness and we can experience strong feelings of happiness simply by changing the way we breathe. If we start working with our breathing, do breathing exercises regularly and are sensitive, the body itself usually takes us to the next step in our development. An interaction comes about, where sometimes we lead and sometimes the body takes over and guides us.

Gradually, we can discover the incredible pleasure of breathing, how to deliberately activate the life energy within us and experience harmony and joy. After having practiced for many years, I would say that it is hard not to feel well and happy with good breathing. But I would also say that all too often I forget this, relapse and have to re-center myself. In any case, nowadays I know how to alter my state of mind through breathing.

You can read more about breathing in Chapter 15 (heart breathing) and Chapter 16 (breathing meditation). In the next chapter we will explore our feelings.

Chapter 8 – Feelings

Exploring our feelings is, in my opinion, the most fascinating adventure we can imagine. Talk about cheap hobby! Wherever we are, we have "ourselves" with us and we will not be bored for one second! I often talk about emotional competence, and by that I mean being able to handle my feelings; feel them, take responsibility for them and not project them on to the surroundings. Although it may be difficult to distinguish between thoughts and feelings – they do give rise to each other – it is essential that we do it here.

Feelings are felt

Thoughts we *think*, feelings we *feel*. Feelings are energy that we experience in the *body*. In our culture, we are very good at intellectualizing our emotions. If you ask someone "how did it feel?" You will often get the answer: "well, I thought ..." We are used to being in the intellect, and respond with an opinion. So we need to increase our awareness of *where* and *how* we experience feelings in our body. The most important thing with feelings is to *feel* them, not necessarily to express them verbally or by action, but to release the feeling *within*, to explore the energy, dare to stay in it (this is how I feel) and based on that, find a suitable approach.

Feelings contain information

All feelings serve a purpose and are positive in that they provide information; they want to tell us something. We can learn to see them as our friends, who are here to guide us. Instead of fighting them, we can invite our feelings and ask to have a closer look. What is it I need to see?

Although all feelings are "good", certain states of mind are more sought after than others. We all want to be cheerful and happy, to feel warmth and love, preferably all the time. In order to stay in this desired state of being, we need to understand and manage the emotions that pull us out of "the good state". In particular, we should pay attention to when we become emotional (over-emotional), here we can be sure to have unprocessed pain within.

Fear, anger and sadness

The most common feelings we struggle with are fear, anger and sadness. When observing them, we can see that they are felt in different parts of the body. Fear tends to go deepest and be experienced in the stomach, anger usually in the shoulders, upper arms, throat/neck and forehead/temples, while sadness is felt in the throat and chest, but also behind the eyes, and it is not so easy to tell what is what. In the brain's emotional center (amygdala) these emotions are very close to each other.

Feelings also have, as we shall see, several layers. Anger can be disguised fear; fear hides vulnerability and so on. We need to get to the root – our deepest need – in order to dismantle them and liberate ourselves.

My feelings are my responsibility

Feelings become problems only when we hold onto them. Here we can again learn from our small children, who have a wonderful ability to switch between different states of mind.

A spontaneous feeling moves like a wave through the body in about two minutes. If we feel it for longer, we have started to work it up ourselves. "I will not forget this" and so on.

The author and physician Deepak Chopra says in *The Seven Spiritual Laws of Success*, that when we respond negatively to other people or situations, we should remember that we are really reacting to our own emotions, and that our emotions are not someone else's fault.

We cannot control everything that happens in the outside world, but we can influence our reactions. *I am the one* who senses and reacts to what happens to me, *I am the one* who produces the feelings in my body. The outside world just triggers things within me. Other people do not make us angry or disappointed. *We* make ourselves angry because of our reactions to other people. It is our own expectations (our inner pictures) that create our reactions. Basically:

Expectation met	= satisfaction
Expectation not met	= disappointment, anger, accusation

Disharmony arises from an internal conflict between my expectations – my unfulfilled desires – and reality. When I can see this, it becomes easier to gain distance from the negative emotions. To see that I do not need to be a victim of my moods. I actually have a choice and can make the changes needed – both in the outside world and in my mind.

Everything we do aims at a feeling

If we scrutinize our motives and aspirations in life, we can see that everything we do is done to produce a feeling. The things that I love to do evoke a sensation im my body. Without it, there is no experience. I strive for material possessions in order to gain a sweet sensation in the body. Money and success provide satisfaction in the body. When we become aware of this, we can learn to bring about the desired feelings directly, without connecting them to an object. This creates freedom and independence. (Then of course, we can buy the things we want, but without depending on them. We know what it is about and are free to choose.)

Practice evoking a feeling that you would like to experience more often – such as joy. You can think of an occasion when you were really happy, or maybe you are happy right now. Relax and feel the quality of joy without relating it to something special. Just sense how joy feels for you. Connect the feeling of joy with your breathing, so that you breathe the joy into your body. Practice this for some time and you will be able to evoke this feeling whenever you want.

We have become used to being happy as the result of something emanating from the outside world. But even if I just think of the same thing and really sense it, the joyful feeling arises and I am the one creating the feeling in both cases.

Personally, I am helped by seeing feelings as energy on different frequencies/wavelengths, like tones on a scale – from low-frequency to high-frequency energy. So mentally, I can run up and down the emotional stairs and practice going in and out of different emotional states.

Remember that emotions such as anger and fear are very powerful states of energy, even if we choose to label them "low frequency". Our dark sides contain huge amounts of energy.

Negative emotions can help us further in our growth by telling us there is something we have to deal with; that here I have *an area for development*. If we solely choose to "devote ourselves" to our anger, depression, or jealousy, we create pain and lose power. If we instead follow the feeling to its origin, we create power. But first of all we need to be aware of the actual feeling, before we can experience what lies behind it.

Anger

”May we not even be angry anymore?” said a course participant once. Of course, we can be as angry as we want to, but it may be advantageous to realize that we create the anger ourselves. Anger is our internal reaction to what is happening. I produce the feeling myself, and I *can* choose another reaction.

Anger is often glamorized by the terms “hot tempered”, “short-fused” and the like, through which we can disclaim responsibility. What we are really saying is: I cannot handle my feelings and I am easily imbalanced.

Anger provides in itself an energy kick, an adrenaline rush, which we can transform into power and action, but in most modern conflicts there are better tools. Anger stresses the body and to be angry often is – according to TV's Dr. Phil – a way to slowly kill ourselves. Anger increases the heart rate and blood pressure, releases stress hormones and ruins many relationships. Anger and accusation are being used as “pain relief” – a momentary reduction of a person´s internal disharmony.

Angry people are frightened people

Anger is disguised fear, even though we may not experience it that way. But if we look more closely at anger, we can see that when we get angry, we feel threatened in one way or another. I have my perception of reality which tells me how things work, how it should be, how to behave. So if anyone chips away at my perceptions or turns them upside down, this triggers a reaction of fear, I feel that my values are being questioned.

We said earlier that all feelings are good, that they show something and we can ask ourselves: does anger give me what I want? Such as joy and happiness. If the answer is no, we can strive to change our approach.

So, what can we do with our anger, if we cannot throw it at others? When we have become angry, it is important that the anger is released, so we can free ourselves from it. Well, in the short term, we can always throw crockery, beat the mattress, strangle a pillow, call a friend, dance and sing, and so on to ease the pressure. In the long term, we need to work with our perceptions and acknowledge our true feelings.

Imagine that you are angry and are standing in front of another person. Now remove the other person and begin to focus on yourself and your own body. What is going on inside you? Think of it as energy. Your body produces incredible additional energy.

Are you able to use this energy in a constructive way or is it pure lost energy, which means you feel exhausted afterwards? If so, start to explore other approaches.

Anger is a superficial feeling, and once we have reached higher levels in our development, we are angry less often, because we see the underlying motives/needs of ourselves and others. The realization that anger is disguised fear can also help us to deal with angry people in our surroundings, to not get carried away by anger but to stay in our own state of mind and help the other person to regain balance.

Fear

Fear is a powerful emotion and we are caught by the thought and image that contains the strongest feeling. Therefore, negative feelings often take over and we are steered towards what we absolutely do not want. It is claimed that 85 percent of the decisions we take are based on fear, because we fear the consequences of alternative choices.

We all have blocking self-images, from simple obstacles to strong phobias, fears of various "things" to a "fear of being afraid". We can see our fears as development areas, as mis-learning. Our entire society is built on fear and if we want to evolve to a higher level, we need to re-learn, and change our internal images. The essence of mental training is that we learn to deal with our fears without having to change the outside world. We change our inner experience.

We do not need to know when our blockages occurred. Even if we did know, it does not mean that problems automatically disappear.

We still have to take action in the present and it is less frightening to transform our fears than to continue to live with them. 90 percent of what we are worried about never actually happens.

The psychological fears (created by the psyche) – from light concerns to anxiety and phobias – are basically the same conditions, but with different strengths. In all these cases, we need to change our inner picture and build new neural connections in the brain, thus changing our interpretation program, and create a new context where we see ourselves able to handle what previously felt threatening.

Some fears are clear, "distinct" and easily identifiable, such as "I am afraid of dogs, because I have been bitten by a dog". Other fears are more deceptive and hide under concepts that we might not associate with fear. We saw in the previous chapter that most of what we call stress is fear and that anger is disguised fear. Even concepts such as laziness, poor character, lack of creativity, procrastination, listlessness can mask fear – that I doubt my abilities and do not dare to pursue my dreams and go for what I want at heart (such as, fear that I am not intelligent enough, do not have the right training, would never make it, and so on). There are many unidentified fears behind our loss of enthusiasm.

Seemingly harmless things, like missing the bus, can start the body's alarm system and put us into a state of panic. One of my students told me that she was extremely afraid of being late. She knew how the fear started in childhood and she could intellectually laugh about it all, but her body still reacted with panic when she got into situations where she was likely to be late, which meant that on finally arriving, she was completely drained of energy.

Phobias

When fear is stronger than the danger warrants, we usually call it a phobia. A phobia can build up fast. A friend developed, in mature age, a phobia of the telephone. The origin of this was that she was once called by her mother, who told her that a good friend of them both suddenly had died. The woman became very upset and felt that she could not continue the conversation, because she was overcome by breathlessness and nausea. The next day when she spoke to her mother again, the same feeing came back, and she began to associate the feeling with the phone. This eventually developed into a general phobia of telephones and she refused to answer the phone. To call in itself was not a problem, but the sound of the telephone ringing triggered the feeling of panic. It may be added that earlier she enjoyed talking on the phone.

Phobias – to varying degrees – can cause much trouble and sometimes even be disabling, but they are usually quite easy to overcome. We can see it as mis-learning, where we have connected two things, which actually are not related to each other. In this case, telephone and panic.

The combination of relaxation/visualization training is an efficient method, where, during deep relaxation – and at our own pace – we can begin to get closer to what we previously feared. Through regular practice, we can program a new inner picture (a new conditioning), which will eventually be integrated into our self-image (Chapter 21). Our nervous system has difficulties in differentiating between what happens in so-called reality and what we only imagine. Thus, we can practice different situations at home in peace and quiet before we expose ourselves to them in real life.

Conscious breathing to deal with feelings

Each feeling has its own breathing rhythm. The way we breathe reflects the feeling behind. All emotions feel better when we breathe *with* them. It is usual that we hold our breath to keep emotions in check. When we breathe with them, we experience more of the feeling. Sometimes we even need to strengthen the feeling in order to identify what it stands for. To breathe with the feeling – deep abdominal breathing to the physical place where we experience the emotion – means that we release it, gradually, and can begin to let go of old pain.

The exercise in Chapter 7 – *To breathe with our feelings* shows how you can use your breathing to free yourself from painful emotions.

Love your fear

When we work with our fears, it is important that we treat ourselves with compassion and tenderness. Love your fears! If we criticize ourselves for our shortcomings, we activate defense mechanisms, and no development will take place. We need never break down the defenses; we release them voluntarily when we no longer need them. So have warmth and affection for what you carry with you! The day we can laugh at our fear, the first victory is won. Once we have laughed at a phobia, for example, the connection to the old picture will never be as strong again. When we recognize our fear, it wears off. When we deny it, an imbalance (a falsehood) arises in the body and we become tense.

Although individual phobias and fears are often easy to access, there is – in my experience – in all the hundreds of things we can be afraid of, an underlying common catastrophe feeling, that "something dangerous" will occur. This feeling stays within us even if we get over the individual fears, and when we explore this catastrophe feeling closer, it seems to always be about perishing, or being annihilated; a fear of the transience of form, a fear of death. We are so caught up in the intellect and the world of form, that it easily leads us to believe that this is the only reality. This means we are unfamiliar with the formless world and fear the disintegration of form.

The emotional layers

This underlying catastrophe feeling is probably what caught my interest the most and has been the focus of my "exploration" for many years. The person who led me down this track – I understand in hindsight – was the psychiatrist Viktor Frankl with what he calls "paradoxical intention", depicted in the book *The Doctor and the*

Soul, among others. He exposed people to what they feared the most. If a person thought he would get a heart attack if he went outside the door, then his task was to go out and "let the attack hit him", until he was no longer able to be scared.

Frankl talks about many – often funny – episodes where people had to expose themselves to what they feared. People with "trembling phobia" – who began to tremble in social situations if someone watched them – got the task to tremble more. To say: let them see trembling like they have never seen before. Yes, of course they did not succeed in trembling, when what they feared was allowed, and even encouraged.

This gave me the idea to follow the *feeling itself* and expose myself to all my feelings, in the desire that there should not be a single internal thought or feeling, that I could not get close to and manage. This started what I later referred to as "the emotional layers" and is the most revolutionary thing I have ever discovered. It was a real eye-opener and transformed my whole perception of reality.

It all started when I let my inner witness observe my anger and I soon realized that I was actually not angry, but sad. It felt very threatening to me, because at that time I saw anger as strength and sorrow as weakness. It took time before I could accept that I really was sad and move on to explore the sadness and what lay behind it.

After having practiced this on myself and clients for many years, I have seen that the pattern is more or less the same no matter what is concerned. It is the most liberating approach I have come across – to follow the fear to the point where it dissipates and turns into the opposite. Instead of working with the hundreds of situations that may provoke fear, we can work directly with the underlying basic fear.

The pattern is described in the following table. We can of course start with whichever feeling we want. Here I will begin with anger as it is an easy feeling to study. The important thing, when working in this way, is to go deep into *the emotion* – it is not enough to observe just the thoughts. It is *the emotional energy* we study and follow, without putting it into a context. At the very moment we go into the emotion we experience only its energy aspect.

Note that in order to work with emotions in this way – you should have developed an inner observer (Chapter 5), so that you can simultaneously experience *and* observe what happens. You also need to find a peaceful, undisturbed time and place, so you can relax and focus all your attention inwardly. Place one hand on your stomach, so you have contact with your breathing and continue to breathe throughout.

The words below are only suggestions. If you follow your feelings, you of course select the words that apply to *your* experience.

Explore the feeling of, for example:

Irritation/anger/accusation	Follow the anger and *feel* what is behind it.
Sorrow, sadness, disappointed, hurt?	What is behind that feeling?
Rejected, abandoned, overruled lonely?	Go further. What is behind it?
Inadequate, not sufficiently loved/appreciated, worthless, "nothing"?	Feel the "nothing"!

At the level of "nothing" (the void), we often resist, want to turn away, flee, do something else. Maybe you feel like disappearing, dying, becoming nothing, being engulfed in a total emptiness. But if we explore the void further, surrender to this "nothing", we can experience how the painful emotion dissolves and is transformed into complete peace. When we go deeply into nothing, we become everything!

If we follow a feeling far enough, in the end only "nothing" is left. There the shift to the coherent state of mind takes place. It is therefore important not to resist, when we experience threatening feelings such as worthlessness or "nothing". It is the *resistance* to feel that hurts – not the feeling itself. The more we can let the feeling free inside us, the faster it disappears. The tension between opposites (pressure and counter pressure) ceases, the pent-up energy is dissolved and we are in contact with pure Being, the oneness which is beyond duality.

If we give in to superficial emotions, such as anger, we miss the entire development potential. Anger usually wants to accuse and take the cause outside us. Sadness gives us a deeper contact with our inner being, makes us softer, opens us to the realization that the feeling/problem is within me and that I myself can change my experiences.

If I, for instance, am afraid of being rejected, this will affect many areas of my life. I will experience it at work and in relationships, without always knowing the true cause. Here we can work directly with the underlying basic emotion. That which takes us out of the harmonic flow.

Fears, phobias and anxiety we only experience in a detached state of mind; and as long as we are in a negative emotional state, we will not be able to make contact with the whole. We simply need to learn how to reach a more coherent state.

Working with the "emotional layers" demands a lot of courage at the outset. It will take us to a "point of annihilation", where we feel that if we take another step, we will die. The most natural thing here would be to escape back to safety. But if we proceed, the pain transforms and is replaced by deep peace. In this state, it is easy to observe the part that was afraid, thinking it would be annihilated, and see that it is only a part of the ego, our unconscious self.

A kingdom

Why would we want to expose ourselves to this? Because here we can regain a lot of life-energy, which is blocked in the body. The basic fear comes from a separation from the wholeness and this gives rise to much unnecessary suffering. People kill themselves (and each other) because of emotional pain. It is also the source of much escapism such as alcohol, drugs, shopping et cetera – ways to temporarily deaden feelings of emptiness and emotional pain.

There are also studies which show that, for example, survivors of cancer and other serious diseases, are those people who are able to really feel all their feelings, both positive and negative. Jeanne Segal, Ph.D. and author with over thirty years experience as a clinical psychologist, writes in her book *Raising Your Emotional Intelligence* that through her research, she could see that the people who survived serious diseases the longest were able to both feel through all their feelings and express them, which also helped them to build closer ties to other people. These people were also in touch with their spiritual side; they received inner guidance, which they felt was an important part of the healing process.

When we try to escape from something, it starts to chase us. So we need to stop, face what we fear, welcome it and deal with it. Were not many of our childhood stories about exactly that? The heroes having to endure terrifying trials before they could get "the princess and the kingdom". It is the same here – for those who dare venture into the menacing void – a kingdom waits on the other side.

Once we have passed the critical point – the terrifying abyss – which separates us from wholeness, peace and joy, life is forever changed. We know that there is something more – something bigger – and even if we lose it, occasionally forget, we still have the insight and can always "connect" again. We have to repeat these exercises until we voluntarily let go of our emotions and allow them to pass, without resistance, through the body.

Naturally, we will end up in the fragmented state anyway. But we can see it, and the security we get by realizing that we can take care of our emotions and transform them, gives indescribable freedom and a huge energy gain, as the blocked energy is released.

Nowadays, I do not need to go through all the layers. Usually the shift happens much earlier. If I go deeply enough into a feeling of sadness, it transforms directly into warmth and love.

So we need to take 100 percent responsibility for our feelings. Realize that we *have* feelings, but that we are not our feelings. I can see that my feelings come and go, but *I* (the observer) remain.

To take full responsibility for all of our feelings may sound tough. But we can take responsibility for what we experience in our own body. Feelings are our internal reactions. A course participant once said that it sounds as if people could behave in any-way possible, hurt me and I would just accept. But that is not the question. The more we work with ourselves, the easier it is to calmly set the limits for what we are prepared to accept, and more easily see what is our own "rubbish" and what belongs to the other person. Moreover, people who are in contact with their hearts are not intentionally hurtful.

Our behavior reveals our internal state. As soon as we open our mouths – even if we talk about others and other things – we are telling the story of ourselves and where we are in our development. We act from our own subjective perception of reality, and therefore our actions and our views are always a reflection of ourselves (of our own interpretation program). A person who appears unpleasant, who has a need to hurt, is trapped in his/her own pain and tries to lessen it by putting another person down. A person in harmony has no such need.

My best teacher is the one who is able to disturb my peace

An over-used expression, maybe. In other words, we should welcome the people and situations which make us upset – see them as an opportunity to increase our awareness of what is within us. How can I use this for my growth; to see my behavior and free myself from old baggage? The more we clear out, the more joy of life can flow in.

Never try to *force* results. It is important to let the process take its own time. We cannot let go of everything all at once, but have to take one step at a time. What we would rather keep hold of is usually what we need to let go of the most – our most cherished illusions that we often have no desire to get rid of. But if we want to develop further, we have to take responsibility for those parts of ourselves we previously may not have seen or not wanted to acknowledge.

We cannot *think* away emotional wounds. Positive thinking is good, but will not calm strong emotional storms. Memories and feelings that we have not worked through remain inside as blocked, "bound up" energy. The body still remembers even if I alter my thinking, I must also take care of my feelings in depth. (See also physical pain in Chapter 14.)

Of course I can put plasters/cosmetics on the wounds by trying to create an environment where I would not have to face the unpleasant – through constant assurance that I am loved, and so on. Most people avoid the "black hole" – through activities, by not exposing themselves to certain situations/people, by not being alone – but this is restrictive. Sooner or later, we must face our fears in order to become whole. Many different events/people can trigger the critical point. Practice identifying the situations/people that cause the feeling of facing into the abyss, but work directly with the emotion. Focus on the *emotion*, instead of the hundreds of events that can trigger it. When something has happened, ask yourself the question: *what did it arouse in me*? Are there other people/situations that can trigger this feeling? For example: I "disappear/drown" in the demands of work, family and others. Even everyday events can bring the same feeling of going under, of not being enough.

If we lose touch with our center (and with the observer) our emotions can easily take over and control us. We can feel as if we were going to die or go mad, as if they could go on forever. When we are in the middle of an emotional storm, usually the only thing we can do is to stay with it until the storm abates. Afterwards we can still and center ourselves and return to a good state of mind. And from there, we can in peace and quiet relive the situation and look at it more objectively, observe it and discharge it. What did it arouse in me? The very awareness of/presence in the process of reliving the experience starts the healing.

If we get stuck in an emotion, we give it the energy to continue. In order *to be affected* by something, we must identify ourselves with it. It must have something to "take root in". With the perspective of a good witness, we can observe our feelings without identifying with them, both feel them and be able to stand outside ourselves. Let the feeling come forward, feel through it and let go of it.

If you are unable to take care of the feeling when it arises, *change posture*, breathe deeply and do something else. In order to get rid of the feeling in the long term, *try not to move at all* (this reduces the feeling) and start exploring. Ideally, we should – when we lose our internal balance – be like a tightrope artist: stand still, breathe, and restore the balance, before we take the next step.

Eventually, it becomes easier to sense, for example, a feeling of sadness, and release it by breathing *with* it and letting it pass through the body. To be able to welcome all thoughts and feelings, knowing that we can take care of them and transform them into a higher frequency.

This also applies to tears – to welcome our tears. They have been given to us for our usage. Tears heal, but we have to *be present* in the crying, to indulge and let the tears loose. Reluctant or restrained tears will not remove the "congestion" in the system and will not have the healing effect. You need not be afraid of getting caught up in tears, they dry up after a while and leave behind a pleasant feeling of relaxation. See your tears as a tool for liberation and healing.

Even difficult memories can be dissolved. With determination and practice, we can eventually come to terms with what has happened to us in life, accept that it occurred and is part of our history, without having to accept the treatment to which we have been exposed.

We should remember that joy and happiness is a state of being. Happiness is not "over there", is not out there, it is within us and we can learn to elicit the state of mind that we desire.

Chapter 9 – Subpersonalities

"I'm not myself," said the poet and dramatist Kristina Lugn on TV[1] and after a pause added: "and for that I am grateful". This sparked great laughter in the audience and even at our house. But in most cases we would probably just want to be able to be ourselves.

We can work with our limitations in many ways, and we can do it directly through observation – in other words, by using our inner observer. But if you like working with images and forms, subpersonalities is a fun and fruitful way to identify strengths and weaknesses. I became immensely fascinated in this area during the late 80's when I came in contact with *What We May Be*, by psychiatrist Piero Ferrucci, a book on Psychosynthesis – where one works a lot with subpersonalities.

Working with subpersonalities helps us to integrate opposites within us, identify our internal troublemakers and reach greater inner consistency. Opposites and paradoxes may perhaps make life more interesting and also serve creative purposes – they can be an incentive to express ourselves in different ways. For example, how would Ingmar Bergman's films have looked if he had not had his "daemons"? But we will inevitably experience insecurity if we identify ourselves only with the parts of us that shift and change.

Subpersonalities, or subselves, (sometimes called personas or masks) is the name for the elements within us that – because we have not had the opportunity to be ourselves fully – have become distorted and no longer express our true needs. However, subpersonalities are not a collection of unrelated parts existing within us – under the surface is our center, our true Self.

1 Epiphany Concert from Berwaldhallen, Stockholm (2007).

Each subpersonality represents a need in me. But if some parts of me have conflicting needs, there will be imbalance in the whole, resulting in disharmony and reduced energy flow.

In Psychosynthesis, the many parts of our personality – our different needs – are often compared to an orchestra, an ensemble of actors or the crew of a ship. In order to function, we have to integrate the elements so that they play the same tune, play or work for the same purpose. It would not work if all members of the orchestra played their own piece of music. We must make the parts cooperate, not fight each other. It is not about repressing or disposing of any one part. They should remain inside, but some parts should not be allowed to take over and control the others. We need to develop a strong conductor/director/captain who can make our subselves cooperate for the common good – the bigger picture – and together become more than the parts.

Working with subpersonalities means identifying elements within us that have been distorted, given too much space and have started to dominate us; and to find symbols for these, so we can label them. We should then more easily be able to recognize them and bring them to the surface, and thereby transform them. Once again we need look out for recurring thought- and emotional patterns; old programs that we easily get stuck in. See what they stand for, and whether they benefit our well-being or hinder us.

Common subpersonalities

In our culture we often have a strong inner critic/judge/faultfinder; and if you have a strong critic, there is often also a strong rebel. "You are too fat," says the critic, "you have to lose weight!" Whereupon the rebel quickly stuffs in two cakes.

The inner critic is often perceived as someone who sits on our shoulder, constantly commenting on everything we do. The critic is sometimes mistaken for our inner observer, but the observer never criticizes. Being in the constant presence of a critic is destructive, so identifying your inner critic is usually a huge relief. In other words, being able to see that this is just *one* of many voices inside; and that

I can choose to listen to it or not. We can pat ourselves on the back and say: "I hear you. Thanks for your interest" and then leave it – if we so wish.

We often have inconsistent elements within us, each wanting to assert its views and needs. Other contradictory conceptions I have encountered over the years are for instance the Slave-driver and the Lazy One, the Bohemian and the Pedant, the Duty Man and the Pleasure Man, the Adventurer and the Security-addict. The more clearly we see these conflicting needs, the easier we can strike a balance between them.

Other examples of common subpersonalities are the Whiner, the Wiseacre/Clever Clogs, the Avenger/Avengeress, the Devil, the Saboteur, the Geisha, the Victim and the Martyr. Certain subselves are more ingrained and do not so easily come forward, such as the Vulnerable and the Small Inner Child.

The Victim is often the last subpersonality we are willing to release, as without it we can no longer blame anyone else. The Martyr/Victim looks for love and appreciation through the "poor me", who says "see me, listen to me, see what I do, how I sacrifice myself. Appreciate me, love me." But this strategy is doomed to failure. The Martyr generates guilt, which is the whole point – to control the surroundings by making everyone feel bad – but if there is something people do not want to feel, it is guilt. The Martyr is therefore rarely loved, so it is better to fulfill our need for attention and confirmation through other means.

The solution is to *acknowledge* these parts so they dare to show themselves. Accept that I house these "inner guests", start to get familiar with them and their real needs. To see both sides of a contradiction helps us to balance it and eventually be able to see what lies beyond. On a deeper level the opposites come together. In short – to see, accept and acknowledge. Then they lose power, their outlines begin to soften and they will transform by themselves.

Limited perspective

By observing ourselves in different situations, seeing how we react, which views we express, we can identify areas where we tend to take on a role, a mask, not fully be ourselves. For instance, occasions where I think I need to seem smarter than I am. Then reflect upon what these situations arouse in me.

As long as I see life from the viewpoint of one, or another, of my subpersonalities and only identify myself with the individual parts – instead of my center – my perception of reality will vary depending on whom inside me is in charge at that moment. When I can see the various parts more clearly, and also sense a deeper level within myself, I can take a step aside, watch them and more easily make them work together – for the benefit of the whole.

Sometimes, it can be confusing to discover parts of ourselves not seen before, and which we do not appreciate. We may want to distance ourselves and it may take time before we fully accept these sides. However, without acknowledgement, they will become even more deeply rooted. We will get stuck in duality, in "pressure and counter-pressure". It is necessary that they are made apparent, that we recognize and welcome them; so we can begin to dissolve them. There is a reason for these patterns; they are parts within me that have not been fully expressed. They have a legitimate need that I have to acknowledge – and they contain energy to be released!

Identifying a subpersonality

Sit or lie down comfortably, relax your body and think of a prominent characteristic in yourself, something that is "typically you". Let an inner picture emerge which represents that part of you – it could be a person, an animal, an object or similar. Do not try to conjure up the image, let it appear by itself.

Observe the picture without judging it in any way. Allow it to be just as it is and to change if it wants to. Feel the sensation that the image is conveying.

Let your subpersonality express itself. If you want, you can ask questions, such as: What is important to you? What are you afraid of? What are your real needs? Why are you in my life?

Give your subpersonality a name, symbolizing what it wants to express.

Write down the information you receive, so you can look back on it and more easily identify this part of yourself in the future. Get familiar with this subself until you can recognize it when it shows up in everyday life.

Then repeat the exercise with some of your most common traits, so you get a clearer idea of the characters that live inside you.

As we become more aware of these elements and contradictions within ourselves, we can talk to them in everyday life and harmonize their energies; for example when Pleasure Man wants to go out and sunbathe and Duty Man has decided it is time to clean. If I choose to go out, it is important that I am not accompanied by a chattering Duty Man who will ruin my day, but make it clear to him/her that there will be time for cleaning, and that I take full responsibility for the decision to enjoy the sunshine.

Transforming a subpersonality

In order to transform a subpersonality to a higher level of consciousness we can use images of ascent, like visualizing a mountain. We simply take our subpersonality with us and begin to climb the mountain, and by the time we get to the top, the figure tends to change by itself and regain its original shape.

As an example, I can explain how I got rid of the "Protestor". The Protestor got her name because, during my childhood, I had a very strong desire to protest. Earlier I had interpreted this as strength and freedom to speak up, but when I started working with myself, I discovered that I was protesting just for the sake of it, and that I was controlled by it. I simply named this part of me the Protestor and read about how to change this side of me by taking her up a mountain.

Curious as usual, I set out. The Protestor was sore and obstinate and did not want to come along. I had to struggle and pull her up. She spat, hissed and kicked about. When I finally got her up the mountain, I turned for just a second – and when I looked back at her again, I found an angry little girl sitting with her heels stuck firmly in the ground, wildly protesting: "I don't want to, I don't want to, I am *never* allowed to decide." It was me at 3-4 years of age! And I said to her – of course you can have a say and decide and we talked for a while. Then I took her by the hand and we walked together down the mountain.

It was a strange experience for me because it was the first time I had done this kind of exercise and probably had my doubts about the outcome. The Protestor disappeared almost immediately out of my life and was the easiest subpersonality to transform.

More difficult was my "Little Miss Sprinter" subpersonality, the part of me that always thinks it is urgent and that a disaster will occur, if she does not hurry up. She has the ability to imperceptibly take hold of me and suddenly I see the world through her eyes and get the idea that it is very urgent – an imperceptible shift from my center to her perspective. Nowadays, I notice her more quickly, I know from where she arose, I see her needs, and can take countermeasures; in this case, just to sit down and for my inner eye observe her endless struggle. Then she calms down. This part of me contains so much energy and loves to have many balls in the air, but she has also caused me a great deal of trouble. I need to constantly keep an eye on her, otherwise she may carry me away.

If you want to transform a subpersonality, you can use the following exercise. Select a subpersonality you are already familiar with and that you would like to know more about.

Sit or lie comfortably and begin to relax your body. Notice your breathing until you feel calm and peaceful.

Imagine that you are at the bottom of a mountain together with your subpersonality. It is a brilliant day and you both start walking up the mountain. Look around while you walk, take time to enjoy the nature, see the colors, listen to the sounds. Maybe you hear birds, a small babbling brook or the sound of a distant waterfall.

Enjoy the beautiful day. Feel the freshness in the air – see how the view gets wider, the higher and higher you go.

Watch your subpersonality while you walk. Is it changing in any way?

When you reach the top, allow the sunlight to flow over both of you and reveal a deeper level of your subself. Let your subpersonality express itself. Does it want to convey something to you? Share what it has to say and see if it changes further.

Do not be disappointed if nothing happens. Often we have to do these exercises many times before we experience change. We also need to make sure that we no longer have any opposition to our subpersonality; that I have fully acknowledged this aspect of myself. Nor should we exaggerate in our hunt for subpersonalities, but rather be satisfied with a few distinctive features, that we want to change. Other elements can also appear of their own accord later on.

Larger units

Since we view the world differently depending on the subpersonality in which we currently find ourselves, life can easily be confusing if we are not in contact with our inner core. Decisions made by a subpersonality can cause internal conflicts and it is important that we can connect to our center to gain perspective. If we sense that we are not centered, we can ask for time to consider and perhaps sleep on it, so we have a chance to reconnect before taking important decisions. If I am anchored in my center, I will have the same views tomorrow as next month.

By working with individual aspects of ourselves in this way, we can get them to merge into larger and larger units. We are able to rise above the parts, achieve a more coherent state and transform their energy. It is *good* to have a healthy critic/supporter that guides me; it is *good* to be clever and so on. We can more easily see the real need and what was distorted. See what comes from love versus fear, what comes from joy, true desire and pure eagerness to get things done. See what is driven by the ego – fear of not being good enough, being inadequate, rejected and so on – and needs to be transformed to a higher level of consciousness. This will give increased vitality and deeper meaning in life.

Chapter 10 – Transpersonal development

There are many paths up the mountain's peak,
but the view from there is always the same.

Chinese proverb

The Self or our higher Self describes the part within us that always stays the same – other names are our authentic Self, our transcendental Self, our center, the essence, the source, Being, pure consciousness or our heart point (which we will come back to later). Yes, a dear child has many names – an impressive amount, when considering the difficulty of describing the state, but they all aim to depict the higher intelligence that we have the potential to reach. Or as Piero Ferrucci puts it in *What We May Be* – "our true essence beyond all masks and conditionings".

Transpersonal psychology or "height psychology" is a term for the teachings that make use of the spiritual dimension for our development. Instead of dwelling on, and going deeper into the problems at the personality level, we look for solutions on a higher plane. By utilizing a higher state of consciousness – with a broader perspective – experiences can be transformed, seen in a new light and brought to a higher level.

The transpersonal Self and the pure consciousness are often portrayed in literature as the same dimension, and although these levels merge in the end, I think it is useful to distinguish between them here.

I therefore choose to divide them into two levels:

Firstly – the transpersonal Self, because we often relate it to ourselves and experience it as a higher form/identity – a level we can reach and at the same time be human beings engaged in everyday life.

Secondly – the pure universal consciousness, before it took any form.

I see the Self as still a "formed" energy – in contrast to the non-formed energy of pure consciousness – and use the transpersonal Self as a term for the level of development where we are in contact with our spiritual intelligence (SQ) and where we also have a conscious, intuitive communication between the personality and the higher intelligence. (See also the description of the transpersonal Self in Chapter 3, *Levels of identity*.)

But the division into levels is not the interesting point. It is the intellect's division of something that is actually not divisible. At these levels, it is the *experience* itself that is the explanation (or that which makes all explanations unnecessary) and I guess the main point is to get it so clear and understandable that we can make use of the different states of consciousness, experiences and insights.

The next step in our development

More and more people seem to have transpersonal experiences and one explanation for this may be that it is the next step in our human development. A shift in our perception from the parts, towards the whole; a raising of consciousness because we have reached a more coherent state with a greater balance between the different parts of our personality.

I once read that the word eccentric in the original sense means to live outside one's center (ex center) and that a few hundred years ago it was considered a mental disorder. Today, probably most of us in the West would get this diagnosis. Or "no one at home" as the native said when he looked the Westerner in the eyes.

As pointed out earlier, we cannot receive lasting happiness and fulfillment from the outside world. That kind of satisfaction needs to be continually replenished. A new job, new partner, new house and new activities – it never ends. Without contact with our higher Self, we will always live in a state of deficiency. We can ease the sense of emptiness with new "things" and activities which give short-term distraction and an energy boost, but soon we are back again and have to buy ourselves some form of relief.

Our ongoing activities are often a substitute for the essence; an escape from the pain of being separated from the whole. When we are in perfect harmony, *what* we do is less important; it is more about *how* we do it. Most probably, the lack of contact with the essence causes most forms of addiction; a way of trying to fill the inner emptiness from outside. Our imperfect personality is constantly busy trying to reach a perfect state – consciously or unconsciously.

Our natural state

I wrote earlier that there is a point inside us where there is always total peace. It is probably not really a point, but we experience it often as a "point of harmony" – a unifying center – deep within us, where we can experience a state of wholeness, boundlessness and that we are part of everything. A state where we just "are" and can observe what is happening from a more all-encompassing perspective. Where we can "let it be" without identifying ourselves with one thing or the other and look at our daily tasks in a more compassionate way. See how we often get stuck on the superficial level, how we are *so* caught up by the small things that we believe the details to be the whole. By observing this through the intelligence of the Self, we can gain a distance and better proportions in our individual lives and the world at large.

To be in contact with Being is our natural state. The spiritual intelligence, SQ/VQ, is our original intelligence (before earthly influence) and when in contact with it we can move beyond our "normal" way of thinking, if we wish. We all experience glimpses of this higher intelligence, moments of clarity, aha-experiences, which can be very enlightening, but often disappear in seconds. Often such a powerful experience that we think our whole world is changing and then, twenty seconds later, we do not remember what it was! If we want to capture these moments, we should be quick to note them down. In order for insights of this kind to become integrated and for us to make use of them in everyday life, they need to be anchored in the intellect as well. So, paper and stubby pencils in every pocket is a must!

Although contact with Being is a natural state, *consciously* living in alignment with our higher Self is a lifelong process. We may have "filters" of varying strength, which help or hinder this perception, but we must also *choose* to open ourselves up to these levels. It is a question of a conscious development, where we voluntarily begin to give up our ego. Where we *want* to change ourselves. We see our higher potential, get a glimpse of who we are meant to be and our personality willingly aligns with the Self.

When we are in our everyday mind, it can be difficult to explain these states since reality appears so differently in different states of consciousness. We have to experience it; otherwise it is all just words and may sound "fuzzy" to many people. But fuzzy and mysterious is often what we call things that do not agree with our current perception of reality, what we do not understand. As soon as we understand, we call it knowledge and the step between the two is sometimes only a matter of seconds – an aha-*experience* and I have gained an insight!

No bird flies too high
when flying with its own wings.
Freely translated from
William Blake

Authentic power

Authentic power comes from the Self and is boundless. It arises from contact with the essence and gives a deeper meaning to our life and our mission. It gives us a broader perspective, helps us to see our deeper values and make choices that are in tune with our higher purpose. A kind of alliance between the personality and our higher Self. When the personality is "in sync" with the Self, it does not "fight", but fulfills with delight the vision of the Self and gains the power to resist temptations that are not in line with our long-term purpose (that only cause us to lose strength). From the vantage point of the

Self, we can see what needs to be dealt with in our personality – but also see that in a deeper sense, we are already there – and this inner security and trust will guide our behavior and our actions.

Our self becomes more coherent the higher levels we reach, more integrated with the source. We become more energy self-sufficient and are less dependent on the people around us to fill our needs. We are able to fill ourselves – in the coherent state we are constantly refilled, and when in contact with the Self we cannot experience stress, anxiety or loneliness. Fatigue occurs when we close ourselves up and are cut off from the source. The presence, the contact with the whole is felt even physically; the depth of the breathing, the relaxation, the lightness, the clarity – often a feeling of delight in the chest, in the heart area.

In contact with our transpersonal Self, we can more clearly see our own and other people's motives, without being caught up emotionally, becoming angry or sentimental. Being able to accept and let it be. Realizing that other people also have a higher Self – as wise as mine – and having confidence in the ability of others to find their own solutions. Rip up your scripts for other people – as Gerald Jampolsky, M.D. and psychiatrist, tells us in *Love is the Answer.*

Depression

Our higher Self never gets depressed – it is not affected by earthly matters. Surely then, a spiritually-developed person could not be depressed? Of course they can, but it means they lost contact with their spiritual dimension at that moment. It is impossible to be in both a coherent state (in contact with the essence) and depressed – which implies a fragmented state. It is therefore important to pursue a lifestyle that allows us to constantly maintain contact with the whole – through meditation, nature or other energy sources. Deep peace and joy produces healthy hormones, and our nervous system will change over time if we have regular contact with the essence. Personally I notice, when I have been neglecting my meditations for a while, that I return to the personality level and begin to identify myself with it – with a more limited view as result.

We cannot experience anxiety when in touch with our spiritual dimension. The first step should therefore be to restore peace and thereby also alter the chemical balance in the body. Being in contact with the whole provides greater protection against worry, depression and anxiety. We can just speculate how much depression is due to people being stuck at the level of "worthlessness/nothingness" (see Chapter 8 *The emotional layers*).

We will not fall into the darkness as long as we identify ourselves with the light – as long as some part of us is in the light. There, by using our inner observer, we can watch the darkness without being engulfed by it. I began this book with the words "what do you do when the road you are traveling suddenly comes to an end" and you are hit by confusion and darkness. If we go further into the darkness, we encounter the light. The problems exist within us. *So do the solutions.*

Viktor Frankl puts special emphasis on the importance of the spiritual dimension for healing and being the cure of neuroses and depression. Getting distance to problems by raising ourselves to a higher level – often with the help of humor (which puts us in a coherent state).

We should also remember that our nervous system has difficulty distinguishing between imaginary and real dangers. We inevitably become part of what we participate in, and people who often see scary movies, violence and the like are said to more easily become depressed. (Fear puts us in a separate state.)

Spirituality and religion

People have always sought a larger context, a meaning in life, the underlying truth. Many are intimidated by the word spiritual and associate it with religion. But spirit is the same word as respire, to be in contact with your breathing. The Latin inspirare (to inhale), high spirits, to be inspired, and thus be in touch with one's spiritual intelligence, the essence. We can reach this contact whether we belong to a religion or not. We do not even need to know how to read and write. We can still be highly spiritually developed. It may even be an advantage – children and so-called "primitive people" live in contact with their spiritual side. It is our natural intelligence that we are born with, but which is often extinguished when we are "schooled" in the currently-prevailing conception of reality.

Spiritual development has no connection to religion or the church, not automatically anyway. Religious people can be highly spiritually developed or not at all. One can have beliefs (IQ) but lack the inner growth. We can see this within the church, where there is at least as much controversy as in other areas of society.

Our spiritual dimension is infinite, and exists before the "form". Religion, however, has form – it is *formed* by people and has rules and orders. As humans, we can choose to belong to some form of religion, but we can also choose to cultivate our spirituality without forms, through contact with the essence.

The most important thing is that we choose those words/symbols that hold the deepest meaning and have the strongest resonance within us; symbols that help us to reach a higher state. The difficulty with the *word* God is that it has been affected both by religious interpreters and by the scientific perception of reality and can lead us to perceiving God as something outside ourselves, thus putting us in a separate state. As a course leader I prefer using "a higher intelligence" as the name for what is above all belief systems, then everyone can participate and feel at ease.

We all want to be in touch with our SQ and experience peace, joy, creativity and spirituality. We can choose the symbols that help us attain this state beyond duality and choose the faith – no faith is also a faith – that gives our lives the highest meaning. The universal intelligence pervades everything and everyone, and stands above religions and divisions such as "my God" and "your God" (at the same time as all religions probably see themselves as spiritual and this dimension is also the origin of all religions).

Irrespective of the symbol we choose, we need great awareness and willingness to actively and consciously listen, in order to live in alignment with our innermost nature. It gives us a deeper understanding which permeates our thoughts, feelings and actions and gives us a larger context.

The good, the true, the beautiful, the one

Most of us strive to find and express our "truth". We can see this in the artist looking for the true expression in his paintings, the musician in his playing, the actor who seeks the authentic expression in his acting. It often involves a de-layering towards simplicity. The painter wishes to express his intention in a single stroke. A movement towards the center, the heart of the matter.

Much has been written about the creative anguish people can feel and that creativity benefits from a degree of "suffering". Even if internal conflicts can be a driving force to express ourselves (and even if we can feel frustration when we are not able to bring about what we want), we are still in the very *creative moment* in contact with our spiritual, creative intelligence – and this intelligence is always there for us.

Seeking one's truth means that we have to walk the path ourselves. For as long as we have not explored our consciousness, we are what Krishnamurti calls "second hand human beings", living in a perception of reality we have learned from others.

The more our identity is in Being (the one we *are*), the less important it is to be acknowledged by the outside world, in order to feel appreciated. We become less vulnerable and can focus on what feels meaningful and leads to growth, both for ourselves and others.

To "cross our tracks"

For most of us, development towards the higher Self is not a straight path. Just as we are heading our way to new heights, we fall back to levels we thought we had left for good. We "cross our tracks", old things catch up with us and we have to work with parts of our personality that we have not yet developed. Sometimes it can feel like we are back to "square one" but the mere fact that I now can call my situation square one means that I have gained a new perspective, in other words, grown.

Our inner work brings up barriers and limitations not seen before and in comparison to our ideal self-image we may feel extremely inadequate (sometimes totally worthless). We all have blind spots that take time to see through. Dead ends where we get stuck. But with perseverance and patience we can eventually reach a new level with more intense natural flow and greater alignment with the essence.

Before we reach a new level of maturity, we often go through a period of disorientation. We shed our skin, long for the previous shell and do not see that the weakness we feel is the beginning of a greater and more genuine power.

It is important that we clear ourselves from lower energies, before we go too high. Otherwise, the discrepancy between the different elements within us can be too great and cause unnecessary confusion. So we need to work on "two fronts" to slowly but surely create a more coherent identity. Taking responsibility for actively raising ourselves to higher levels of consciousness while also clearing the internal debris, that pulls us down.

While it may be painful to scrutinize oneself, the pain is probably necessary for us to start our inner work. *Only the one who is suffering asks "why"*, said the Indian spiritual teacher Ravi Shankar in a television program. Those who feel good rarely ask themselves, "why am I so happy?", and in periods where most things work well, it is easy to forget that we should maybe still move forward in our development.

Release the genie from the bottle

At the personality level, we are all different, but the more we evolve and identify with our higher Self, the greater the similarity; the closer to the "source", the larger the unity. We leave the personal viewpoint and see life more from a universal perspective.

When we go far enough inwards or upwards – whichever image we prefer – opposites move closer together and transcend to a higher level. Piero Ferrucci describes the unity of opposites like this in *What we may be:* "Like the two sides of a gothic arch, they approach each other as they mount, till they converge and fuse into a *synthesis*" creating "a new psychological reality which is more than the sum of its parts."

Once we are in contact with our higher Self in everyday life the experience of the world and life becomes more hologram-like.[1] Even if we experience the parts, focus on one thing, the whole universe is there in every part. The whole makes the background to our experience of the parts, and makes the world and our personal self more connected. As we know, "whole" stands for the coexistence of opposites.

The all-embracing intelligence is a loving intelligence that offers other solutions to our problems than when we use only the intellect (IQ). The realization that we are part of everything often gives rise to a desire to contribute to the good of the world. One wonders, how can I use my talent to contribute to a better world? Find solutions that benefit the whole (in which we are also included) and we can experience a great freedom when we realize that there is actually no winning or losing, as everything eventually comes together.

When in contact with Being, we are not as sensitive to individual situations and have greater distance and tolerance to everyday burdens – a sense of peace, whatever happens. I have often read about "a peace that passes all comprehension". I have always thought that this sounded a bit theatrical, but it is true in as much as we cannot understand or reach it with the intellect. This is a state of completeness beyond duality, and therefore nothing can be seen as "better". Thus, there is no other place to yearn for. Actually, we only need to open ourselves to this peace. Attune to it. It is there as a background all the time, but we might not notice it.

If we want to know how much of our security and identity we place in the outside world, we can try to take away – piece by piece – work and hobbies for instance. Who am I? Remove partner, children. Who am I then? Take away friends, my home. Who am I? In the end, I am only my consciousness.

How much peace do I feel? If I am in deep contact with Being, peace will remain intact. This level is not influenced by changes belonging to the physical world/reality, but can observe the coming and going of forms and see that one part of me is still there. Of course, this does not mean that my earthly self would not grieve and be affected by such losses, but I can gain relief from having an overall perspec-

---

1 Hologram, see Chapter 11 *The holographic model.*

tive, bringing in a higher dimension. Even if I cannot reach peace at that moment, I know I will be able to reconnect to it.

Chapter 11 – Consciousness

Pure consciousness, before it has identified with any form, empty of content, just vibrating energy, all-encompassing and nonlocal – nothing and everything. How can we describe that? Thinking logically, this chapter should be blank.

As I write this, I am reading an article[1] on the Russian Andrei Linde, one of the world's leading cosmologists and good friend of Stephen Hawking, where he speculates "that our description of the universe may remain incomplete as long as we do not solve the mystery of consciousness. Perhaps our inner reality is even more real than the material world outside."[2]

Many scientists believe that consciousness may be the primary reality, out of which the secondary material reality emerges. Consciousness could thus be the basis of our entire reality, so what could be more interesting than trying to broaden our understanding of that?

What is consciousness?

So far, nobody has been able to identify what consciousness is, and no scientist has found its location. The pure consciousness is not static; it is living, dynamic, beyond thought, beyond form, and therefore difficult to "pinpoint". Nor has it been possible to find consciousness in our brain, even if we use our brain to be conscious of consciousness. Fortunately, we do not need a *definition* of what consciousness is to be able to make use of it.

---

1 The Swedish journal Forskning och Framsteg (April 2007).

2 Author's translation.

Even though no one has been able to definitively "prove" what consciousness is, there are many "theories" and also models of explanation.

Peter Koestenbaum, Ph.D., business and leadership philosopher and former Professor of philosophy at San Jose State University in California, writes in his book *Is There an Answer to Death?* that we humans live in two worlds, "the universal and the particular", and that in addition to being physical beings, we are also spiritual beings. He means that when we talk about a term like pure consciousness, we cannot use analytical, logical thinking. Clarity and accuracy belong to the material world, while the cosmic consciousness is "everything". "Being, like consciousness, is an indefinable term", says Koestenbaum.

In the magazine Alpha Omega, Ervin Laszlo says that in modern science there is no longer a clear distinction between the material world and the energy world. "Life and mind are mutually interrelated elements within an overall process that is very complex, forming a harmonious creation. Space and time are united into the dynamic background of the observable universe."[3] He says that matter is no longer believed to be "a fundamental property of reality" but has been replaced by energy and interconnected fields as the basic elements in the universe. "Cosmos is a seamless whole, which has evolved over eons, and has created conditions for the emergence of life and thereafter consciousness." He adds that modern science is now beginning to confirm the ancient Eastern understanding of the inherent unity of everything.

In her book *The Quantum Self*, Danah Zohar speaks of similarities between thought processes and quantum processes and she believes that the quantum vacuum has the same physical structure as the human consciousness, a Bose-Einstein condensate, a process that seeks the most complex combinations and is "the most coherent form of order possible in Nature, the order of unbroken wholeness".

She writes: "The crucial distinguishing feature of Bose-Einstein condensates is that the many parts that go to make up an ordered system not only *behave* as a whole, they *become* whole; their identities merge or overlap in such a way that they lose their individuality

3 Author's translation.

entirely." Danah Zohar says that she believes such a Bose-Einstein condensation among neuron constituents to be "the physical basis of consciousness".

She also gives an interesting insight into how this fusion of identities could come about and describes it as a dance of vibrating molecules which – at a critical frequency – would vibrate as one unit, as one dancer with one identity.

To me, this sounds very similar to the Eastern description of the Hindu God Shiva, where "the cosmic dancer" Shiva, through his dance, maintains the dynamics between the diversity and unity of the universe.

Fritjof Capra, atomic physicist with good knowledge of Eastern philosophy writes in *The Tao of Physics* that the Eastern perspective's foremost characteristic is the awareness of the basic unity of everything, that all things are seen as "interdependent and inseparable parts" of the same cosmic whole; "as different manifestations of the same ultimate reality".

He says that this basic unity is now one of modern physics' most important revelations. "It becomes apparent at the atomic level and manifests itself more and more as one penetrates deeper into matter, down into the realm of subatomic particles." He believes that this unity is going to be an important aspect when comparing modern physics and Eastern philosophy.

Does everything have a consciousness?

Everything probably does have a consciousness, in some sense of the word. Why else would the things we study – even *objects* – react to our observation?

"In atomic physics", Fritjof Capra writes "the scientist cannot play the role of a detached objective observer, but becomes involved in the world he observes to the extent that he influences the properties of the observed objects." He also refers to Professor of theoretical physics John Wheeler, regarded as one of America's foremost in the area, who considers this understanding within quantum theory to be its most essential feature and has therefore proposed that the term

”observer” be replaced by ”participator”. Capra adds that besides this, quantum theory may also need to include the human consciousness in order to describe reality.

The author Eva Dahlbeck, citing a large number of scientists in her book *På kärlekens villkor*, writes that according to later research, humans are an inseparable part of nature and that we are ”governed by the same laws as everything we observe. And not only that! We contribute to the existence of everything, and everything contributes to our own. In order to thoroughly crush our illusions of an absolute existing matter, we can note a further finding in recent studies of reality: it has been shown that nature does not exist without our observation; that nothing exists without being observed, without taking form in a consciousness.“[4]

According to Eva Dahlbeck, the explanation of this is said to be that “everything – even all that is visible – is made up of energies, types of power centers, which make up atoms, and atoms in turn take shape only through the energy transfer arising from our observation.”

She also says that there are leading scientists who believe “that quantum theory has solved the mystery of consciousness and its relationship to the material world, they mean that reality comes about when information reaches the brain of the observer. Driven to extremes, this idea means that the universe may become tangible only when someone perceives it – that it is created by its own inhabitants!”

In an interview,[5] Avery Solomon, mathematician and philosopher, says that ”nothing is objective in the eyes of the viewer and knowledge, therefore, is always fragmented and colored. What we have named knowledge to this point is faith and the spiritual reality called faith ... may in fact be the real knowledge”.

“The world, says Avery Solomon, is given, genuine. It is our version of the world that is constructed ... Knowledge is the filter through which your consciousness is watching. The question is what our consciousness would see if the filter was not there? Or rather,

---

4 Author´s translation.

5 The Swedish newspaper Svenska Dagbladet (October 10, 1999), *Allting är ett enda stort medvetande.*

would the world exist without the interpretation? And how would it then look?"[6]

This is definitely worth reflection! But let us proceed and look at a model which has had a big impact, namely

The holographic model

This theory – presented by physicist David Bohm and Karl Pribham, Ph.D. and world-famous neuroscientist – has been of great importance for the new paradigm we are considered to be entering. The theory embraces the belief that the universe could be a hologram.[7]

If universe is a hologram – in which case our brains are also holograms – then it is highly probable that we humans, in certain conditions, can gain access to a higher intelligence.

Here, I want to refer to the now-classic book *The Holographic Paradigm and other Paradoxes*, compiled by the philosopher and psychologist Ken Wilber, where Wilber and others cite Karl Pribram:

"Thus, if the brain did function like a hologram, then it might have access to a larger whole, a field domain or 'holistic frequency realm' that transcended spatial and temporal boundaries. And this domain, reasoned Pribram, might very likely be the same domain of transcendental unity-in-diversity described (and experienced) by the world´s great mystics and sages."

Pribram believes that our brains perform "mathematical calculations" and that without the brain's ability to convert, we would experience the world on the frequency level. He also says that our brain could have a type of "lens" which can transform these frequencies into the reality we normally perceive.

Our brains would thus build up our physical reality by transforming these frequencies; and by going beyond everyday consciousness and its limited capacity, we would be able to make contact with the "invisible matrix" that is the basis of our reality.

6 Author´s translation.

7 A hologram is a type of optical storage system, like a photographic plate, which can store information so the whole picture is in every part. If you were to cut out a part of the picture and enlarge it to its original size, the whole picture would be found in this part. The part is in the whole, and the whole is in each part.

The void

While it may not appear so in our everyday lives, it seems that most of the universe is a void. A void filled with highly concentrated energy, containing the possibilities of everything that can happen. Every*thing* is created out of no*thing*! By making contact with this void, we can, by means of *experience*, gain a deeper understanding of the underlying oneness, from where everything originates and to which everything returns.

I remember one time – during meditation – when I came to the insight that the wonderful state of nothingness and pure-being that I was then experiencing, must be the same void that could feel so frightening when in a state of anxiety. Could this beloved, yearned-for state be the same void that can be such a horrifying experience when we are approaching the point of annihilation (Chapter 8). Could it really be like this? Yes, the void is probably the same but we approach it from different states of mind and therefore experience it in completely different ways – connected or separated. From a state of love or from fear. When the void feels threatening, we have lost touch with the whole and can feel as if we are to be disbanded and destroyed; which is probably what happens in that we are "disbanded" from the ego for a moment. But if we explore the void further, the experience turns into a deep inner peace.

Thinking and consciousness

"Thinking and consciousness are not synonymous. Thinking is only a small aspect of consciousness. Thought cannot exist without consciousness, but consciousness does not need thought" says Eckhart Tolle, scientist and author, in *The Power of Now*.

Krishnamurti writes in *Freedom from the Known* about our human consciousness: "A living mind is a still mind, a living mind is a mind that has no centre and therefore no space and time. Such a mind is limitless and that is the only truth, that is the only reality."

Krishnamurti was a very good friend of David Bohm. They had profound conversations – preserved in book form – and both considered that thinking hides and distorts reality.

Obviously we have to turn the concepts around and realize: it is the consciousness which makes it possible for the brain to create our physical reality, consciousness is the foundation of our thinking. Thinking can only exist within what is already known and does not have access to domains beyond time and space, so solving the mystery of existence by thinking would probably be impossible.

The thinker is doomed

Renée Weber, Professor of philosophy, says in *The Holographic Paradigm* that the illusion of a personal thinker is related to time and death, that the thinker is death-bound, but consciousness is not.

The more our identity is in Being, the more we can understand that death may not exist the way we normally see it, that it is actually an illusion based on duality. Life and death: the ongoing build up and breakdown. Breathe in, breathe out. Moving beyond duality may help us to a greater understanding. For me, it makes a huge difference when I can experience this on a deeper level, even if I am often absorbed in everyday life and forget the wisdom. But we can always go within and reconnect to the coherent state of mind to get a higher perspective on life. Pure consciousness is eternal and thus beyond death.

Peter Strang, M.D. and Professor in palliative medicine at the Karolinska Institutet, Stockholm Sweden, who has been with many people on their deathbed, says in a TV interview (as written down by me): During life, many people fear death, but when death approaches, people suddenly realize that they will soon die and in the last days all worry is gone. They find something out which makes all anxiety disappear. They become a little bit absent in a positive way. Many sense the presence of a deceased relative, of their father or an old grandmother, and see them being in a peaceful place. He also says that when a person dies, the energy in the room becomes dense and charged – a positive force. Something happens and, it may be imagination, but it happens every time.

An "aristocrat in living"

Maybe we can reach this peaceful state of mind during our lives by moving beyond duality. Peter Koestenbaum writes in *Is There an Answer to Death?*: "With the discovery of the dimension of the eternal in us, a great peace descends over our existence. "He believes this could be the experience that gives mankind the freedom we seek and that when we have integrated this insight in our daily limited lives we can live as "a free person and an aristocrat in living".

Koestenbaum says that we can choose to see reality from the individual perspective only "which gives us existential, social, and political reality"; but we can also choose to open ourselves to "the universal or cosmic consciousness (or The Eternal Now) that runs through us, and this is a choice that gives us immortality".

To die from the form can be frightening. But the more we identify with the eternal dimension, the easier it becomes to free ourselves from the bindings of the physical world, to accept that the body and the ego die, but that consciousness is eternal. Do you recall the metaphor of the waves in the sea in Chapter 2; that we can distinguish every single wave but also see that they are an inseparable part of the sea, in constant change.

What if the waves – just like humans – were to see themselves as individuals and compare themselves with each other. Some larger and more powerful, "waving" in a better way; others smaller and more average. From our point of view, we can easily see that they are also parts of a larger whole – connected and separate at the same time, both wave and particle.

What if the waves – when nearing rocks and land – become scared and anxious and think; help, I am going to break apart, I will be finished, wiped out. We can say; no, you will not be wiped out, it just seems that way, you will return to the sea. Yes, but I will not be my own wave anymore. No, we say, but that does not matter, *it is the same sea!*

What if the same is true for us humans – that we have both a particle aspect and a wave aspect and when we die, we once more become part of the infinite sea of energy.

We see it in nature all the time. Flowers that die, only to return again. The very *intelligence* of the flower is still there.

There is no scientific model
that can explain all,
but we can reach inner states
where everything feels explained.

The truth

Maybe we cannot find "an ultimate truth", partly because a "definition" belongs to analytical thinking and it would define consciousness to be separate from something else and therefore not the whole; partly because the universe is alive and the truth has no "defined location". *Everything* is probably a part of the truth, and there are truths at different levels. The truth I experience in everyday life – such as matter and diversity of objects – I will not find at the theta level, where duality has ceased. But the stone I drop on my toe hurts just as much even if I have learned that most of it is empty space.

For my own part, there is a dimension that I can only experience in my *body* – during deep relaxation. The smallest "action", like moving a muscle, interfering in my breathing or observing "actively", makes it disappear – or more accurately, I have separated myself from the total experience. I must be 100 percent the *receiver*, only perceive it, only *be* it. There is just pure vibrating energy, no self or form of identity, no limits to my body, just pure bliss. Naturally, I have tried to explore this condition. Little by little, on different occasions. But to reflect on it, even in the smallest way, means that I have already separated myself from the whole!

According to the Eastern perspective, the ultimate reality is beyond all forms and therefore cannot be described. It is the essence from which all things take form. The Chinese call it *Tao* – the unity beyond *yin* and *yang* – and they say “the Tao that can be told is not Tao”.

Even so, most highly developed people seem to end up with the same “eternal truths” – through inner experience. The closer to the source, the greater the objectivity. There is a big difference between the ego’s black-and-white view and the calm observations of the Self. So even if we cannot find an ultimate truth, we come into contact with more universal laws the closer we get to the source.

Maybe, despite both Eastern and Western theories, we have to accept that a *conceptual* truth cannot be found; be content with only *experiencing* what is beyond words, and be grateful for having the resources to reach inner states, where we can perceive everything as explained.

Finally, we can return to our circle model in Chapter 4 and note that we can only reach the two inner rings in a coherent state of mind, where we perceive the world as interconnected. The outer rings we can either perceive from a coherent perspective – when we are in contact with our center – or from a fragmented perspective – when we see things from the ego’s point of view.

Chapter 12 – A holistic world view

If everything is one big consciousness and *if* we accept the thought that the universe could be a hologram – that everything is interconnected in an inseparable whole, that the energy world is the primary reality from which the secondary, manifest world emerges – what would this mean for our view of the world, for our identity, for our sense of a personal self?

Let us play with the idea! If the consciousness of humanity is essentially one, this means that we are all each other on one level. The saying goes "every man for himself", which would then mean the same thing. We are each other and everything we do influences everything else in all eternity. What I give out will come back to me.

What would this perspective mean for our view of relationships or of love, for example? Well, a complete revolution in rethinking.

What would it mean for our understanding of life, if we were to accept that we are co-creators of our reality and our life situation – both individually and collectively?

What would it mean for our view of health if we accepted that through our thoughts, emotions and actions we can contribute to our health?

We would have to realize what complex beings we are, what resources we have access to and what powers we can develop.

The web of relationships

If the whole exists in every part and every part is in the whole, we are, to some extent, involved in everything that happens and we can never disconnect ourselves from this web of relationships.

We would all be cells in the same universal organism, and every thought, choice and decision would affect (and be affected by) this universal system. Consciously or unconsciously, we communicate with everything around us and are part of all that exists. I have, therefore, a responsibility for my communication – to know what I contribute to the larger unit – but also realize that I am affected by, and am an inseparable part of, the surroundings – whether I like it or not.

Peter Russell, M.A., mathematician, physician, psychologist, and Honorary Member of the Club of Budapest, uses the concept "synergy" to describe the cooperation of all living things. He writes in *The Awakening Earth* that synergy cannot be reached through force or strain, that the single parts in the system work towards their own goals but "in a way that spontaneously supports each other". He says: "An excellent example of a system with high synergy is your own body. You are an assortment of several trillion individual cells, each acting for its own interest, yet each simultaneously supporting the good of the whole ... When for some reason synergy drops and the organism as a whole does not receive the full support of its many parts, it becomes ill. When synergy is lost altogether, the organism dies."

We have to realize that it is of little benefit then to starve certain parts of the organism and over-indulge others. Besides my own individual ambitions, I also need to consider the "larger system" – contribute to a viable world. What is the use of working for my own good, if the larger body is not healthy and in balance. Everything is connected and if the larger body dies, then we all go the same way.

In other words, we need to expand our awareness of the relationship of all things – understand more about our interconnection. In the Western world, we are often strongly focused on the individual. But the development of a personal self differs from one culture to the next. In certain societies, for example in Africa and Asia, people have not developed an individual consciousness in the same way as in the West, but rather see themselves in relation to others. A person *is* something only in relationship to family, relatives and so on, which also brings with it a responsibility for all those relatives; but in many cases also punishes whole families for the wrongs that an individual member has committed, which may seem strange to us. Apparently, we need to be aware of both "the parts and the whole."

Danah Zohar brings a quantum-physical perspective to our relationship-awareness and talks about our "wavelike self", a more fluid self than the denser "particle" identity. She also calls our spiritual level the quantum Self. Stephen Wolinsky writes in his book *Quantum Consciousness* that we will not find our true selves in the "part(icle)" reality.

We have adopted a great number of quantum-physical expressions in our language, such as quantum leap, quantum thinking, quantum Self, quantum logic, quantum memory, quantum consciousness and quantum psychology. Does this also imply that we have already opened our minds to a broader awareness of the interconnectedness of all things?

Transforming the "room"

"Primary reality may be a frequency realm" suggests Ken Wilber in *The Holographic Paradigm.*

"Could it be", asks Eva Dahlbeck, "that in the whole of the human species, there is a built-in predisposition to an extended sphere of experiences, to some more or less adjacent frequency ranges, which have not yet reached their common connection?"[1] Maybe, she writes, the broadened consciousness will be the normal state of mind for the future human.

The consciousness of humanity is one and has to be transformed if we want to change the world, says David Bohm. We have to redesign the room, says Danah Zohar in *ReWiring the Corporate Brain*, meaning that most changes – both personal and organizational – are about "shifting the same old furniture about in the same old room" and then we are surprised that nothing has actually happened. "Real change, fundamental transformation, requires", writes Zohar, "that we change the underlying patterns of thought and emotion that created the old structures in the first place. It means that we have to

1 Author's translation.

redesign the room. Stronger still, it may mean that we have to tear the old room apart and start anew."

If we want to change our reality, we have to go beyond the old frames of reference and open ourselves to new levels of consciousness; establish new neural connections, "rewire" our brains.

A balanced brain

In other words, we need to bridge the gap between the rational, analytical thinking and the associative, intuitive understanding. Improve the balance between our different intelligences (Chapter 5) and be able to unify our IQ, EQ and SQ. We need to develop a more balanced brain – a brain capable of interpreting a holographic universe.

In our culture, we are expected to understand reality through the intellect – from a fragmented state of mind. But the fragmented state gives us a narrow view of the world, as seen from a national viewpoint, an occupational outlook or experienced by a subpersonality, for example. For as long as we see the parts, forms and events without seeing the underlying unity, we are trapped in this limited-reality illusion – often called Maya in the East – that the material world is the primary reality.

The fragmented state generates pain and gives rise to many of the problems in society – competition, struggle for power and confirmation, fear of not having enough, focus on differences rather than similarities.

I believe we can make it easier for ourselves by adopting the concepts of quantum physics, such as the wave/particle duality, even when it is about our inner being. To see the separate, individual aspects as particle-like, and the coherent, relational state as wave-like. To better understand that nothing can exist on its own without its surroundings, that nothing is separate but just seems that way because it appears in its particle aspect. But if we look more closely, the outlines blur and we can see that it is connected to its surroundings – the part is in the whole, and the whole is in each part.

If we explore the "part" deeply enough, for example an emotion, it will dissolve and return to the whole, to the sea of energy. And vice versa, if – when in a coherent state – I start focusing on something separate, it will appear in its particle aspect. Separate or not – it depends on where and how we look. Everything is intertwined.

For my own part, the terms "fragmented" and "coherent" state of consciousness have helped me a great deal in my development; and throughout this book I have chosen to show how we can make it easier for ourselves by more clearly seeing how we shift between the states of either fragmented/individual or coherent/relational. How the fragmented state gives rise to the illusion of loneliness, abandonment, of not being sufficient and the catastrophic feeling of being "nothing" (Chapter 8); while the coherent state gives rise to unity, participation, belonging and being part of everything.

What if I, Marianne, in my particle aspect can be separated from all other particles, but in my wave aspect am connected with everything and everyone. So that even if I am a separate body, I can still be part of all on the wave-level.

What if our consciousness constantly shifts between the wave- and the particle-state without us realizing it. That we, depending on the situation, are more or less "wave-" or "particle"-like.

What if the aspect I experience depends on love or fear. When we are nervous or scared, we feel alone and separated from others and from the whole. When we feel secure, we transcend more and more to our wave aspect.

Personally, I experience, when I stay for longer periods at our country house and open myself to nature and the greatness of life, that after some time I am more and more in tune with the bird song, the sounds of the forest and the sea. Borders become more fluid and I feel part of everything, just like a cell in a larger body.

We can easily experience this state, for instance during a sunset by the sea; how we shift to a higher state of consciousness, blend into the whole, unaware of time and space, until we are woken, maybe by a voice calling our name, and suddenly we are back into the body, to "reality", aware of being a separate individual, aware of time, watches and obligations of various kinds.

The quantum vacuum as an information field

According to Ervin Laszlo, we can see the quantum vacuum as an information field, where we can connect through our brain to the waves in the field and receive information, for example during meditation or other alternative states of consciousness, where we are open to knowledge not available in our everyday consciousness. He says that there is an ongoing communication between our inner being and the outside world. Everything that goes on in our mind makes a wave pattern in the vacuum field, while our mind is constantly influenced by the subtle pattern spread out in the field.

According to David Bohm, we can learn to be "antennae for more subtle forms of energy – for the cosmic level".[2] Our brains need to become more sensitive. They are now too preoccupied with the conflicts in civilization. He means that our limited way of thinking causes our problems and that we need silence and stillness to be able to alter our brains in a more fundamental way.

As we develop and reach higher energy levels, we will become more sensitive because parts of our nervous system, which previously lay dormant, are now activated and we can see and understand things that we did not notice before. We often have a greater demand for nature, stillness and silence – while at the same time we realize that loneliness is an illusion – we are part of everything. Those who have once experienced the sacred silence can no longer experience loneliness, write authors Elisabeth Haich and Selvarajan Yesudian in *Selfhealing, Yoga & Destiny*.

Stillness and silence are the door openers. The outer stillness and silence help us to reach the inner peace which enables us to perceive the communication that is going on within.

2 Radio Sweden: *Sena vanor* (1996).

Intuition

The more we think, the more materialistic we become, says Krishnamurti, because thoughts are matter.

The intellect deals with the parts – structures and analyzes. Intuition understands the overall picture. It comes to us from a higher dimension of consciousness – without the involvement of the intellect. Intuition often feels self-evident: "Why haven't I seen this before?" In enlightening moments we get the answers as flashes of total insight.

As we develop our sensitivity to the intuitive, intuition will become an increasingly reliable tool for the interpretation and understanding of life.

Personally I experience that the more I develop my SQ, my intellect changes in that it calms down. I no longer have the same issues as before and other associations are awakened, other neural links are activated. While impulses are changeable, carry us away and can be premature, intuition is calm and clear and of a more durable nature. True intuition is followed by a strong certainty and eventually tends to manifest in the outside world.

Connecting to the cosmic consciousness requires very little from us, but we will not reach it when under pressure. We can rush through our whole life without – on a conscious level – making that contact. A relaxed body gives a relaxed mind, and vice versa. Relaxation and meditation help us to develop our intuition and to reconcile the opposites in life; to repeatedly return to the unbroken wholeness, "take off" from there and thus more easily handle our everyday reality. The inner stillness and silence is always there for us, even when the outside world seems chaotic.

The overall goal for mankind today, what we seek and long for the most, seems to be contact with the whole, the coherent state; in other words spiritual development. The security in identifying with Being, the underlying oneness. It gives us a broader view of life and of our world. It opens the door to more mature solutions and a greater will to take on responsibility.

The wisdom society

The search for meaning, vision and higher worth seems to be leading us into a wisdom society, from outer knowledge to inner wisdom, from information to transformation. After the hunter society, farming society, industrial society and the information society, the time has come for the transformation society, or *trance*formation society, as Lars-Eric Uneståhl puts it. Author Gary Zukav writes in *The Heart of the Soul*: "Learning to see our inner experiences as primary, and our external circumstances as secondary, is the new frontier for the human species."

Inner security is replacing outer security. Instead of changing the outside world in order to feel better, feel valuable and successful, more and more people are working on finding their inner security. As we said before, it no longer works to chase external rewards. We are beginning to see that we are only chasing our self-created images of success and miss the inner development that gives us true strength, security and well-being.

Our society is still in its childhood. Until now, most of human history has been about fight and survival, to master the outside world. Now we are entering a new phase, where power struggle is coming to an end, both individually and societally. It has been a long time since anyone "won" a war. We are beginning to grow out of those kinds of solutions. Unfortunately, it is still the best "warriors" that make it to the highest positions in our society, and so-called "ordinary people" often seem to have reached a higher maturity than the one our leaders possess. But as we, at grass-root level, expand our consciousness, we will also be better at choosing our leaders.

Changing the world through inner growth

Outer peace through inner peace. Utopia? Hardly. Utopia is within us. We can choose to explore our inner selves and reach the states and the frequencies that give us joy, harmony and satisfaction.

Changing the world through greater happiness, security, true motivation! Quite an appealing solution, in my opinion. No adverse side effects. A win-win situation. And so far untested on a larger scale. Outer revolutions and frameworks will soon lead to new conflicts. Inner development leads to growth – an inner transformation of humanity, a collective higher level of consciousness with an entirely different life- and world view as a result.

The critical mass

The phenomenon is known by several names, among others, the "hundredth monkey effect". In physics it is called phase transition and means that when a sufficient number of electrons form in a certain way, other electrons follow and form in the same way.

This appears to apply to us humans as well; when a sufficient number of people take a particular approach – reach a certain level of maturity – their energies tune in to the same frequency, a type of harmonic vibration, which makes others act in the same way.

This has been used to explain sudden – seemingly improbable – changes, like the fall of the Berlin Wall. How could this happen so quickly, when the resistance had been so solid? Well, you could say the wall was already mentally torn down.

A viable world

We have the ability to solve the problems of the world by changing our approach to life, our way of thinking. Apparently we are free to create whatever we want, all the time. There is nothing actually stopping us. The barriers are within us.

Let's sum it up! If nothing can exist on its own accord without its surroundings, if nothing can exist without first having originated in a consciousness; then only what we collectively focus on could exist. We would actually be contributors to what manifests in the world.

What would the world be like, if we only focused on what we deeply, from *our hearts*, desired – meaning, a focus from a high energy state? Ponder that for a while – or a whole life. The thought makes the mind spin.

This perspective on life would also end the way we see ourselves as victims. We would have to realize that we are co-creators of our reality and that there is a reason for what happens to us; realize the importance of having a clear intent, which sparks forces that create what I want to achieve. An approach like this would substantially increase our motivation to observe our thoughts, explore our emotions and be clear on what we are creating.

Even if we are not capable of understanding everything, all of us can – if we so choose – by expanding our consciousness, get as much of an intuitive understanding of the underlying, creating principle, that we are enabled to solve the problems of humanity, both individually and collectively; and together create a viable world.

The more we can embrace that on one level we are each other and express different aspects of a larger unified whole, the easier we can appreciate our various talents and gifts; see that we have different purposes in life and realize the importance that we – each and every one – get the opportunity to develop our natural gifts. That we can complement each other without competing – together the parts make the whole – and that we can co-exist and grow together.

This would create infinite possibilities to change our world, to transform our collective thought, our collective consciousness. We are creating the world *now* with every thought, every choice, every decision, individually and together. What if we could add all our natural gifts for the common good. *There are no boundaries to the progress we could make.* Unfortunately, humanity might not be mature enough for this. But at least, we will have to realize that we are *fellow beings* to a much greater extent than we ever imagined.

Even if quantum physics is a young scientific model and some might say it cannot be compared with the thousands-of-years-old Eastern thinking in matters of wisdom, I believe that it is quantum physics' way of explaining reality which will appeal to the West and also be used as a gateway to Eastern thinking. Why? Because quantum physics conveys its message in a vocabulary which we Westerners (in particular Western men) find easier to comprehend. In my courses I have noticed how much easier it is to speak of these matters in terms of modern physics, than it is to use Eastern "gurus" – which has a tendency to make the participants squirm in their seats.

Chapter 13 – Quantum psychology

The first time I came across the term quantum psychology was in 1992, in Danah Zohar's book *The Quantum Self*. Some years later, I read Stephen Wolinsky's *Quantum Consciousness* where he expands further on quantum-physical and Eastern train of thoughts, on David Bohm's, and others' ideas that everything is connected. Quantum psychology can also be seen as a continuation of directions within psychology which assume that there is an underlying whole; as seen in Roberto Assagioli's Psychosynthesis with the higher Self, Viktor Frankl's Logotherapy with an emphasis on finding a higher meaning in life – and C. G. Jung's Collective Unconscious, among others. Quantum psychology thus proceeds from the emerging world view which gives rise to a paradigm shift also within psychology.

In quantum psychology, we no longer see "the self" as something isolated and separate, but in relation to its surroundings, entwined with the underlying whole. The self is a part of consciousness. As David Bohm says: "The proposal that mankind is 'the many' is valid up to a point, but beyond that point it fails". The many eventually blend into one and in the end everything appears to be one big consciousness.

Quantum psychology studies the underlying field or the unchanging background, often compared to a movie screen. The screen on which the whole of our life's story plays out, while we are so preoccupied with our own activities that we rarely discover that underlying whole. We are so used to compartmentalizing our lives, to seeing the world divided into individual parts, things and events. But are there really any borders not invented by mankind? If we look down from space, we can see that there are no actual borders on the *Earth* itself – the borders exist only in our minds. "Cosmos is a seamless whole."

In quantum psychology we practice being aware of this unchanging whole in our experience of the world – being aware of the space between objects, the silence between words, between notes. Seeing the *energy aspect* in everything – in thoughts, feelings, concepts, language, matter, sound and silence, and seeing the void as a living, vibrating energy. When we learn to include this space in our experiences, we gain a wider picture of reality, a stronger capacity to observe "particle reality", matter and the thought processes that arise in consciousness. We get a distance that makes it easier to choose what we want to identify with and to avoid unconscious identification with one thing or the other.

Sit comfortably and relax, look around and practice noticing the space between things – the energy world. See, listen to and feel the space – the vibrating energy – around us. With practice, you can be just as comfortable with the energy world as with the manifest world.

Our concepts restrict thinking

"Because our representation of reality", says Fritjof Capra in *The Tao of Physics*, "is so much easier to grasp than reality itself, we tend to confuse the two and to take our concepts and symbols for reality."

Our fantastic language, which gives us so much, also locks us in a restricted reality, with its precise formulations and definitions of what something is, or is not. It keeps us trapped in our current perception of reality. What we observe depends on our concepts. Our language reflects our individual and societal maturity level – it reflects the reality we are capable of understanding and language develops as *we* develop.

Thinking involves separating oneself from the whole, but we can still be aware of the whole. Einstein said that everything is a void and that form is condensed void. We "condense" the void, when we create the concepts. Our concepts and ideas are condensed energy. What we see and experience depends on our conceptual world; and our conceptual world we have learned from others. When I realize that my reality depends on my interpretation and that my *conceptual world* contributes to that interpretation, I can start to question and think things through rather than just let everything slip in without reflection. I can start to see that my opinions are just forms of energy.

> *Once you realize the approximate nature of all concepts, then you can really love them, because you love them without attachment.*
>
> Fritjof Capra quotes a Buddhist monk in *The Holographic Paradigm*

Let us reflect on an everyday term such as *full time*. For many, this is associated with a certain number of working hours per week and this idea holds our whole working life "prisoner" – rather than making it clear how many hours I need or want to work, according to my situation and my needs *right now*. Or the term *retirement age*. Plenty of research today suggests that people with a flexible retirement age actually live longer. Why should we all retire at the same age? Why do we need age as a criterion at all? Out of practicality? Yes, but consider the creativity that would be released if people were allowed to think freely. Why do we need a word such as retirement at all – what are we retiring from? From a job position? Yes, but that is only *one* part of life. And the word *work*, what does that mean? Most often paid work, but paid work is only *one* part of the work we do. Isn't everything we do a type of work? The closer we come to our true purpose in life – that is, doing the things that we love to do – the word "work" often means the highest form of freedom – in other words – presence.

Reality is indeed built on concepts, but we can choose the classifications ourselves. There is nothing that is "set in stone" – we can form the concepts we wish to, we do so all the time. Our intellect needs the conceptual ideas, they give us good information, but we also need to see through them; realize that we label things ourselves and that we are free to break up the frameworks we wish – individually and together.

Reflect upon which concepts you bind energy to. Perhaps, some to an extent that they rule your days and your life.

Language can limit or free us; it can be loose and without reflection, or vigorous and creative – an expression from my deepest Self. We can choose the conceptions that resonate within us and give us a meaningful existence. A living "inspirational" language is – when used consciously – a fantastic strength-giving instrument to everything we do and create. Words are symbols made up of energy on different levels of vibration.

Once, when my husband and I took a midday nap, I had – on waking – an experience where I was outside the "real" world and able to see how our reality was made up of concepts, how we build the world on our constructs. It was as if everything was laid out on a tray of possibilities and we were given the opportunity to create and choose the content and model of reality. It was a remarkable experience, and the most amazing aspect was that in the middle of the sunlight and while it was happening, I was able to explain to my husband what I was experiencing. Thus, I found myself outside the conceptual world but still able to explain with words!

How, and from where does a psychological problem arise?

For something to be experienced as a problem – I must *define* it as a problem. If I do not *see* it as a problem, then it actually is not a problem, is it? I am not trying to be funny – I am really trying to explore.

In order to formulate a problem I need my intellect, I need language and duality. There has to be something that is better or worse, right or wrong. I have to see the world as fragmented.

For as long as we are in the world of intellect and language, this is just a play on words; but beyond language, there is another reality. When we are in contact with the essence, it is not possible to see things as problems. We can observe the course of events, but not see it as problematic – rather as events that have not yet found their solution.

In order for a problem to exist, we need to give it energy – time and space. Space for it to exist and a certain duration over time. Can a problem still exist if we do not give it energy? When we are completely anchored in the present moment, it is not possible to experience problems.

When we create a problem, we only see a small part of reality. We have an altogether too limited view and are not able to see the underlying order. Our intellect misses the entirety; the simplicity. Psychological problems are conceptual problems that arise through their "labels".

Well, this might seem like a play on words, but personally I find it very interesting to see that my problems do not reappear on every level. It makes a very big difference for me if I know that they do not exist *as such* but are only in my perception. Even if they do not automatically disappear from daily life, I can more easily choose how much space I want to give them.

> *The significant problems we have*
> *cannot be solved*
> *at the same level of thinking*
> *with which we created them.*
> Albert Einstein

Problems are the "gold" – a gift. It is by solving our problems that we grow. "To solve another´s problem is, in fact, one of the greatest disservices we can possibly render", says business leader and author Rolf Österberg in his book *Corporate Renaissance: Business as an Adventure in Human Development*. Then we do not allow that person to grow.

The solution to a problem is always found at a higher level than where it arose, so when we have solved our problems, we have widened our consciousness and grown.

We can turn it around and look at the problem's opposite – what possibilities the problem may hold; thus focus on solutions. One of the best phrases I have adopted and which I always pass on as soon as I get the chance, goes like this. You say kindly to yourself: "*it will be interesting to see how I solve this."* It gives me strength right away, and transfers my energy to finding solutions. We need to give our inner self a picture, a vision, for it to start looking for solutions.

We can also mentally project ourselves to a future where the problem is solved, and ask ourselves: how did I do it? In this reverse perspective, it is substantially easier to get past obstacles and to instead see solutions.

During meditation, for instance, we have the opportunity to experience reality without it being filtered through conceptual thinking. During deep relaxation concepts like right and wrong, good and bad, change. They transform to being just "different" and gradually come together. We can follow a problem from the unbroken whole to the intellect, and then back to the "sea of energy" – the underlying wholeness from where all of our problems take form, and to where they return.

The conclusion is that problems exist and do not exist – at the same time. It all depends on where and how we look, from which state of consciousness we are observing.

What if, the more we are in our "intellect" – the more we think and analyze, the more dualistically we experience the world and the more "problematic" our view of the world will be.

What if it is true that all problems arise from thoughts of separation.

"Skip the story"

One of the fundamental findings, says philosopher and author Colin Wilson in the foreword to *Quantum Consciousness*, is that all mental conditions are basically forms of energy. Some of them we see as good, some as bad. But, by simply experiencing them as energy, the false sense of identity is taken out of the situation.

By leaving our intellect behind, even just for a moment, we can experience the world from its energy aspect without putting names on our experiences. Describing or labeling diminishes the experience, separates it from the whole and puts it into a "form". Instead, we can choose to focus on the very energy fluctuations in our body – see how different events trigger different sensations, release different reactions; and allow us to have the experience without putting words to our feelings, just to feel the energy. Focus on the energy of the emotion, rather than on the story, people, or situations, without thinking about *why* I feel like I do; just observe the reaction itself.

Emotions give rise to flow or blockages in our bodies (comfort or discomfort). We can see our emotions, thoughts and concepts as "bound" energy. Every time we repeat a habit or an interpretation, we attach more energy to that neural connection, until it becomes so natural and strong, that it feels as if something actually *is* a certain way. For example, if I were to repeat, time and again, that I am worthless, or valuable, it would gradually feel more and more like a "truth". I have a choice – I can continue to attach myself to – or begin to detach myself from the interpretations that do not benefit me. It is basically the same energy that gives rise to all concepts and labels.

An exercise to move beyond the conceptual world: sit comfortably and at peace; relax and try to experience a feeling without putting a label to it, just experience the sensation itself, sense that it is made of energy.

Relating feelings to an object

We spoke earlier about the significance of retaining a distance to our mental images and ideas, and that it is important to be able to detach our feelings from the object – to be able to sense a feeling without linking it to something else. The more we can avoid this habit of relating – attaching a certain emotion to a certain situation or person – the freer we are to choose the mood we want. We focus only on the sensation in the body, not on the *object* causing our reaction.

Eventually, the story – which is just *one* way of interpreting reality – will become less interesting. I can instead start focusing on the internal reactions that my interpretation program gives rise to. Feelings arise within me and signal how I process my energy.

Excitement or anxiety

When we are in a coherent state of mind, our emotions flow comfortably through our body because we allow their natural course. In a fragmented state, it is sometimes harder to interpret and separate feelings from one another. After my own crisis, I remember that it was difficult for me to distinguish between excitement and anxiety. I saw excitement (pleasure) as anxiety (pain). Inner peace was what I wanted the most and every energy fluctuation inside felt threatening.

We said above that for anything to become a problem or an internal conflict, we must create a dichotomy within. We create force and counterforce (pressure and counter-pressure) inside ourselves – even if we are unaware of it. With anxiety, the pressure has become stronger than we can manage. We build up a tension until the unwanted state becomes overpowering and threatens to destroy us. Most of our energy has now transformed to anxiety – the threat – whatever it looks like. To regain our strength, we need to explore the anxiety, "enter into" it and "be" it, the energy is then released and the anxiety abates. Like a battle between two sides – if you become the opponent the dichotomy ends. Peace is restored.

An example of this is one of my clients, who could clearly see this dichotomy and that she gave all of her energy to what she called "the horrible monster". I asked her to enter into the monster but she did not dare to. I asked her again to be one with the monster and after a short silence, my client exclaimed with surprise "I can't do it – it just disappears!"

If we explore this state of mind, *become one* with it, we unite the divided energy and reach a more coherent state. Note that it is the energy of *the emotion* we have to explore, it is not enough to work with just the intellect – I will not become emotionally aware by *thinking* about my feelings. Remember that we should have developed a good inner observer to be able to work in this way.

We can also manage anxiety with a good breathing technique (Chapter 7), but this needs to be properly integrated, otherwise we become drawn into the emotional storm and forget the tools we have. The more observant we become, the easier it is – at an early stage – to breathe through our emotions and dissolve the tension before it intensifies.

When in harmony, we can call forth an unwanted emotional state, observe it and see that we are capable of going into it, dissolving it and in this way undramatize it all. This gives well-needed security and knowledge that it is my own energy I am taking back.

On the level of the Self, we are beyond the duality and therefore do not get stuck in these problems. In the coherent state of mind, we are able to see that the division is created in our mind, but that our consciousness also contains levels of unity. This is the quickest and most powerful way of coming out of an unwanted state. By making contact with the connected state instead of looking in the story for explanations, we can replenish our strength and make the changes in our life that may be needed.

Resistance

If we try to get rid of or change our emotions and resist what we feel, we create "force and counterforce" within. Instead, we can study the resistance and see that it is just energy. See that fear and painful feelings are energy and nothing we need to resist or try to control. (It is the resistance against feeling that is painful, not the emotion itself.) The more we try to avoid pain, the more we suffer. Observation makes the resistance fade away.

Try to refrain from searching for "reasons why" – especially reasons outside yourself. See that your ideas are just energy, made of the same base-energy that created everything else. Notice how willingly we seek to avoid, do something else, find excuses and so on. Persevere in your observations and the resistance will slowly abate – in the same way that small, unruly children stop being noisy, when not given fuel such as tellings-off and the like.

If you feel that you get stuck, concentrate on the "deadlock" or what emerges from within you. See that even this dissolves – resistance dissipates if we explore it. Say yes to the opposites and they come together. To love and embrace negative thoughts and emotions makes them disappear faster than if we try to banish them.

Look out for restrictive patterns. For example, a few years ago I noticed within myself an insidious phrase that kept repeating itself: "it's no use anyway". Well OK, I answered, then it does not matter. But my inner self protested: yes, it does matter!! That little hidden phrase was really energy-draining and so ingrained, that I had not noticed it.

Sometimes, our memories are so highly charged that we need to relive them, before we can release them through observation alone. The turbulence they create inside is so strong that we simply cannot manage to take on the observer role without reliving the memory one more time. Maybe we need to share; maybe we need to go through "the layers" and above all breathe- and feel through the situation several times, bit by bit. Every time we work through our past events, we release some of the pent-up energy and let go of the emotion. Gradually, they no longer start the inner-scenarios and we notice that we can talk about it all casually. It becomes like an old film we have seen many times – very familiar, but no longer engaging – "that was then!"

To leave something behind is not the same as shutting it out – it is about releasing, and letting it return to the sea of energy. As long as something has form, it is still there. We need to let the form dissolve and return to non-form.

Ask yourself: what do I need to leave behind me, that does not lead to my "higher good", that does not lead to growth? For instance, a dependency on the likes and opinions of others.

Sit comfortably and relaxed. Allow yourself to feel an emotion that you would like to leave behind. See where you sense the energy-increase, observe it and breathe to the place where you feel the emotion. See also Chapter 7 – "To breathe with our feelings."

There is no place we can escape to where we don't have our emotions with us. We can't leave our emotional baggage at home.

Escape

Escaping from our emotions can take many forms, such as work- and shopaholism, perfectionism, addiction to food, sweets, alcohol and drugs. Anything to take the focus away from ourselves and avoid confronting our inner pain. But sooner or later our inner catches up with us – there is nowhere we can go without taking our emotional life with us.

Every crisis and dead end can be seen as a reminder to begin to explore my deeper feelings. To see the bigger picture and that every trial I am subjected to offers possibilities for growth and to reach greater harmony with my core.

What do I attach energy to?

When I can see that the reactions in my body are due to my interpretation and the way I manage my energy system, I can start to choose my behavior. Do I want to carry on attaching energy in my usual manner, or am I prepared to "step out" and create new forms; forms that allow my consciousness to expand and grow. Maybe even refrain from creating new forms; just identify with the whole and let the energy-of-life flow freely through my body.

Practice seeing the world from the energy aspect, see and feel the energy in worry, stress, the TV programs you watch and the food you eat. See how your energy fluctuates depending on the situation, your thinking and so on. Evaluate the TV-program by how much energy it gives you – do you choose programs that are energizing or draining? Do you feel strengthened and refilled afterwards?

Do you have an excessive sweet tooth? Where do you experience the craving? In your mouth, your stomach? Try to stop eating – just for a little while – and see what happens. What do you feel? Where?

Put up with it for a while and see that the craving is only pent-up energy and that the sweets stop you from experiencing the underlying emotion. What is it really about? My Swiss-friend's grandmother explained *her* sweet tooth like this: "my mouth is so bored!"

Are you drained by other people? Ask yourself: *what in me makes me give my energy away to that person?* Notice *what* you feel and *where* it arises in your body.

Use spare moments to observe your emotions. Notice what you feel and start to identify where in your body different emotions occur. See that the situations can be new and countless but that the emotional reactions are old and ingrained/habitual. Practice studying them without identifying with them – see them as energy that you can bind and dissolve yourself. Gradually it becomes easier to simply "step out" of your reactions and allow the energy to pass through your body.

As we develop our ability to observe, we can use what happens as lessons, as "powers of enlightenment". Negative thoughts and emotions tell me that here I have an area for development; that I need to free myself from opinions, beliefs and reflex patterns. We do not need to search in the past for reasons and explanations. If we have issues within, that are not dealt with, they will reveal themselves *in the moment.* Remember that what contains the most pain also brings with it your biggest potential for growth.

Taking full responsibility for our experiences also means refraining from laying the guilt on ourselves; otherwise we can easily end up in the victim-role which activates our defense mechanisms. We are all doing our best and choose the solutions that seem the most suitable at the time. If we see things differently later in life it means that we have developed – seeing things differently is the "price" we have to pay for our growth.

Often, we need to dissolve our blockages mentally, emotionally and physically. We can cognitively change our inner image, but we have memories in the body which also need to be healed. To free ourselves mentally is often the easiest, our emotions lie deeper and even when we have liberated ourselves from the emotionally-influenced reaction, we can still feel residues in the form of physical tension. The body is reacting to "old information".

Every pattern we identify is a step towards liberation. When we see that our reality is made up of highly temporary forms, a freedom to attach and detach these forms comes about. We can see that our self-image is a result of the boundaries that we have set up in the boundless consciousness and that we can transform this image ourselves.

Including the space in our experiences "dilutes" the story and makes it easier to see through constructs and beliefs, to gain a perspective on what I previously created; be able to let go of ingrained limitations and cherished beliefs. Happily enough, we just need to *see* and acknowledge what is within us; not try to change ourselves or anyone else, not analyze or seek explanation – just observe. Observe the thought, but also its parallel in the body. Where does the thought attach in the body.

When you are in harmony, practice watching how you give energy to various ideas (condense) and how you can dissolve the energy and let it return to the sea of energy.

Body posture

We spoke earlier about the importance of good posture for proper breathing. The posture is also important for our ability to take in higher energies. When we are depressed, the body will easily bend, but if we have a straight posture with chest high and eyes to the sky, it is hard to be downhearted.

We quite simply need to help our bodies absorb and be able to hold higher energies, through our posture, breathing and the way we move – to open ourselves fully to these energies. When we are tense, we close our body and do not get the replenishment and flow of energy that we need.

An Indian guru who visited Sweden to speak to business people said that if we are tired at the end of the working day, we have not been using our energy in the right way. Well that is probably true, even if it may sound a little strange to us Westerners. Energy needs to flow freely, and relaxation is more important than we may think, for higher energies to be able to flow in and refresh us.

We can do an interesting little exercise which shows the importance of posture to our way of looking at life.

Sit on a chair and think of a problem. It does not need to be the worst you can come up with but something in-between. Bend over, look to the floor, think about the problem – feel the hopelessness, misery and powerlessness. When you have thoroughly absorbed the feeling, let it go. Straighten up, keep your chest high, look to the sky and smile so that the corners of your eye crinkle. Keep that posture, look up, smile and think of the same problem again.

Did you experience a difference? It is hard to see anything as hopeless when we have a good posture and an upward glance.

The Upper Limits Problem

In their book *Conscious Loving*, Gay, Ph.D., and Kathleen, Ph.D., Hendricks, best known for their work in relationship enhancement, write about "The Upper Limits Problem". They believe that we cannot tolerate feeling good, for too long. Throughout history, humans have been more accustomed to fight and flight and cannot manage too much positive energy for a longer period. Everything becomes unbearably good and we start looking for faults in ourselves, in each other and the outside world, and so begins the journey down again. A lack of trust in the life process and that we are worth feeling good. We need to expand beyond these limits. By moving to a state beyond duality we can see these forces, free ourselves from past conditioning and train our bodies to manage higher vibrations. Luckily the body then becomes more sensitive, which makes it painful to fall back into the old, unhealthy energy patterns.

As we mentioned earlier, we need to work on two fronts – make sure we raise our vibrations, and clean up our inner debris.

Thoughts and feelings of gratitude, love, compassion and the like take us to higher heights. We can compare these feelings to the seven deadly sins (wrath, greed, sloth, pride, lust, envy, and gluttony) which all come from a detached state of mind, from the ego and thus a lack of contact with our higher Self.

The two states of "detached and connected" appear in many descriptions, expressed in various ways.

Gerald Jampolsky suggests in *Out of Darkness Into the Light* that there are only two voices and that we create suffering or happiness, depending on which voice we choose to listen to. Susan Jeffers, Ph.D., writes in *Feel the Fear and Do It Anyway*, that she believes "there are only two kinds of experiences in life: those that stem from our Higher Self and those that have something to teach us. We recognize the first as pure joy and the latter as struggle."

The cause of our problems seems to lie in the feeling of separation and detachment from the whole. We live like caged animals in a reality that is too limited – in other words, we are limited by our *own* concept of reality.

But at a certain level, duality does not appear. There are no boundaries at the "quantum level". Stephen Wolinsky says that when we make contact with the whole our view of life transforms – what unites is strengthened while the pain of being detached diminishes.

Flow

Feelings of flow belong to the whole and cannot be experienced as "separate", as something which has an opposite. They are characterized by flowing freely through the system, without friction; all disturbances and blockages are gone. Our body works in harmony with all its constituents and with its surroundings. In a state of flow, we experience life without labels and limits.

The psychologist Abraham Maslow, who was one of the first to study peak experiences, says that these moments were characterized by pure joy. All fear and doubt was gone. Even the awareness of ourselves disappeared. All detachment in the relationship to the world ceased.

Flow is often related to extraordinary performance, when we are on the limits of our capabilities, but can also be experienced directly through Being, where we can reach a state of perfection and harmony with the essence.

Recall a time when you were in harmony with the essence, your boundless flow. What did you do? How did you experience it?

If everything is connected and everything is basically energy, we need to be properly skilled in managing our own energy system. My thoughts are energy – I need to be able to observe them, to see what I create. My emotions are energy – I must be able to enter into and step out of different emotional states, be able to stay centered without being drawn into unwanted feelings.

My well-being, my health, my whole life is about how well I master my energy system.

Chapter 14 – The energy system

In Eastern cultures people have, for thousands of years, worked with themselves directly on the energy level, for instance by using the chakra system. The word chakra is Sanskrit and means wheel or whirl and is used to denote different energy centers in our body, which are also seen to represent different levels of consciousness we can reach. When exploring our inner being we can benefit from an awareness of this energy system.

Here, I will cover the energy system only on a broad level – showing similarities between the chakra system and Maslow's and others' theories, and how big the agreement between East and West is even in this area. For those who would like to immerse themselves further, there are excellent books on the chakra system, which is a comprehensive model of explanation.

The energy system provides information about how we process energy in our body – where we have tendencies to block the energy flow and also the experiences that might cause these blockages.

The chakra system

The chakra system is about the life force that flows through us. Usually you work with seven energy centers, or energy wheels, that are thought to lie along the spine and be related to our different needs. Different organs and glands are also connected to these centers and each center is thought to vibrate in a certain color.

Our development is considered to move from the lower to the upper chakras, but to facilitate comparison with the following models I will start from the upper. A short description could look like this:

The crown center (seventh chakra) is located at the top of the head and represents universal consciousness, awareness of the whole and that we are one with everything.

The gland is the pineal gland and the color is violet or white (the combination of all colors).

The brow center (sixth chakra – also called the "third eye") is located between the eyes, level with the eyebrows and slightly inside the head. It represents our spiritual nature, intuition, ideas and visions, and evolves as we acquire the ability to see larger contexts and the underlying meaning of our experiences.

The gland is the pituitary gland and the color is indigo-blue.

The throat center (fifth chakra) is located in the throat/neck and is the center of communication. It represents our ability to express ourselves. When we are in balance, our voice has resonance and we can easily find words. When imbalanced, we have difficulty expressing ourselves and our voice becomes tense and thin.

The gland is the thyroid gland and the color is turquoise-blue.

The heart center (fourth chakra) is located in the middle of the chest, level with the heart and governs our relationships, love, giving and taking. When in balance we are loving, empathic and feel confidence in life. In imbalance we are reserved and cold. Physically we can experience the imbalance as pressure in the chest.

The gland is the thymus gland and the color is green.

The solar plexus center (third chakra) is located in the solar plexus just above the navel and represents our will and force, but also the need for control and power. It is sensitive to influence from the outside world. On this level, the inner struggle, "the big battle", between the ego and our higher Self is fought. Here we have the opportunity to make contact with our authentic power and the will that emanates from the Self. When fear takes over, we can easily end up in a power struggle and a pursuit for external power and control. Blockages in this center are experienced in the abdominal region.

The gland is the pancreas and the color is yellow.

The sacral center (the second chakra) is located slightly below the navel and is related to creativity, family, sexuality, reproduction. In balance we are creative and feel reverence for life. In imbalance we easily become egotistical, maybe violent and also more inclined to take advantage of other people.

The glands are the gonads and the color is orange.

The base center (first chakra) also called the root center, is located at the base of our spine and is related to our understanding of the physical dimension. It anchors us to the earth and represents survival – fight or flight. Our inner journey starts here, and at this level we are the most unaware of our potential. We act from our ego, perceive the world as mainly material and see life as a struggle. When the base center is in balance we feel safe and "at home" on earth. In imbalance, we can experience the world as alien and threatening.

The gland is the adrenal gland and the color is red.

The three lower centers belong to the physical world and the three upper levels to the spiritual world. The heart chakra is the centerpoint, connecting the lower centers to the upper.

It is worth noting that the chakra model is, and has been used also in the West, for example by C. G. Jung.

Maslow's hierarchy of needs

We can compare the chakra model with Abraham Maslow's hierarchy of needs, which is often described as a pyramid or a staircase, where our development takes place from the lowest step and upwards – from our basic needs to our highest potential. The original pyramid is made up of five levels; a sixth level, self-transcendence, has later been included. Here too I start from the top.

Self-actualization	to reach one's full potential
Esteem	respect and appreciation from oneself and others
Love and belonging	friendship, love, fellowship
Safety	personal safety, economic security
Physiological needs	food, drink, protection from heat and cold

I recently saw the following version that has seven steps, just like the chakra model.

Spiritual fulfillment
Intellectual fulfillment
Self-expression
Love
Self-esteem
Security
Survival

The chakra model is thousands of years old and probably the forerunner to the Western models. As we can see they express themselves in roughly the same way, even if the chakra model emphasizes the energy aspect. So this is a widely accepted development model, where the evolvement is seen as ideally moving from basic to higher needs.

More recently, I have heard raised voices for the view that our true basic need is to be in contact with our higher Self, the universal intelligence, and thus be able to process energy through love and trust. We see for instance, that small infants die if they do not receive bodily contact and loving care, even if the physical and material care is perfect.

We are all free to choose the, or those, model(s) of explanation that resonate most within us. We can make use of detailed divisions as the above, or choose to see these divisions as just energy, which in the end become one and the same energy. If you wish, look again at Chapter 3 and compare with the three levels of development: the ego, the personal self and the transpersonal Self.

Regardless of which model of explanation we prefer, we can stick to the two states: ”connected” (love and trust) and ”separate” (fear and doubt). We can start to notice how we manage the energy in our system and practice putting ourselves in those states of mind that allow the energy to flow freely and that give a real “spin” in the centers.

Health or sickness

As we saw earlier, it is not events, people or situations that make us lose balance. It is our inner ideas and the way we process energy in our body. Every painful emotion is a sign that we react out of fear and doubt and, as we saw in Chapter 8, *The emotional layers*, the fear/shame of being worthless are the basic causes of our emotional pain.

We experience feelings differently depending on where they arise in our body and how we manage them. When energy passes through our body in fear and doubt, we experience tension and discomfort. When the energy is released in love and trust we experience comfort and feelings of flow. By noticing where in the body tension is felt, we can gain an insight into which kind of experience may have caused – and is causing – blockages in our system. If we often have a pain in the stomach, back, chest or head, for example, we can take advantage of the divisions in the model in order to better understand what we need to change in our perception to allow energy to flow more freely.

If we ignore our painful emotions for too long, they strain our body and may cause ailments, pain and eventually sickness. Therefore it is important to process these emotions. Medicine can help in the short term, but if I do not learn to address my emotions in a better way, the symptoms will return. Psychological pain gradually turns into physical pain and manifests in the body – the real medicine is to enter into the pain, then the “form” dissipates and returns to flow.

We can easily perceive certain types of pain as only physical, that they do not have an emotional element. Some years ago, I fell and hit myself hard and as a result had so much pain in the tailbone (coccyx) that I had trouble both walking and sitting. After a couple of weeks, I contacted a good friend, who is an osteopath, and explained my dilemma. He said, this will not go away by itself. You should come to see me. In the end he helped me, but the pain returned. When I wanted my third treatment he said: "Marianne, you have sufficient knowledge to take this pain away yourself. Find out what this pain stands for". Confused, I went home and realized that, despite being used to "going through the layers" and being good at dissolving *emotional* pain, I had not thought of the possibility that this pain could have an emotional element. After all, I had only fallen! I explored the pain and what emerged was grief and a whole range of emotions. After a while the pain disappeared and did not return.

Later on, I practiced this method on other forms of pain; for instance after an operation, and it worked in the same way. If I go fully and lovingly into a painful emotion, it dissolves! But I can add, that I often forget this knowledge and simply note that; ouch, I have a pain in my shoulder and run off happily without thinking I can do anything about it, just trust that it will pass, which it generally does. But if we have recurring problems somewhere in our body, it can be worthwhile taking a closer look at what it stands for (and of course confirm that no medical attention is required).

Instead of focusing on the external circumstances, we change our way of processing energy in our system. Only we can do that job. No one else knows exactly what you are experiencing or how you manage your energy system.

Emotions arise all the time. If we do not feel them, it means that we have become unaware of them and need to train our sensitivity. As we said earlier, it does not help to just think of our feelings, we need to *feel* them. Fear and doubt cause painful emotions, while love and trust generate harmonic feelings and well-being.

If you have difficulty in sensing your emotions and do not feel anything in the beginning, observe anyway. Start practicing the ability to feel. Go deeper into your body and into the "physical sensation" itself. Where do you experience your emotions? What do you feel? Make it a habit to regularly scan your body. See also Chapter 8, Feelings.

Everything begins in our consciousness and it is important that we can reach the level beyond duality, beyond the division into "sick

”or ”healthy”. In this way we create a free zone where sickness does not exist; and make contact with that part within us which is not affected by these constructs.

If I am diagnosed with a certain illness, I can – after I have created a picture of what I need to do – mentally ”erase” the diagnosis so that it does not get a hold, gain an identity within me, and start to live its own life and manifest in my body. If we repeat that we have a certain illness, the notion becomes more and more ingrained and will gradually become part of our self-image. But what we need to identify with is the *image of healthiness.*

We have to use all of the resources available to us – conceptual, emotional and physical – to be able to understand, feel and dissolve our blockages, to gain an insight and be able to transform the energy from debilitating to nourishing. This applies regardless of whether it is about our health or other objectives.

The lesson?

Could it really be so simple that our well-being and development is about how we master energy? Making sure that energy can pass through my body with trust in the life process. And what should we do with those things that happened earlier in our life? The same applies to our past! If we have unprocessed emotions within, they will reveal themselves in the present and here again it is about releasing our past in love and trust *now.*

For my own part, life is infinitely more manageable from the basis of a “fragmented” versus “coherent” state of consciousness; whether I manage my energy from fear or from love. The events of the outside world are no longer the most important; it is about how I *master* them.

Even if this sounds simple, life will continue to provide challenges and we need to be continually observant in order to stay aware of our feelings and accompanying thoughts, to have a good breathing pattern, good posture; and above all to make the *choice*, to choose an approach where I am willing to examine my reactions, my views et cetera.

When we work directly on the energy level, we have already left behind labels such as "guilt" and "shame", and realize that what is stored in my body are unprocessed emotions due to my reactions and the only one who can process and dissolve them is me. To come to terms with what happens, and has happened, and to forgive oneself and others takes us to a coherent state. Exploring our negative sides is an underestimated joy, when we fully realize the reward.

Do you sometimes wonder what your life would have looked like if you had made other choices? It would certainly have looked different on the surface, other events, other people, but the underlying challenge would still be the same: to heal the parts of the personality that are not yet in balance, and gain harmony with our innermost source; thus reach our highest potential.

What if our experiences are not the most important, but instead the *learning* we can gain from them; that the outer experiences mirror our inner being.

What if our experiences mainly serve the purpose of giving us the opportunity to transform energy to a higher level of consciousness.

Power struggle or cooperation

The explanations above can also be used on the societal maturity. Individually and socially, we are considered to have reached the stage represented by the third energy center. Even if certain individuals have reached a higher maturity, most of us and society globally, are still at the level of the second and third chakra, with violence and power struggles.

A sufficient number of people should now have attained a level where we are mature enough to see through the fear, which is the driving factor behind the need for external power and control, and be able to transform it to inner power and security, and thereby begin to take a step towards the higher wisdom of the heart (the fourth energy center).

This inner struggle is often marked by crises and breakdowns. But by understanding the underlying reasons – the essence behind our needs and wishes – these breakdowns can instead be breakthroughs to a higher level of development.

To conclude, I would like to refer to the message given by Gary Zukav and Linda Francis in *The Heart of the Soul*: "The journey you are on is toward wholeness. Why try to find detours? Why delay your arrival at a destination that is far more satisfying, fulfilling, and enjoyable than where you are now?"

We can see the energy system as an inner guide, providing us with immediate information on whether we are in contact with our essence or have fallen back to more immature levels.

Chapter 15 – The heart's intelligence

It is said that the longest journey we can make in life is from the head to the heart – to move from a fragmented to a coherent perspective – the real paradigm shift in our inner being.

The brain is usually seen as cold and clear while the heart is warm and blind, but by learning to make our heart and brain work together, we can develop "the wise heart and the loving mind". When we are rooted in the heart, our brain works at its optimum. When we understand life through the heart's intelligence, we cannot experience stress or fear. Nor can we be bored or *see* problems as particularly problematic – we *see* them more as another path, holding other experiences and possibilities. Our heart can accept this, but in most cases the brain cannot, it wants to control the outcome, and the more we try to control, the more stressful life becomes. (Fear closes the heart chakra.)

The heart muscle is apparently the first organ formed in the body. An "information"/intelligence that makes the first cells organize and form the rest of the body. This information is linked to consciousness – the "non-local" consciousness that exists in every part of the universe.

The heart may in fact be our true knowledge center. The heart takes up electromagnetic information from the surroundings via the central nervous system, information that our five senses cannot register. This information is processed in the heart and sent up to the brain in the form of intuition.

As we saw in Chapter 14, the thymus gland is related to our heart center and the thymus gland is also considered to be the location of our sense of self. When we point to ourselves to say "That's me" or

"I did it", we are pointing to the thymus gland. If we were to point to our head, it would seem as though we had done something crazy.

The heart rhythm influences our brain

At The Institute of Heart Math, in California, research is done into the heart's intelligence and how positive and negative emotions affect our heart and heart rhythm, and here we can gain further evidence of the importance of expanding our heart center.

They suggest that the heart has a central function and that – in addition to pumping blood – it has its own nervous system that can feel, remember, and operate independently of the brain. Neurocardiology has discovered that more signals are sent from the heart to the brain than vice versa. Our heart communicates with the brain in four different ways – via the nervous system, biochemically through hormones and neurochemicals, mechanically via the pulse and electromagnetically (electric signals generated by the heart's contractions). Information travels from the heart to the brain and from there via the sympathetic and parasympathetic nervous system out to the rest of the body.

Our heart rhythm also affects the way our brain works. Emotions of frustration and anxiety make for a disharmonious rhythm that blocks our higher brain functions (we resort to fight- or flight-behavior), while feelings of love and appreciation provide access to clear and effective thought processes. It increases our memory-capacity, our problem-solving capabilities and puts us in contact with our core values.

At The Institute of Heart Math, they have also designed a computer program, by which we can gain direct feedback on our heart rhythm via a sensor on the index finger (or the ear lobe). Through this technology we can detect how our breathing and different emotions affect our autonomic nervous system, and thereby the curves on a screen; see which type of breathing and which emotions make the heart rhythm harmonious (coherent), resulting in beautiful sine waves – or disharmonious (incoherent), resulting in a chaotic pattern on the screen.

The incoherent pattern indicates that the sympathetic and parasympathetic nervous systems are out of synch. That the two systems are "fighting" with each other, accelerating and braking at the same time, inhibiting access to our higher brain functions which makes us inefficient and uncertain. Thus, preventing us from using our talents in the best way possible.

Feelings of love and appreciation, on the other hand, ensure that the two systems cooperate. Focusing on our heart activates the parasympathetic nervous system, making us calmer and more balanced, and improves our ability of recovery and healing. A harmonious state which facilitates the heart's work; our heart gets the vital flexibility needed to swiftly change tempo; speed up when we need to run or slow down when we are going to sleep. Stress disrupts this rhythm and longer periods of stress can negatively affect the heart's flexibility.

We can affect our heart rhythm ourselves by transforming our emotions and improving our way of breathing. Emotional responses are learnt. As noted earlier, we interpret most things based on previous experience and if we have been used to emotions of anxiety, frustration, anger and the like, these are the neural pathways we have been exercising; whereas if we often experience positive feelings like love and appreciation, these are the pathways we are exercising. Once learnt, everything we experience falls into the old familiar track – the pathway of worry or of trust. The systematic influence of positive feelings eventually transforms our nervous system – we can thus develop our pathway of trust, so that we begin to interpret our experiences from a state of love and trust.

When we "think" with our heart, EEG and ECG oscillate in the same rhythm; respiration and blood pressure follow the same pattern. When our brain and heart cooperate, we become more focused, more creative and reach a higher intelligence. A coherent heart rhythm provides a state where we perform at our optimum – physically, emotionally and mentally – where we are in the "zone" (flow) and everything works with ease and harmony. The increased coherence puts us in contact with resources which normally are not available to us.

The most important change we can make is to alter our emotional condition. By consciously practicing breathing through our heart and putting ourselves in a state of love, we can remain in this harmonious mood for longer and longer periods. Heart focus is our most energy-saving mode of function, the whole system works as one harmonious unit and connects us with our higher intelligence.

Heart focus/heart breathing

Sit (or lie) with a straight back and free "bellows" to make your breathing easier. Start by breathing deep into the stomach a few times and relax your body. If you like, add a few "spine-flex breaths" (Chapter 7).

Prolong your exhalation slightly. You can count to 5 on the inhalation, 8 on the exhalation and rest for a count of 3, as described in Chapter 7.

Focus on your heart center in the middle of your chest and imagine that you are breathing through your heart, that the air is flowing in and out through the area around your heart. Breathe calmly and slowly and find a smooth and natural rhythm.

Add to this a positive feeling. Recall a situation where you felt really good and relive that feeling. It could be an experience of beauty, a memory of a loving relationship, the sight of a small child – something that makes your heart melt.

Sense it and become familiar with the feeling of being in a heart-focused state.

Solving problems through heart focus

Take a moment to identify "the problem" and the thoughts and feelings around it.

Prepare yourself as described above. Focus on your heart center and imagine that you are breathing through your heart. Add a posi-

tive feeling and when you have reached a loving state of mind, ask yourself: how can I handle my problem in a better way?

Listen to your heart – your inner voice, your intuition!

The Self – our "heart point"

The heart's intelligence operates outside our conceptual system – beyond duality – and has a transforming capability. We gain the wide-angle we need to be able to see things from a higher perspective and find solutions on a higher level.

When in a heart focused state, the energy comes from our higher Self – our deeper intuition and wisdom – and we gain a harmonious interaction between our heart and brain. (Lately we have gained yet another concept/label – heartfulness – for this state, where we are deeply rooted in our center).

As we said earlier, it is our feelings that make our brain work, and what could be more important than being in contact with the highest – the feeling of love. Love in this form is self-generating and does not require replenishment from outside. It comes from within and arises when we do things we love doing, feel feelings of love, gratitude, trust and appreciation. It comes from presence and contact with the whole. Our capability to love depends on the state of mind we are in.

This state of mind is characterized by simplicity, clarity, pure joy and often a warm feeling in the breast. It is also a state of generosity as here we do not have so many personal needs, we have found what we sought. In order to successfully remain in this state for longer periods, we need to free ourselves from negative thoughts and draining emotions, which effectively take us back to lower levels. It is a choice we need to make – over and over again. It requires a clear intention and a lot of practice.

Both love and sorrow open our heart center. We only mourn what we love and true sorrow is love. When centered in our heart, we see the world from a loving perspective, can see our own and others' endeavors and see that each and every one of us do everything to the best of our ability on every occasion. Pity (which attaches to our own unprocessed emotions) transforms into compassion, which comes from the processing of our own inner pain. We recognize our own struggle in others and know that we have also been at these stages and fall back into them occasionally.

Note that emotional awareness is not the same as being *emotional.* So called "emotional people" often do not know what they feel. I recently heard on TV someone being called an emotional person – as an excuse for him being imbalanced and unable to master his feelings.

Love and fear cannot be experienced simultaneously – they exclude each other. Everything we embrace with love – thoughts, emotions and more – is transformed to a higher level. Transformation takes place in the acceptance, and resistance is gone.

The day when we can love our fear, our weaknesses and shortcomings so much that we can remain in a coherent state, they will disappear. They cannot survive in a connected state. Then, we can experience *all* of our feelings from the heart, without leaving our center, without ending up in a separate state. What earlier brought about fear can now be experienced through the perspective of love – as a loving sorrow for our imperfection, for the feeling of not being enough, not being sufficiently loved or appreciated. Through the perspective of love, we now experience this with warmth and tenderness – like a parent tenderly observing a child's struggle, knowing that it has to have certain experiences in order to develop, and we can feel an unconditional love for life, ourselves and others.

We said earlier that we can make it easier for ourselves by realizing that there are only two states – fragmented and coherent – that is, fear and love and grades thereof. If we go deeply enough within ourselves, in the end there is only love. The unconditional love is a powerful force that changes our understanding of reality – we realize that we are related to everything and that this everything affects everything else. There is really no separation; the whole is interwoven with the parts!

Chapter 16 – Meditation/Mindfulness

The best way to capture moments is to pay attention.
Jon Kabat-Zinn in
Wherever You Go There You Are

Meditation has often been seen in the West as slightly mystic – an unworldly activity that people devote themselves to in Eastern cultures. But meditation is about reaching our natural state of Being and wholeness – a state we can easily lose sight of due to our hectic lifestyles and one-sided focus on the material reality. Meditation is actually nothing we need to learn, it is more about refraining from our habit of identifying with the more superficial part of our consciousness. I wrote earlier that the word eccentric is supposed to have meant to live outside one's center – meditation is the opposite, an aid to living from our center.

At the same time as our material prosperity has increased, people's inner dissatisfaction has also increased. It is extremely contradictory to hear people say that they have so much to do, that they "do not have time to live". What is living, then? Well, what we probably lack is the actual rooting in Being, in the whole; that which gives us the very spark of life. Regular meditation helps us to keep continuous contact with our center and prevents us from remaining in a fragmented state for such a long time, that we allow our view to be clouded and relapse to a fragmented outlook.

Meditation has received a boost in the West through the concept of mindfulness, thanks to, among other things the great book *Wherever You Go There You Are*, by Jon Kabat-Zinn, M.D. But regardless of whether we choose to label it meditation or mindfulness (or heartfulness), it is all about contact with Being. Meditation will get a higher status in our society, as we can nowadays make use of research methods that are accepted in the Western world.

Here, I will discuss meditation as a tool for reaching a coherent state, making contact with the oneness, our permanent identity. How, by nurturing our conscious awareness, we can reach an increased alertness of both the inner and the outer world and be able to observe and transform experiences in our everyday life. If, while reading this book, you have practiced your inner observer, have watched your thoughts and feelings, become more aware of your breathing; then you have already started to cultivate this alertness. The difference with meditation is that you do it in a more "ordered" form.

Health-giving effects

Meditation has many therapeutic effects and is said to:

- lower adrenaline and cortisol levels
- lower the blood pressure and heart rate
- increase the presence of alpha- and theta waves in the brain
- increase the production of melatonin
- increase our ability to handle stress
- improve the immune system
- improve the body's self-healing capacity
- make us happier and more harmonious
- raise our DHEA levels

DHEA (dehydroepiandrosteron) is an aging hormone, which is at its highest level in our mid-twenties and reduces as we become older. During meditation, increases of up to 43 percent of this hormone have been recorded, and regular meditators are usually regarded as having a biological age of 5-10 years below their chronological age, in other words functioning as 5-10 years younger.

Brain scanning

By using so-called brain scanning, it has been possible to study what happens in the brain during meditation and it has been established that the activity in the left frontal lobe – the part which makes us happy and positive – increases. This increase remains even after meditation. At the same time, the activity in the right frontal lobe – which regulates fear and aggression – decreases. There is much here to indicate that new neural links are formed, which transform the brain so that we habitually become more positive and optimistic and gain an increased capability of experiencing feelings of happiness, while fear and aggression are reduced. (Optimists are said to also have a lower blood flow in the amygdala, compared to pessimists).

Two challenges

There are many ways to meditate, but most meditation techniques have the same main purpose – to focus the thought on one single thing and block everything else out. This gives our nervous system a deep rest, much deeper than with normal sleep. The cerebral cortex activity reduces and more primitive parts of the brain are activated. With EEG we can measure an increase of alpha- and theta-waves in the brain.

In my opinion, there are only two "difficulties" with meditation: firstly, to actually stop and sit down, secondly, to do what I decided to do beforehand. The method I choose is less important, but if, for instance, I have decided to solely observe my breathing for ten minutes, *that* is what I should do and nothing else.

We should probably start to meditate only when we feel the real need for it. Our mind tends to be reluctant and needs to be trained so that we do not drift away when feeling resistance, restlessness or are making ourselves bored. It therefore requires discipline from the beginning, until meditation has become a definite *need*.

Personally, I started to meditate after having trained mentally using cassettes and CDs for more than a year. I had read a great deal about meditation during my education and wanted to try it out, without knowing so much about it in practice.

I simply sat down on the floor with crossed legs and focused on my breathing. I did not experience anything special the first few times, but it was pleasant, I was curious and continued. So then, on one occasion, something happened in my body – I felt as if I was being moved very rapidly into my stomach and it felt as if there was a large "ball" of calm and clarity there. This was something new and extremely agreeable and naturally I wanted to experience it again. It became the goal for my next meditations which of course created a barrier against achieving it. Eventually I let go of the idea and the feeling of well-being began to come more often. It became a natural state which I was also able to take with me into everyday life.

I have continued to meditate in various ways, not always so orthodox, I have more allowed it to develop out of my own needs. The need for a calm, pleasant feeling in my body, to experience the wholeness behind thoughts and feelings, and in this state, to be able to explore the inner and the outer reality.

I also use meditation to put questions to my inner being, to receive guidance from a deeper intuition than we normally experience. It gives me access to an overall perspective of what is important and helps me to rise above details and fragmentation. Since we live in a duality in our everyday consciousness, I believe that we need meditation to be able to reach higher states of consciousness and discover the unity that lies beyond separation.

Peaceful or indifferent

The overall purpose of all meditation methods is for us to be able to retain the elevated state of mind, also in daily life.

Course participants sometimes ask if you do not feel indifferent to what is happening, when being so peaceful. This is not the case. The peace emanates from a deep rooting in the Self and a loving trust in the life process, where we are in full contact with our feelings; while indifference comes from a lack of emotional engagement and a lack of contact with our center – in other words, from a separate state.

Moreover, we will still be upset – at least in the superficial part of our consciousness. But after meditating for some time, we might experience that we will still become upset on the surface but that it does not reach deep within – in our center there is still peace. The more we start to identify ourselves with this point of stillness, the longer we can live in this inner peacefulness.

Types of meditation

The most common forms of meditation among us Westerners tend to be observing our breathing or choosing a so-called mantra, a sound to repeat. But we can also choose to observe a burning flame for example, meditate on an inner image, listen to an external sound such as a running stream, or simply contemplate what is going on within and in the outside world. Personally, I often just clear my mind of thoughts, observe my breathing and devote myself to "just being".

It is less important what we choose to focus on, the challenge is doing what we decided to do in the first place, to center the mind on that instead of being distracted by other things and letting thoughts run round your head. Thoughts will come, but with practice we can let them come and go without engaging in them. Just re-establish our focus on what we have decided. (If we engage in our thoughts, we give them energy.)

Meditation should be characterized by simplicity – it is all about contact with Being and nothing should be simpler than that! But we need to be aware of a few things. In my view the most important thing is to have posture and breathing which allows energy to flow through the body.

Posture

Sit on a chair – or *even better* – on the floor with crossed legs, as this gives a good base. Place a pillow or something similar under your bottom, about 20 cm (8 inches) high so that you have a downward sloping angle from the thighs to the knees. This is partly to make it easier to sit and improve circulation and partly to give good positioning of the back. It is important to keep the lower part of your back straight and also make sure your neck is straight (no vulture neck), so that energy can flow freely through your body. Good posture helps us to sharpen our attention and also put us in a receptive state. Hands can be placed on the knees with palms facing up or down – this gives differing experiences. Experiment a little. You can also keep your hands in your lap, lightly held together. I always place my hands so that one is resting on top of the other, palms facing upwards with the thumbs facing each other. This is, I understand, a so-called mudra,[1] but nothing that I have learned, my hands just seem to place themselves naturally. So keep trying until it feels comfortable.

You can rock your upper body gently back and forth until you find the position where your body holds itself. Your eyes may be closed or half closed – the latter can help us to stay alert.

Make sure your chest is raised so that your breathing is free and easy. "Sit in a way that embodies dignity", as Jon Kabat-Zinn suggests, adding that his students then intuitively know how to sit.

Of course, we can also lie down. It depends on what we want to accomplish. I perform many exercises while lying, such as guided meditations and breathing exercises with recorded instructions on CD. But for certain purposes, sitting meditation works better – the vertical positioning of the spine facilitates our "connection" and receptivity.

An old Indian proverb says that if you are emotionally upset, *sit up* – even while you are sleeping!

Time and place

Usually, we meditate for about 20 minutes. Certain teachings are very strict about this, while others allow more freedom and say to use the time you have at your disposal – seven minutes is better than nothing at all. Of course, we go deeper if we sit for a longer period, but with practice we can benefit from even shorter sessions. At the beginning, it can be wise to decide in advance how long to meditate,

1 Mudras are special hand positions used in Buddhism and Hinduism.

as our restlessness can easily make us want to do something else. Expect thoughts to arise, trying to take your attention away from the task at hand.

Nowadays, I stop when I am "done". And how do I know when I am done? My eyes open and I feel ready to return to everyday life. On rare occasions I can sit for up to 45 minutes, but usually around 20-30 minutes.

As usual, we have to try it out, find what feels good, but not overdo it; that is, using meditation as an escape from everyday life. When meditating, we quickly enter into timelessness, and in this state no time or rush exists, but if you have decided beforehand how long you will sit, you usually sense when it is time to stop. Finish the meditation calmly by making contact with the surroundings, look around and ground yourself, before moving on to other things.

We can make it easier for ourselves by having a set time for our meditation, for example in the morning or evening – or both. But not too late, as we then easily can fall asleep. Remember also that best is to meditate on a relatively empty stomach – preferably before eating, rather than after.

As we said above, an experienced meditator is seen as being biologically 5-10 years younger than their chronological age. We are considered to live longer and be healthier. *So, we do have time to meditate*! We have everything to gain – not just a longer life in better health, but also a more enjoyable life – a life in deeper harmony with our core.

Choose a place that feels calm and comfortable. If we want, we can choose a special place that we always use and add some rituals like lighting a candle, using scents and the like, but we can also just sit down and see if the place feels good. Different places in the room and in nature have different energy vibrations, so if one does not feel good, try to move just a little bit. It can be an advantage to not restrict ourselves too much to one particular place, but rather be able to meditate wherever we are.

As I wrote earlier, a certain amount of discipline is required at the beginning and we need to meditate regularly until it has become a habit – one we do not want to be without. Just like physical exercise – it takes a while to establish a good routine. Then we long for it!

Breathing meditation

Maybe the choice that feels most natural. Breathing is always with us, we breathe while performing all activities in everyday life. We do not need to rearrange anything and there are, like we saw in Chapter 7, many health benefits to be gained with good breathing.

If you choose breathing for your meditation, prepare yourself as above and begin to observe your breathing; how you breathe the air into your body and how it flows out. Allow your breathing to go deeper, so that you are breathing into your abdomen, but without drawing in too much air. As light and natural as possible – let the breathing just happen inside you.

To start with, it can be easiest to train breathing while lying down and you can also benefit from counting your breaths, for example, on exhalation count 1, on the next exhalation count 2, and so on, until 10; then start again from the beginning. If you lose count, restart from 1 – in this way you will train your awareness. Focus on the exhalation and make sure that it is smooth and calm. Feel free to extend it somewhat, relative to the inhalation (see Chapter 7). Continue to focus on your breathing. If thoughts come, just turn your attention back to your breathing. With practice, the mind calms down and you can observe your breathing without having to count breaths. Just be one with your breathing – it often becomes so light that you barely notice it.

You can observe your breathing in the abdomen or at the nostrils. At the beginning it can be an advantage to observe it in the abdomen, to ensure you have good breathing. Later on, it is a matter of taste which one you choose. Often breathing becomes more natural if we observe it at the nostrils and let it take care of itself in the body. It is all too easy to be "helpful" and unnecessarily interfere with the breathing.

The "OM" sound

A mantra is usually a sound without any obvious meaning, so that we do not start to reflect on it unnecessarily. But if we prefer, we can also choose a word that has a meaning, such as "peace", or something similar.

The most commonly-used mantra worldwide is the OM sound (pronounced ooohhhmmm), which has a fascinating history that I would like to share. In his writing *Die Bedeutung von OM*, the Indian yoga teacher Selvarajan Yesudian writes that the Sanskrit syllable OM embraces the whole universe. Everything that exists emanates from the vibrations of the OM sound. OM is regarded as the oldest sound and everything that is radiates from OM – like the rays of the sun. Everything we see, feel and can touch is condensed vibrations of OM – the absolute highest reality. In Hindi, OM or AUM is a synonym for God. It is also the same word as AMEN. We humans are a manifestation of OM and the OM sound is therefore considered to have a beneficial effect on our body. It is thought to give peace, take away negative energies, imbalances, and also strengthen the body's self-healing capability – as the body is a condensation and manifestation of OM.

There are different opinions of how OM should sound. In my view it is good to do it on exhalation, since this will be extended. OM can be expressed either silently or loudly. In either case and after a while our body is usually filled with delightful vibrations – repetition of the OM sound raises our vibration frequency. During this meditation we can choose to focus our attention on the brow center or the heart center (see Chapter 14).

I would also like to propose the sound "Aaah" as a morning meditation – pronounced on the exhalation with an open mouth, loudly or silently, depending on where we are. "Aaah" has a wonderfully rejuvenating effect on body and mind.

If you choose to meditate on a mantra: sit comfortably and prepare yourself as described above. Start by observing your breathing for a few minutes. Then begin to focus on your mantra – for instance OM (ooohhhmmm). Finish as described above.

Observation

To be affected by something, I have to, as we discussed earlier, identify myself with it. By instead taking on the observer role, I can gain access to the part within me that only witnesses everything that happens. I can then watch the world from my center without getting "stuck" in irrelevant details, opinions and judgments. If you have been developing your inner observer (Chapter 5), you have already trained your ability to observe life without valuing, judging or becoming involved – neither in the positive nor the negative aspect. Just being aware of the duality, of both extremes of our interpretation, and refrain from identifying with either of them. In this state we can – as Stephen Wolinsky puts it –watch "the mental parade".

From here, we can calmly and firmly observe what arises in our consciousness without being drawn into it, without thinking thoughts around it, without trying to change anything. Just let it emerge, watch it, acknowledge it, welcome it and thereby transform it (in love and trust). We are able to free ourselves from anything that comes to the surface. By taking on the observer role, we can watch even the negative without feeding our interpretations. In this way, we can deactivate old neural links and have the opportunity to see our existence in a new light. The most important is not what has happened to me, but how I experienced it – and I am free to change my interpretations.

You can use the posture described above also during observation. When this is learned, the body and mind know instinctively what to do and we automatically enter a state of heightened awareness.

Start here too by observing your breathing for a few minutes. Then either notice what emerges naturally or something you previously decided to observe – for example, a reaction you would like to relive and study more closely. If you encounter resistance, do observe this in the same way – without being drawn into it. See that it is just energy.

We can anticipate that the ego will protest, defend its point of view and can see changes as threatening, can be afraid of entering the unknown and leaving its familiar reality. We must have the patience to let go, one bit at a time – not because we have to – but because we choose to. We choose a higher level because we see that it will give our life a deeper meaning and more comfort. But we should also make sure that we do not create new constraints – such as having to pretend that I am more mature than I am, or satisfying some inner need to behave in a certain way, which all can force me into a new prison.

Making yourself independent of the outcome

An exercise that I usually use if I have become a little too fond of a certain outcome, is to imagine a set of scales, where I place the desired result on one side and the alternative result on the other. I then mentally move from one to the other, watching both scenarios until I can accept and experience both outcomes as equally good and see that both are created by essentially the same energy. Then I can continue to work for what I want to accomplish without worrying about the alternative. As long as we are dependent on a certain outcome, we are not free.

Moreover, we do not always know what the best solution is. A good way then is to affirm "the best solution for all concerned". This often produces some amazing twists and turns.

> *Those who behold the horizon every day*
> *will never become narrow-minded.*
> Anders Källgård, M.D. and author

Stillness of thought

According to Deepak Chopra, meditation is a way to prolong the space between thoughts. We spoke earlier about the importance of being able to *observe* our thoughts, to be conscious thinkers. But there is also an advantage in being able to go beyond thought and experience the world without interference from the intellect, discover that there is something beyond thought and begin to see the "screen" that we mentioned in Chapter 13. When we can successfully still our thoughts, we can discern that screen – first by glimpses and then more like a connected whole. The screen is a complete void, the unchanging background where we can "be at rest within ourselves".

Funnily enough, stillness of thought was one of the first things I came across when I started to read about personal development. One of my first books was by Krishnamurti, in which he writes about moving beyond thought. It sounded very strange to me at the time and I was struck by the idea that if nothing else, I would at least think "now I'm not supposed to think". I was completely stuck in my thoughts, but had never reflected, or even noticed it.

Driven by my curiosity I decided to explore it. Krishnamurti was considered to be the wisest man in the world, so I supposed he would know what he was talking about – and I will never forget the first time I succeeded. I was sitting in our garden when suddenly my mind became totally quiet. What I remember the most is how all the sounds suddenly became much stronger. The birdsong was deafening and everything around me became so intensively *alive*. It was an overwhelming and almost shocking experience.

So how can you free yourself from thoughts? It comes of its own accord when you have practiced meditation for some time. The mind calms down, thoughts become slower and sometimes stop. The space between thoughts expands and becomes larger. If you want to experience the feeling of being free of thoughts for a moment, just say to yourself "I wonder what my next thought will be" and then wait. Was it silent for a moment? Observe the silence and when the next thought arises, ask the question: "Where did that thought come from?" The answer, of course, is that it came from you. You are the thinker! We can also, if we wish, "lock" the thought by fixing our eyes at the root of our nose, between the eyebrows.

Thus, we have the opportunity to perceive the world without chattering thoughts, without it being filtered through the present conceptual reality, without putting words to our experiences – only perceive it through the energy aspect. Just note what happens in the surroundings, for instance observe a sunrise, the mist coming off the water, a bird flying away, a fish leaping and leaving rings in the water. We can watch all of this without thinking, just experience it in total serenity. (Until suddenly something happens that makes our mind start to reflect – and think thoughts – around it.)

The space between thoughts is also ideal for goal-visualization. As we saw in Chapter 5, the brain-wave-states alpha, and above all theta, are the most favorable levels of consciousness for anchoring visions and goals. In the transitional stage between thought and non-thought we can take the opportunity to drop our wishes.

The more we work with ourselves, the more sensitive we become. Our mind is sometimes likened to a dam – the calmer the water in the pond, the more clearly we notice every ripple. It is the same way with our mind – as long as it is upset, we are unable to notice our thoughts and emotions, but the calmer we are within, the more we can discern what moves inside of us.

During meditation, we can reach a state of oneness and eternity; moments of complete fusion with the whole, where we experience just a pulsation, just energy vibrations. Only the pure life energy remains. In this state, it is clear that we are part of something much bigger.

But what I really want to stress here is the incredible *rest* I get from being spared the constant thought-chatter. Today, thoughts probably come to me even when I am not consciously thinking, but they are often so weak that they do not reach me. I experience life much more through intuition and my body – through the vibrations that surround us at all times.

Only when we can silence the inner chatter, can we really enjoy being on our own – really "socialize" with ourselves (our Self). When in contact with the whole, we cannot experience loneliness, in the sense of *feeling* alone, here we are part of everything. The silence becomes alive and vibrating and puts us in harmony with the essence.

The inner silence also keeps us in a state of openness and receptiveness, where we can capture the inner communication that is constantly available, if we have our tentacles out and ready.

In the borderland between non-form and form, we can "download" information that is not influenced by our present perception of reality (our five senses). This connected state is sometimes compared to how computers work. If I want to know more than what is available in my own box I need to connect to the larger network – the universal consciousness – to get information.

When our thoughts calm down, we can begin to make out our true inner voice, the communication that goes on all the time without us noticing it.

We can put questions to our inner being and receive answers from a higher level, sometimes in a language other than the one we usually use. Often in the form of sudden moments of clarity and sometimes – when I am stuck on the details – as a counter question, such as: *what is the purpose*? There is often a tremendous power in the answers we receive, often amazing. How then, is it possible to know when the answers come from our higher Self? The criterion for me is the strong sense of ease and certainty. I simply do not ask any further questions. I have my answer and the question has ceased to exist.

Many insights and aha-experiences come to me in everyday life, when I am doing ordinary activities, out for a walk or similar; that is, not during the meditation itself. These insights often affect me physically as well, like an incredible weight in my body which forces me to sit down – often with a sense of both doubt and wonder. "It just can't be like that – it is not possible!" But eventually I come to realize that yes, it is possible.

Sometimes the answers can be more humorous, like some time ago when I became stuck in my thoughts and irritably said to myself that I could not get any further, that I needed a teacher. "You do have me" said the quiet inner voice. "Yes, but then you should give me better ears", I said angrily, "because I do not understand the message". "It does *not* come through the ears" said the gentle inner voice. No, I was fully aware of that, but the reply filled me with laughter and the irritation was gone.

Intuition is mostly sensed as a complete and instant experience – without words and not gradual, not a little at a time. We can learn to feel the difference between the chatterbox and the true inner voice by practicing our sensitivity. When we honestly, from our heart, ask for help to *understand*, we tend to always receive an answer.

To make contact with our inner guidance we can, once again, visualize a mountain:

Sit, or lie comfortably. Relax and observe your breathing for a moment until you feel calm and have peace of mind.

Imagine that you are in a valley and that in front of you is a tall mountain – it can be a familiar mountain or one you create yourself. Now, begin to climb the mountain. You walk upwards in the sunshine, feel the fresh air and enjoy the freedom and the silence.

You are on your way to a meeting. Somewhere along the way you will meet a character – it could be a wise old man or woman, or some other figure. This person/figure knows all about you and feels great love for you. You will be able to have a conversation with this person and ask questions about your life.

You are now approaching the top and enjoying the freshness, the light and bright colors. You can continue to walk the mountain ridge or sit down and wait for your visitor. Eventually you catch sight of a character, with whom you gain a deep contact.

When you are satisfied with the conversation, you wander back down the mountain, taking with you the answers you received. You can return to this place as often as you wish when you have issues that you want to be illuminated.

The person you meet comes from a higher level within you and is always loving. If this is not the case, then you may have received a visit from your inner critic. If so, make sure you relax a little more before you do the exercise.

Sometimes, we have to walk this path several times before we meet our figure. I had to walk for a long time before, quite suddenly, I met the person, who has since been my inner teacher. This exercise was one of the first I tried, and I probably had too much doubt about the whole thing.

The underlying wholeness does not change,
but we change when in contact with it.

The experience of being one with everything

To better understand how this inner information and communication can arise, we can remind ourselves that the universe may be a hologram (and therefore also our brain). Maybe, by going into higher states of consciousness, we can reach frequencies where our brain is able to interpret the holographically-encoded information about the universe, and thereby become aware of our relationship and oneness with all things.

Several of our quantum physicists speak about altered states of consciousness. Many say that they are meditators and have had spiritual experiences which have lead them further in their search for scientific knowledge.

What if our ability to perceive this higher communication depends on how well we train our mind.

What if there is a harmonic base frequency in the universe that we can tune ourselves in to, and thereby reach a greater "co-vibration" with the whole.

Will I become an introvert?

Is it really wise to devote so much time to one's inner being, you may be asking. Will I not become too introverted?

In our everyday lives, we may not need to be too concerned with whether there is an outer world, separate from our inner. It is enough to state that regardless of whether there is an outer world or not, all of our *experiences* take place within us. Everything we see, we see inside us. Everything we hear registers within us. Everything we feel and think, we feel and think inside. We respond to the outer world, but regardless of whether it is an inner world or outer world event, the actual experience takes place inside us. There are outer world *events*, but no outer world *experiences*. However, I can convey my experiences to others and I can *act*.

We constantly walk around in our own darkness or light and we are always free to remake our story, dissolve dark memories, add bright memories and so on. We are our own actor and our own director.

Hence, I create my own life through my interpretation of what is happening, through everything I see and hear, think and feel; through my expectations and intentions, my relationships. No wonder we all perceive the world differently and see different realities.

Wherever I go and whatever I do, I can never experience something outside myself.

Ponder that for a moment!

If everything I can ever experience happens inside me, what could be more interesting than really getting to know this inside. *The stage on which everything plays out*!

Always "at home"

When we are in contact with our center we always feel "at home", no matter where we are. We do not need to rush through life in search of happiness – what we are looking for most of all is within us, waiting to be discovered.

Here, I would like to say a few words about the feeling of love and bliss, which is often experienced during meditation and which is commonly not mentioned in this context, because then we can easily end up doing what I did: start to expect it and thus trip ourselves up.

The feeling of bliss emanates from the very contact with Being, from the whole, from a state of non-expectation, so striving for something actually prevents its occurrence. Instead, it is about just sitting down, without the expectation of anything at all – and thus not separating oneself from anything at all – and in doing so, we can move beyond duality and connect to the wholeness, the oneness. Somewhat tricky? Maybe a little unusual for us Westerners, who often prefer instant results.

Although we may not be completely whole, we can always move into the whole/coherent state and see life from this perspective. Gradually, we are able to be more and more in contact with Being in our everyday lives, to live from our center, from our heart.

As Deepak Chopra puts it in *The Path to Love*: "As you begin to master the art of letting go, with patience, dedication and love, your reality will change." He says that much of the old will disappear and that instead we will find ourselves. A self that is not made up by "beliefs, expectations, and interpretations, for these things come and go. It will be a permanent Self, rooted in awareness and creativity. Once you have captured this, you have captured the world."

A moment of stillness and silence

Getting to know oneself need not be such a big thing. We can get into the habit of taking a moment for ourselves during the day, when we slow down, feel our emotions and take care of the day's negative thoughts before they become a mindset. My interpretations create neural connections in my brain, which will grow into routine patterns, unless I consciously avoid this. Meditation is a great way of detecting and disabling those neural connections, which do not lead to positive development. Neural links are broken when not used; and by being observant, I can consciously form neural links which better reflect who I want to be.

Sit down for a moment, relax and reflect over the events of the day. What has broadened your understanding of life, where have you become stuck in old, outgrown habits. The more we can observe our limiting patterns, the more we can deactivate the old connections and form new ones.

Short moments for concentration

An easy way to train our concentration is to take advantage of short moments, such as waiting at a red light or in a queue. Here, we can still our mind, observe posture and breathing. Use this time for short concentration exercises, where instead of making myself annoyed or bored, I can decide to focus on one single thing and keep doing so until it is my turn. I can choose breathing or an external object, a point or similar; as in this case it is advisable to keep the eyes open.

Cash checkout queues are also a good place to observe our thoughts, feelings and prejudices about people. Here we can learn a lot about our beliefs and our inner dialogue.

Harmonic movements

Posture and movement have a big influence on the emotions we experience. Our movements affect our body chemistry and we can use movements – slow and fast – to reach a more harmonic and coherent state.

We have all heard about whirling dervishes, and rhythmic dances and drumming has been used through the ages to reach higher states of consciousness.

Slow movements demand more concentration and a raised awareness. Walking slowly, for example, sends strong signals to our body to calm down. We can practice so-called meditative walking – walking in places with a calmness which allows us to only focus on the actual movement. After a while the body walks by itself.

In addition to yoga, qi gong and the like, we can use everyday tasks to gain greater harmony – ordinary tasks such as unloading the dishwasher, hanging out the washing, and cleaning – by doing them in full presence and awareness of our movements. Here I have plenty to learn myself. I explained in Chapter 9 about my subpersonality "Little Miss Sprinter", who does *not* have the time to move slowly. However, while writing this, I also took the opportunity to clean the windows and tried to do so in total awareness. Being present in what I was doing, listening to the sounds in the distance made it a very restful time.

A future medicine

The knowledge that we can affect our health through diet and physical exercise is so accepted today that we can get it on prescription. How long will it be before we also can get breathing- and meditation exercises on prescription; against high blood pressure, for example? Meditators have fewer days of sick leave than non-meditators. Meditation/mindfulness is a way of releasing energy so that we can live with less "friction".

Nowadays, we know that our immune system changes with our state of mind and that we can influence our brain ourselves, so that it produces hormones and neurotransmitters that make us feel good. The dependence on tranquillizing or antidepressant drugs could no doubt be reduced in the future, as we learn to attain a greater inner peace through our breathing, our way of thinking, the way we deal with emotions and so on.

A holistic view of reality – with greater understanding of how intertwined everything is, how we are co-creators of what emerges, how we can influence our health and reach states of mind that we did not know even existed – is also going to change the way we see science. We will have to realize that we can only gain certain knowledge through our own experiences, and qualitative methods like self-observation will gain a higher scientific status.

Meditation can also be an aid in recovering from traumatic experiences. An article[2] on brain scanning states that research results have shown "that people with relatively higher activity in the left part of their frontal lobe more easily recover from upsetting experiences. If they are shown a frightening picture of, for instance, an accident, the negative impressions fades faster than with ordinary people, in whom the brain activity of the frontal lobe is dominated by the right part."[3]

---

2 The Swedish magazine Illustrerad vetenskap (Science Illustrated) No 9, 2004.

3 Author's translation.

This reminds me of a man from the emergency services who explained that nowadays, after particularly difficult call-outs, the practice is to sit together and meditate, instead of holding a debriefing session. This provides such a perspective to what happened that afterwards it feels as though the experience was a month ago.

Knowing the results we can achieve through mental training will probably make it more natural in the future to take a daily ”inner shower”. Just as we shower on the outside, it should go without saying that we also need to clean up on the inside. Making sure we take away the ”dirt” before it becomes ingrained, and use suitable “detergents” like meditation, observation and breathing exercises to increase our life force.

It will probably also become more common to take off for longer ”purifications” in nature, to retreats and the like for recharging, a kind of regular “lubrication” of the system. It helps to gain perspective, to be able to see what is important and what is less so. Our high-tempo lifestyle can make it hard to find the time to take care of all of our feelings and experiences as they arise. A common phrase in the office is ”paper jam” when the paper gets stuck in the printer – maybe we could call what occurs inside us a real ”emotional jam”.

Meditation – like all mental activity – changes the brain and we can contribute to the balance within, and live with greater joy and efficiency. Experiencing consciousness in its pure form gives us a broader view of life and a deeper sense of living.

Chapter 17 – Time

Time has been discussed a great deal in recent years and lack of time is a recurring theme. But time seems to be just a concept – one that we humans have created.

Lennart Lundmark, author and historian, gives in his book *Tiden är bara ett ord* a detailed description of the emergence of the concept of time. From the "natural" time – when humans followed only the changes in nature, sunrise and sunset, seasons and the like, and had a need to sort their daily impressions and experiences into some kind of order – via the ancient Greeks, the birth of the clock, industrialism and Taylorism, with its time studies of working life, through to the age of the train and the need for a country- and worldwide time system. He writes that our natural concept of a uniform and universal time has not been formed by deep-thinking philosophers, but by technological and economical changes and once we have understood this, we can start undramatizing the concept of time and make it our servant instead of our master.

The concept of time we have today, where we perceive it as an independent, autonomous phenomenon – something that exists "in itself", independent of surroundings and context – is relatively young and has already been questioned by many.

The question of time

Peter Heintel, Austrian Professor of philosophy, who founded Tempus – a club whose aim is to delay time – said in an article[1] that time really does not exist. "What exists is processes, movements and

1 The Swedish newspaper Göteborgs Posten (April 1, 1998).

changes. Dividing them into bits, measuring and naming them time is a human invention. Measuring all processes with the same yardstick is absurd."[2] Lennart Lundmark says in the same article: "Just knowing that clocks do not measure something out there which proceeds at its own pace gives us a new freedom".[3]

We Westerners commonly perceive time as something outside ourselves. But time obviously measures something within us – our *inner idea* that something is ticking out there. So it is not time that stresses us, but our concept of time.

The linear conception of time

In my opinion, the linear conception of time is what causes problems for us. In our culture, we often have a mental image of time as a kind of road. This makes us believe that we "are on our way" to something or somewhere and that we are also in a *hurry*. We partition time into past, present and future and want to manage as much as possible during "our short time on earth". Life becomes a race towards death.

The linear concept of time is not shared by all cultures. In the agricultural society for example, the circular/cyclical conception was the norm. I am a survivor from that time and see the months of the year as a round dial, with January as 1 o'clock, April as 4 o'clock and so on, and I place all events into this mental dial, from where I can later see when things will happen.

Asians are said to have an image of time which is more like a web, out of which events appear and disappear here and there, which for me is similar to quantum physics' description of the wave- and particle concept; where one can see the quantum field as a web/sea of energy, out of which events arise, gain an identity/particle aspect, then disappear and return to the whole again.

People in Africa suffer a shortage of most necessities that we take for granted, but not of time, and we just need to transport ourselves

2 Author's translation.

3 Author's translation.

to Eastern Europe to see quite a different perception of time and a much greater disrespect for the clock.

Fast and slow time

Thomas Hylland Eriksen, author and Professor of social anthropology at the University of Oslo, writes in his very amusing book *Tyrrany of the Moment* about how he no longer has the time for his research, since he never gets enough uninterrupted time to immerse himself. The time which remains unbooked is barely enough to just answer e-mails, write articles and the like. The breaking up of time into small snippets means that many things are only superficially done.

He also speaks of fast and slow time and how the fast time can be useful for many things, for instance when using technological advances. It is *good* to be able to e-mail to the other side of the world in a moment, but many things definitely do not benefit from being sped up – a symphony for example, or looking after children, the elderly, or maintaining relationships.

Good decisions also take time; require reflection and maybe even sleeping on the matter. I am thinking here of the American Indians, who are said to go out into the forest and sit under a tree to wait for an answer when they have important questions to consider.

Clock time and experience time

Even if time did not exist, clocks do. This fantastic tool that has been given so much space in our lives that it often controls us, rather than the other way around. This gives us a reason to really reflect – both about the legitimacy of accepting this view and to also take action, so that we can live with the *feeling* that it is we who manage our time. For as we saw earlier, it is the very feeling which is the most important in this context.

If we yearn for something to happen, time seems to go more slowly than if we try to avoid something. Our experience of time depends on our state of consciousness and we can influence our own experience of time by learning to move in and out of different states of consciousness. Time exists only in the intellect and we can – when needed – easily move to a state of timelessness.

Meditation helps us to go beyond time and into timelessness and thereby gain a perspective on the concept of time. If we go deeper "into" time, we end up in timelessness. Our personality lives within the concept of time, while the Self is in timelessness. So we could probably say that time both exists and does not exist. It depends on how and where we look – from which state of consciousness we are watching.

It is remarkable that when you one day come to a place where there is no labor-saving machinery, you get so much extra time.

Freely translated from *The Tao of Pooh* by Benjamin Hoff

Time off versus free time

All time is of course free time. Freedom is an inner state, a feeling that I can carry with me. But if we book up too much of our time, we can easily end up with a sense of lacking time – in other words, in a detached state. Most of us would probably need to practice keeping more of our time "unbooked", to let more of our *free* time actually be free, to create the conditions needed to be able to live in a timeless state more often.

I once saw the expression "hockey time" – meaning that we just count the time the puck is in play. We focus so much on the activities that we forget the important "time for just being". Our time off should be maximized with as many experiences as possible.

What if it is all about *deepening* our experiences, so that they give us memories, meaningfulness and recreation. Put us in tune with the essence and restore our inner balance.

As we saw earlier, we lose much of the contact with our feelings when we are on the move and rush, and without feelings we gain no lasting memories. It is the emotional charge in my experiences that determines whether they will stay in my memory.

The main difficulty we face today is probably being able to take as much continuous time off in order to realize how trapped we are in time and in the current concept of reality. Many of us would benefit from a freer approach to time.

Urgent matters are seldom important.
Important matters are seldom urgent.

Haste and efficiency

It is easy to mix up haste and efficiency, to think that we are more efficient if we hurry up. But for the most part it is probably just the opposite. Efficiency is about paying attention – focusing on the right things – and sometimes the most effective thing could be to do nothing at all – to let life come to us and await the right timing.

Time pressure is a trap that takes away spontaneity and creativity. We act like robots and rush from one task to the other, which causes feelings of "must", stress and inadequacy. The rate of change from 1945 up to now is said to be equally great as from 1945 and two thousand years back. Hence, we are exposed to a huge amount of influences, and much job satisfaction and joy of living is lost because people are not able to follow their own pace.

The biggest gain we can make in time saving and well-being is by focusing our energy on what we want, without being carried away by unwanted thoughts and emotions.

"Time is money"

The expression is no modern phenomenon. According to Lennart Lundmark, it was coined as early as 1751 by the author Benjamin Franklin. But the person we have come to think of most often when we hear this expression, is probably the engineer Frederick Taylor with his Taylorism, time and motion studies and assembly lines.

The exaggerated focus on time has undoubtedly given rise to increases in productivity and much of our prosperity. But this forced tempo and increased competition of course makes the competitors also speed up their tempo and as a result everyone needs to run faster. No advantage is gained, apart from the rise in productivity. The challenge now is to strike a balance between prosperity and well-being, since well-being has steadily decreased as prosperity has increased.

A rush to what?

In my courses, I have given participants the task of answering the question "a rush to what?" So far, we have not come up with a good answer. We have to realize that basically, we are not heading anywhere. We live here and now.

Take a moment to play with the idea that time does not exist. What would that mean for you? Would it change the way you live – and if so, how?

What if it is true that time stands still and it is us that move.

Time will linger enough
for those who know how to use it.
Leonardo da Vinci

Time as a gift

Wilfrid Stinissen, Ph.D., Carmelit friar and author, writes in *Evigheten mitt i tiden*, that we can see time as a gift, given to us for development and growth. Time – with its past, present and future – allows us to interconnect and get a general view, to gain insights and give new meaning to past experiences. It gives us the opportunity to make new choices. He also says that we can gain time by using it well. By being in harmony with my core and my mission, I can use my time in a way that takes me forward and helps me grow.

Maybe we can see time as a helpful companion, giving our life structure and meaning, but which does not possess any energy/power *per se*. It is us that give content to time and we can make sure that this content is meaningful.

While writing this chapter, I was forced (under intense internal resistance) to give up my goal of when this book would be finished. Life gave me so many other things to deal with and I could not take away other tasks. I managed to get a stomach ache before I saw the absurd situation – I had become stuck in time pressure while writing about the time that did not exist! The deadline, which initially provided structure to my work, had become a burden and I had to let go of the date I was aiming for – to allow it all to emerge at its own pace.

A new way of viewing time

In Chapter 13, we spoke about how our conceptions keep us trapped in a limited reality, through their definitions of what something is, or is not. In the world view/perception of reality that is now emerging, our view of time will change. We will see a paradigm shift here as well.

"The concept of time is a construct that exists only in our consciousness. And there is nothing wrong with that, as long as we do not try to turn it into something else",[4] writes Lennart Lundmark.

Tragically enough, it seems that the faster everything goes, the less time we feel we have. We really need to "see through" our concept of time. Time exists in the intellect and helps us to put structure and order to our existence. We need the uniform time and the clock to coordinate our activities and for our communication – but we can choose our *attitude* towards time.

Concepts change constantly and our conceptions are basically just "forms of energy" in our consciousness. If we accept that there is no

---

4 Author´s translation.

objective time, what kind of meaning/energy would we then wish that our concept of time contained?

What we can predict is that we will have a concept of time that is more related to the issues at hand, more related to our inner clock, our inner rhythms. Flextime, computers and other technological tools have led many of us to become more independent of time and location when performing our work. The difference between work- and leisure- time has already begun to blur. For many professions, work hours will be of less importance as the basis for income. In the future, increasingly more people will be paid for the accomplished result – how much *time* a person uses to achieve this result, will be of less interest. Time will quite simply not be the yardstick.

Our internal image of time

Even if the overall view of time is now being questioned, it will take a while before this has any impact on society at large. But in our private lives we can immediately make some major changes. In addition to more firm steps like making sure we create more unbroken time, do not book our time so far in advance, and see which of our activities lead to our goals, we can start to change our *internal* image of time. With a calm and harmonious image/feeling inside, the body's alarm system is not so easily activated, even if the outside world is just as "messy" as before.

Feel free to use a pen and paper for the following exercise, so that afterwards you can write down the information you receive from within.

Sit, or lie comfortably. Relax and observe your breathing for a while, so that your body and mind calm down.

Now be aware of the concept of time. What does time mean for you? See if you can find an image that represents your idea of time – a symbol of your relationship to time. Connect to the feeling that the image conveys.

See also whether you have different images of time for different situations. What is your image of working hours like? Of vacation time? Do these two images differ? Sense the feeling that the images convey.

Take your time and when you are done, straighten up and open your eyes. Note down what you learned about your internal images of time.

If time images appear that you would like to change in some way, for example an image of work as a treadmill, a clock with hands spinning as fast as a rocket or a holiday image that you are not happy with, you can change that picture for one that better captures the essence of what you would prefer – for instance, a sun that slowly moves across the sky, a calm lake or a joyful time together.

If you want to program a new time image, enter into deep relaxation, evoke your ideal image and begin to associate it with the situation you want to change.

Sit, or lie comfortably and begin to relax your body. Observe your breathing for a while until you feel comfortable and in harmony. Evoke your ideal picture/feeling and start to transfer it to the situation you want to change by linking the new image to that situation.

If it is about your workplace, see yourself being there while at the same time keeping your desired feeling. For example, you can link your desired feeling to your office chair. If you do this regularly – until the new image feels natural – your inner time picture, and thus your feeling for your work situation, will change.

Continue to explore your inner time images, for instance while in traffic jams or waiting at the checkout, and replace them with images that symbolize the feeling you want, that improves your well-being.

Dare to think for yourself

Time is obviously a concept that we have created ourselves from the rhythms of nature and our time consciousness is learned like all other concepts. But since the lack of time appears to be by far the largest single source of stress in the Western world, there is every reason to explore it further.

Time is apparently just a way to measure events and thus no shortage in itself, but when morning comes, most of us have already "sold" our time – we are so booked up that there is rarely any time left for spontaneous ideas and creative thoughts. The feeling of lack of time is due to our fragmented perception of reality and is actually a lack of contact with the essence, because when in a coherent state we cannot experience "a shortage".

If we explore time a little more, we end up in timelessness. If we go deeply into time, the separation disappears – our belief that time exists outside ourselves, living its own life. Meditation/mindfulness, relaxation and the like, help us to make contact with timelessness and Being, to gain perspective on time, to question why we accept only the intellect's perception of time; thus allowing us to take a more personal and flexible attitude to time. Learning to live *in* the time is to live in the present moment, in a coherent state.

My own relationship with time has changed during the writing of this book. I have had to create unbroken time, large, uninterrupted chunks of time, to be able to write regardless of time and the clock – regardless of whether it is night or day, weekday or weekend. I have had the privilege of spending long periods in timelessness, with only sporadic visits in the so-called reality.

The more I have thought about the idea that time might be just a human construction, the fonder I have become of the "concept". I have come to really like time – it is a clever construction, which we should give the appreciation it deserves – use the absolute time where it works best, and use other yardsticks when they fit better.

The division into past, present and future is a useful one, when we know that this division is only an aid to the intellect (the intellect and the thinking need the concept of time in order to work), but being aware of its relativity should allow us to reconsider and perceive our entire existence in a new way.

Once again we can ponder the quote by the Buddhist monk in Chapter 13: "once you realize the approximate nature of all concepts, then you can really love them, because you love them without attachment".

Wilfrid Stinissen suggests that we should view time as a spiral form: "The spiral is a synthesis of the cyclic and the linear. Everything comes back, and yet everything is new, since it happens on higher and higher levels."[5]

While we can see that the universal time has created so many possibilities and much progress in the world, we need to have the courage to adapt time more to our own rhythm, to live more in the present. Allow ourselves to sometimes work a lot, sometimes less, to take care of children, study, do something else for our development. We need to rethink, but above all: *dare to think for ourselves*!

Next time you look at the clock, dear reader, remember that it only measures what we humans have agreed that it should measure!

---

5 Author's translation.

Chapter 18 – The Now – authentic presence and happiness

"Always say 'yes' to the present moment. What could be more futile, more insane, than to create inner resistance to something that already *is*? ... Say 'yes' to life – and see how life suddenly starts working *for* you rather than against you" writes author Eckhart Tolle in *The Power of Now*.

Yes, what could be more foolish than resisting something that already is, that has already happened. Still, this is just what we mostly do when we get stuck on things in our everyday lives, get irritated, are in a hurry and the like.

Always now

When we organize our experiences in a linear fashion, time appears as past, present and future, but strictly speaking, it is not possible to experience anything outside the present moment. It is *always* now. Yesterday was "now" when it occurred. It was "now" 2000 years ago, it was "now" when we were born and it is going to be "now" when we die. There never was, and there never will be a time that is not *now*. The past is experienced *now*. Planning for the future is done *now*. When the future is here, it has become *now*. We experience everything in the now – the present moment is all that exists – everything else is thoughts, dreams, memories et cetera, that appear in the present moment.

How long is the now? The moment? The intellect would like to divide the present moment, prefer life to consist of an infinite number of small "nows". But that is once again a conceptual construction.

When in contact with the whole we can experience that the present is *eternal* – one single eternal now and in this now I reside. My task is to stay present in this now – as here lies the power and the potential for development.

Thought escapes the now. If we always spend our time in the intellect, we live in a mental construction and miss the experience of the present moment – the only real moment. We need time and intellect, clocks and diaries in order to function in this world, but we can still live with an awareness of Being and the now.

Krishnamurti tells us that we must learn to "die" from yesterday in order to meet every day as new, to experience life with a fresh mind – as if it was the first time I had seen it.

Eternity is in every moment and
every moment holds all eternity.

Authentic presence

The moments we are able to be completely in the present will convince us that the now is the reality – the raised vibrations in the body, the peace, ease and joy, the feeling of eternity. Wilfrid Stinissen puts it like this in *Evigheten mitt i tiden*: "Time stands still ... The clock continues to strike, but we are no longer synchronized with it. We no longer live in what passes by, but in what is permanent, the eternal."[1]

I saw somewhere the phrase *authentic presence*, and I think this is the best expression I have seen for this presence, where we are in harmony with the essence, the whole.

We can see how present we are by estimating our sense of inner peace.

1 Author's translation.

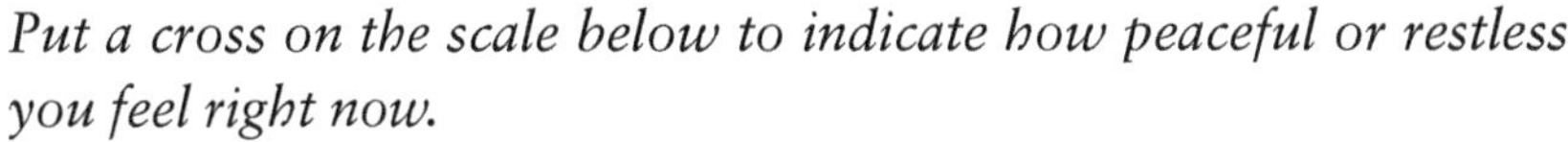

Put a cross on the scale below to indicate how peaceful or restless you feel right now.

1__________________________5__________________________10

Restless, impatience	*Inner peace*

The degree of inner peace corresponds to the degree of your presence in the moment!

Feelings of well-being come of their own accord when we are present. Presence raises our vibration frequency and gives a heightened feeling of life.

Stress makes us lose contact with the present moment. We are often enraptured by the future and an impatience to be ”there” instead of ”here”. This means that we leave the coherent state, take a much too long-term view, making us ”shorten” time and causing us to feel that everything clashes. We can ask ourselves: *what does this moment demand of me*? In most cases, not so much.

We saw earlier that our memory is affected negatively if we lose contact with our feelings, and often a bad memory is the same as bad presence. When anchored in our center – our memory is good.

To live our everyday life with total presence in the now – to live in the eternity that exists in every moment – is often referred to as ”enlightenment” in Eastern teachings.

Life never repeats itself –
we repeat ourselves.

The lessons of life are learnt in everyday life

We can see life as an exciting inner journey, where existence provides the situations and people we need for growth and development, to make our behavioral patterns visible – if we choose to see them. To strive for a lifestyle that prevents us from creating new burdens and new pain. To make sure we have the opportunity for reflection and presence enough to see the meaning in what happens to us; to be able to take care of our experiences when they occur (or when the old catches up with us) and be able to use them for our growth. As we said earlier, we do not need to *search* in our past for reasons and explanations. If we have unprocessed emotions and experiences within, they will manifest themselves in the present moment. *Guaranteed!* If we are observant, we can even see that the mistakes we make *now*, happen because of what we need to learn *right now.*

Regardless of the measures for growth we choose to take (such as observing what happens, meditating, breathing through and the like), we do it in the present moment. The now is all we have and all we are ever going to get.

Sounds simple, doesn't it? If the present moment is all there is, why do we not go there directly and skip everything else? Why do I write 17 chapters before getting to the heart of the matter? Well, to succeed in staying in the moment – reaching authentic presence – we need to be able to observe our thoughts (to go beyond them), master our emotions (to let them through), notice our breathing, posture and so on. Often, we are so trapped in our physical reality, with all the mundane tasks and responsibilities which call for our attention, that we are unable to keep contact with the present for longer moments. We need *to practice.*

Practicing presence/mindfulness

Practicing to be present in the moment is not so much about *what* we do – rather *how* we do it. We do not need to worry ourselves to death in finding the optimal exercises – it is the very *presence* in the exercises that is the key. It is all about quality training – in other words, the *degree* of presence in what we do. Training to be present is about training our senses and it is often enough to perform simple exercises, such as drinking a cup of tea in total awareness or touching an object and really paying attention to the feeling against your skin. We can slow down our movements, go for a mindful walk, listen to the sounds and really *notice* the surroundings. We can observe our breathing and posture, practice being focused in our heart. We can eat a mindful meal – smell and taste!

An easy way to reconnect with the present – with the moment – is to listen to sounds. Take a few deep breaths, relax and start focusing on the sounds you become aware of. For example, the whistling of the wind, the birds singing, other people's voices. Notice how your awareness follows the sounds as they arise. If disturbing thoughts come, let them, but do not focus on them. Go back to just listening to the sounds around you.

Do something practical, like washing up, in a mindful way. Feel the water, the washing up liquid, run your hand over the porcelain. Discover the pattern of the plate. Feel how pleasant it is to just be here and now, in thought, feeling and action.

Personally, I feel that I am helped by doing things in the "right" order, to sense the energy of the different tasks, adapt them to my own rhythms and choose a good structure during the day. It helps to keep me present in what I am doing, instead of already being on the way to the next task.

If we are deeply rooted in the present, we feel peace and joy in what we do and can start noticing when "friction" arises in the way we handle things. Getting caught up in a separate state can occur in the blink of an eye – something happens to make me irritated or feel pressurized and I lose contact with my center and thereby access to a deeper understanding. I begin to see reality from a limited/fragmented perspective. If I find something tedious and boring, for example, this points to a lack of presence. If I raise my degree of presence, it directly becomes more interesting. The cure for restlessness is a heightened sense of presence.

If you feel that you have lost contact with Being, take a short pause and focus on a single detail. This will help you back to the present moment. What you focus on is not so important, but you can, to further emphasize what you want to achieve, use the same detail every time – like focusing on a ring you always wear. The repetition means that your inner will associate the focusing on the ring with being present in the moment. Add if you wish a couple of spine-flex breaths (Chapter 7).

Contact with the present and the Self gives us insights from a higher level, a wider perspective of life, makes us feel part of a larger reality. The past and the future do not disappear – they are still there – but do not so easily affect or interfere with our presence in the now.

Gradually, we will become aware of when we unintentionally lose ourselves in the world of thoughts and how our state of mind affects our interpretation of life. To remain present in the midst of an active life, in the middle of our daily duties, to accept the present moment the way it is – as if we had chosen it to be that way – to study our thoughts and feelings, provides enough information for us to be able to grow and develop.

Happiness

Happiness can be hard to find within, but is impossible to find outside ourselves. Happiness is a skill that we can learn – it is not a gift we receive from someone else, from outside. Everything we experience, we experience within ourselves.

Many years ago, I saw a picture of a man who dashed through life in his search for happiness. Behind him came a tiny old woman running with a wand in her hand, shouting: slow down, slow down, I will never catch up with you. She was the Fairy of Happiness.

Studies of happiness have shown that 93 percent of happiness has to do with internal factors. Only 7 percent is due to the outside world, like winning money, which one easily might think would bring happiness. It is also shown that happiness rises sharply after the actual winning moment, but after a year the feelings of happiness are back at the same level as before the win – and later on, the happiness is even lower than before. One explanation for this is that we have changed our frames of reference. We make different comparisons to those we made before.

Lasting happiness

As long as we *strive* for happiness, we remain in duality. If there is something "separate" that is happiness, its opposite, unhappiness, also exists. As long as we relate joy and happiness to someone/something special, we run the risk that it will be lost. If we want a more permanent happiness, we have to do away with all notions of what happiness is.

We must free ourselves from the *very need* to be happy. Learn to see the difference between attachment to happiness (deficiency) and enjoyment of happiness (wholeness). As long as I have an attachment to happiness, I also risk being unhappy. We normally experience happiness in relation to a situation/person, but we can also experience this increased feeling of vitality *in itself* without relating it to an object. To free ourselves from the notion that life has to be a certain way for us to be happy. It is not the outside world that prevents us from being happy, but our notions of what happiness is. Often, we search for an image of happiness that we have created ourselves.

When we feel unhappy, we have an insufficient contact with our center, the life-pulse, our deepest values – we do not manage to make contact with the essence. This state is often made worse by incorrect posture, poor breathing and more, which further add to our miserable feeling.

Feelings of happiness are largely about the extent to which our senses are activated. We can compare it to falling in love, when our mind is totally absorbed by the object for our passion, how our vibrations are raised so that it feels like we are floating on the clouds. This happiness, however, often tends to be of a transient nature as we do not manage to stay at such a high level of vibration for longer periods, but by moving beyond duality and being able to live in a more coherent state, we can make our happiness last.

We have the seeds of a more permanent happiness within, a happiness that is not dependent on outer world events, not "object related". Liberation lies beyond duality – by going deeper into Being and drawing energy direct from the source.

Happiness – a skill

To train being present in the moment is to train our ability to experience happiness. Happiness comes from everyday things when we are fully present. Raised awareness enhances the experience. The very presence generates feelings of happiness – the degree of our presence determines the degree of our happiness.

Feelings of happiness resonate in the heart and are about opening our heart center. But probably the most import thing is to understand that happiness comes from within, even if we may perceive it as coming from outside. It is released within us when our parts are in tune – in a coherent state – in a harmonious oscillation with the larger reality.

Joy and happiness come automatically with the coherent state – a state of unconditional love for life itself, as it is. Our ego surrenders to a larger perspective, leaving more room for our spiritual dimension.

We cannot be happier than the state of mind we are able to put ourselves in.

What if happiness is a frequency we can tune in to.

Always as young as the present moment

Our personality lives in the world of form and time, the Self in timelessness – in the eternal now. The pure consciousness has been called the fountain of youth – as young as the present moment. By having our deepest identity in the timeless Self we can avoid identifying too much with concepts like age and aging – thought-forms in our consciousness – and instead have our identity in Being, in the very existence.

We can live and act from a deeper reality, where we are in contact with our inner guidance, feel confidence in the life process and fully accept what is and what has been. This is an "energy efficient" way of living, which reduces wear on the body; we are replenished to the extent of what we give out – extremely rejuvenating for body and mind.

Balance between "being" and "doing"

Feelings of happiness come from the actual presence in who I *am* and what I *do*, and are ultimately about my ability to create a meaningful life – to *develop* in who I am and in what I do, to follow my path and find a purpose in life (Chapter 21).

Our challenge today is probably to find a balance between the non-formed and the formed energy – between "being" and "doing" – to be able to gather energy in being and transform this energy into action.

Author Anna Bornstein writes in her book *Intuition* about C. G. Jung: : "To embrace the diversity without losing sight of the unity, to experience physical forms while being aware of the formless spirit; is how we could perhaps summarize the goal of the psychological development that Jung had in mind for the modern Western individual."[2]

For my own part, I have to realize that my personality holds a sprinter (incidentally my best sport at school), who loves it when life runs at high speed, but who – if she is allowed to carry on – soon puts me in a fragmented state. She is always on the starting blocks, ready to pursue some imagined urgency, but she also contains lots of energy and a thirst for activity. Nowadays she is balanced through contact with Being, where I can reset myself, rest in the present, gain guidance from my higher Self and take a new direction.

Since we will never be "complete" in our personal development, it is a gift to be in contact with the level within us where we are "already there", and from there be able to liberate ourselves from limiting approaches in our present perspective of reality. Being makes the background to everyday life, which then takes on another meaning once we have made contact with the whole.

2 Author's translation.

Chapter 19 – Relationships and love

Love conquers all. Love can move mountains. Love can be something far greater than we perhaps usually consider it to be. Love is the fundamental power/energy that we cannot live without (unlike aggression, for example). We know that babies die without love and touch, even if they are given food and dry nappies.

While reading (for personal growth and for this book) I have come across many descriptions of the "all-unifying force" that scientists are searching for – the theory that could give *one single* explanation of how the universe works – and in several places there are discernible hints that this power could be *love.*

The message sounds familiar, it is not new, but comes this time from maybe unexpected quarters; that we could also get scientific support for the strong power of love – love as the highest working energy, the very principle of life. Several scientists have been on that track, among others David Bohm, who said that this power could well be "love in the sense of some very intense energy…".

What if love is the higher energy that holds the universe together.

Once, when I was driving the car and thinking about the void – the sea of energy that scientists call the "sea of possibilities" – the radio suddenly played the old song *Sea of Love*!

What if the "sea of possibilities" is a sea of love.
What if we live in a sea of love without realizing it.
What if love is the truth.

What do we then do with such big words? How can these insights help us in our often lost everyday lives. Well, if love is the glue of the universe, then love is also what keeps *us* together – from the smallest cell out; which gives a greater harmony between our different parts, puts us in a coherent state, makes us healthier "cells" in the universe.

That love could be the ultimate reality/life force has been long-preached throughout the ages, without so much really happening, so why should it influence us now? Personally, I can think of several reasons:

- The time is right. Mankind does not have so many freely-accessible paths left, if we want to continue living on this planet.
- Quantum physics' explanations of the interconnection of all things towards one single energy can help us to increased understanding of how the universe works. Words like universal oneness simply become more understandable, gain a more "tangible" meaning.
- The personal gain – a richer, more enjoyable life in all respects. More and more people meditate, learn yoga, mindfulness and the like and we are beginning to have our *own experiences* of higher states of consciousness – experiences of being one with everything, and what this means for our understanding of a higher reality.

We obviously live in a coherent universe, a unified whole, where nothing is anything in itself, just in relation to something else. Reality seems to consist of related energies, manifestations of one single, fundamental unity in which spirit and matter are intertwined. Nothing is really separate; everything interacts in this rhythmic, vibrating pattern – in constant motion, and change. Somewhere there is probably a common principle (of motion) which makes all of this work together. If we look around, it is highly likely that love has a crucial importance for most creative processes – from small babies to creative ideas.

If we can accept that we create our own reality, that everything we experience, we do so within, we can start to build truly meaningful and conscious relationships.

Our relationships are the perfect instruments for our development and for finding our authentic power. Relationships bring out the love within us but also our worst fears, such as being rejected, abandoned or not being good enough.

Relationships give us the opportunity to see and work through the parts of us that need to be healed – those parts that want to judge, accuse and the like and want to place responsibility outside ourselves. We know that our feelings do not depend on anyone else, but instead on how we process energy within. My well-being, my joy and happiness are generated within me and every painful emotion tells me that here is something I need to manage in a better way. We can see how such an approach would affect our relationships, our view of love, the meaning of life.

Relationships are ultimately about the potential for us all to become whole, to reach our center and the unconditional love within.

That love exists within us is easy to see when we are in the connected state, but when we fall back into the ego's dualistic approach, we lose access to that wide-screen perspective. The yearning for unity makes us search for love outside ourselves, but the flow of love arises from within us – love comes from being one with the Self.

Love is indivisible and the difficulties first arise when we start to think in terms of separation – "I love this person, but not that person". It is never love that causes our problems, but what we *believe* to be love – or belong to love – like power struggles, jealousy, the "possession" of someone and the like, which all come from fear.

Whenever we do not feel loved and appreciated we are caught up in the separate state. When in contact with our center we always experience peace, joy and love.

Being caught up in a fragmented state therefore does not necessarily depend on our surroundings. We put ourselves in this condition through our own negative thinking, prejudices, old emotional patterns. Maybe I receive a negative comment and feel that I lose my harmonic state because of it, but actually it is due to the feeling of separation that arose within me.

The more we understand these mechanisms, the easier it is to release ourselves from our reactions and the better relationships we can create.

Conflicts

Since we all have our own "interpretation program", our way of understanding reality, conflicts unavoidably arise – which does not necessarily have to be negative. We get the chance to see things from a different perspective, giving us the opportunity to develop.

Conflicts are always about opinions and beliefs. The contradictions are only on the surface level. For anything to become a conflict, we must leave the whole and focus on the parts, meaning we only see a limited part of reality.

Most of our conflicts can be resolved within us – if we were to change the outside world every time we become irritated or frustrated, we would have much to do. For instance, during meditation we can go to our center to regain perspective, mentally move back and forth between the views of others and our own, until it all becomes more neutral.

You could say that the problem belongs to the person, who experiences it in his own body – it expresses itself as irritation, anger, accusations, prejudices et cetera.

Be aware that people sometimes gain energy from conflicts, are "addicted to adrenaline" and become energized by creating dramas. The separate state is painful; accusations and the like provide short term relief from the inner tension.

If we intentionally hurt or accuse someone, we will have bad vibrations in our own body. Praise and appreciation give rise to good feelings, within the giver as well.

We can practice giving feedback instead of criticizing. Criticism activates people's defenses and we could try to create dialogue instead of argument and debate. A dialogue where we listen and see things from the viewpoint of the other person without judging – just to gain a better understanding and spark conversations that *give* energy instead of draining us. Conversations where we feel free to say yes or no – to set the boundaries from our center.

We can consciously try to create win/win situations even when it comes to smaller, everyday situations and ask ourselves if anything can be done better. What is already good? What can we do more of? What needs to be improved? How can we improve? Who does what?

In stressful situations: ask for time to think things over, leave the situation for a while to regain the inner balance. As we said earlier: if we do not ensure that we always take energy from the source, we leave our well-being in the hands of others. I give power to another person to determine how I will feel.

If I am able to remain in my center, I can keep my energy flow regardless of what others think or do. This happens automatically when I am in a heart-focused state. Our ability to understand the perspective of others and be generous is not so much about having a noble personality; it is more about the state of mind we are in. In the connected state we feel confident and generous.

If we too readily take responsibility for the problems of others, we should remember that other people also have a higher Self, and trust their ability to solve the problem themselves. Solving our problems provides strength and growth. If that sounds indifferent, go to your heart and feel your love and trust for the other person's ability. If you like, you can have a mental dialogue with the other person's higher Self and entrust the Self with the solution.

"Difficult" people

If I regard another person as difficult, I cannot have a good relationship. My very attitude separates us.

Instead of accusing others, we can withdraw the projection and ask ourselves: *What is it in me that makes it difficult to accept this person?* We can take a closer look at situations and people we would rather avoid and reflect: *What does my feeling signify? What does this arouse within me?* I can choose to take 100 percent responsibility to heal that part within me.

We cannot change others, but we can create a climate that promotes change. We can begin to see the other person as we *want* to find him/her. The "wrong" person can sometimes be our best teacher, who challenges our perspectives, our interpretations. So-called personal chemistry can be seen to be a matter of maturity. When in contact with the whole it is easy to get on with each other.

If you want to improve a relationship, focus on something positive in the other person. Everyone has positive sides, if you cannot find one in the other person, the barrier is within you. You then have some of your own inner work to do. Once you have resolved it all inside, it will resolve itself in the outside world. The other person will sense your changed attitude (your altered vibrations). Stay with the positive and take the new picture to your heart.

During the process of transforming a relationship it can be easier if we do not see the person for a while, in order to really integrate the new image. Otherwise it is easy to fall back into the same old ingrained opinions.

If instead other people have difficulties in accepting *you* and your path, that is part of their development.

The observer – a built in therapist

Why are my fingerprints always on the dagger in my back? I once read this in a book and it illustrates in a witty way our participation in everything that happens to us.

By using our inner observer, we can watch our reactions – see what lies behind them and see our own part in everything. Feel when we drift over into negative energy, irritation, defense, irony and the like.

There is always a reason for what we do. Behind every emotion there is a need. Behind every behavior and action there is a positive intention. Everything we do aims at meeting a need within us. Observation brings our feelings and actions into focus and helps to set us free from old habits.

The observer's compassion for our efforts makes it easier for us to find the true cause.

Healing a relationship

As we are all connected on a deeper plane, we can never completely leave a relationship – it just seems that way because we focus on the particle aspect. The relationship endures even if we do not see each other; it is just separated on the surface, which does not mean that it has *ended*.

All relationships teach us something – even if some are only short meetings, while others are lifelong. Some bring up more of our "baggage" than others and of course it is then easier if both parties see the "benefit", the gain and development that these relationships offer.

Sometimes, relationships are broken against our will, by death, for example. Or we can be forced to end a relationship because it has become destructive or quite simply does not feel meaningful continuing. In both cases, it is important that we can heal the relationship lovingly on a deeper level.

To be abandoned often raises a whole host of emotions, such as rejection, inadequacy, worthlessness and can send us straight into the abyss (Chapter 8). But it can also help us to go beyond the point of annihilation and in the long term, find our core.

By moving beyond duality and putting ourselves in a loving state, we can heal our relationships; discharge them emotionally, understand that it is never anyone's "fault". Things happen because of where we are in our development.

If a relationship has been broken, I can still heal my own part, so that I do not accuse and carry negative energy in my body. What I feel and experience does not depend on anyone else. I experience everything within, and we can work with ourselves so that we can conclude in harmony. Here we have to be truly honest with ourselves and "vacuum up" the recesses of our inner being. It is easy to believe that we are finished, when the body no longer reacts so strongly, but if we watch carefully, most of it is often still there, in a more subtle form, such as an almost imperceptible shift in the energy flow. Residues of negativity easily hide unseen after the larger anger, frustration and pain has passed. It may take time before we are able to heal a relationship physically, mentally and emotionally and reconcile ourselves with what has happened.

Take on the observer role so that you can watch without judging yourself or anyone else. Just observe your ideas and what you feel. Feel your emotions; they are yours alone and have nothing to do with anyone else. The process of observation discharges and dissolves – if we are willing to take full responsibility.

Bear in mind that we are the ones who will gain from cleansing ourselves from the pain that otherwise drains energy and negatively influences our life and health.

Ideally, we should not break a relationship before we are firmly rooted in our core and can think about the other person with warmth and love; can wish health and happiness for that person with all of our heart. Even if we are not able to love the qualities and behavior of everyone, we can always love their potential, the person they could be, or could have been.

At some point in the future, we will have to leave behind our relationships, and for conflicts that are hard to resolve, we can do a "preliminary" exercise by moving ourselves forward in time and imagining that we are very old. Note that this exercise must be done in a deeply relaxed state, where you can come into contact with your higher Self and move beyond duality.

Lie comfortably and relax your body. Focus on your breathing until you feel completely calm and at peace.

Now imagine that you are very old. You are lying on your deathbed with only 30 minutes left to live. The other person/persons are with you in the room and you have half an hour to express what you want to say. Go to your heart – and in this heart-focused state – say what you want to say.

This perspective usually helps us to go beyond the details and see what is essential in our life and our relationships.

Accept that you may fall back and need to do these exercises many times before it is all released. But it is important to understand that our higher Self, our heart, never accuses. It feels compassion for us and others in our attempts to solve life's problems.

A relationship is completely healed when I, from the bottom of my heart, feel that I can release the other person and wish him/her all the happiness in the world.

Sometimes we are also simply "finished" with a relationship and it comes to an end by itself. We have learned what we could from each other. The relationship has played itself out, it is unsullied and neutral and we can – if we wish – conclude it with love and move on.

Love yourself

This may sound like a cliché, but it is the fundamental condition for us to be able to put ourselves in a coherent state. If we are unable to love ourselves, then we are unable to reach the loving state which is the prerequisite for feeling and experiencing true love.

We have to love others *through* ourselves – by being in a loving state of consciousness. In other words, love ourselves to be able to give it out to others – be able to look at ourselves with compassion and tenderness, before we can look at the other people's struggles with tenderness.

Loving oneself is not the same as selfishness. Selfishness arises from a lack of love, from the inability to love oneself. If we cannot give love to ourselves, we become – not through unwillingness but through unawareness – very demanding to those around us, who are then expected to fill our inner emptiness. Most of us have grown up with *conditional* love, that we should be a certain way in order to be good enough, and often we have integrated these expectations so deeply that we demand them of ourselves in order to feel worthy of love. We need to understand that we have the very source of love and joy within us.

We can learn to see the difference between superficial love and inner love, to distinguish between deficiency-love and true love, and learn to love consciously. What makes us unhappy is not what happens on the surface, but losing contact with the essence and not being able to see the underlying whole.

Romantic love

"What is it, that can make a person leave everything and at the same time feel as if they had won the first prize? That, almost from one day to the next, can make people reevaluate and want to exchange their whole life: their home, their money and even their children?" This question comes from a series of articles published in a Swedish daily newspaper[1] and the answer is of course – the big passion!

Passion/romantic love gives us temporary freedom from thoughts and feelings of separation, takes us beyond duality, but also forces us to meet our deepest fears, like being rejected or abandoned, not being good enough, not being sufficiently loved.

Gary Zukav gives in *The Heart of the Soul,* a hilarious and drastic description of our search for "salvation" – our hope of finding the perfect partner, the one who can make us happy for the rest our life and save us from our own inner struggles. He writes: "The breakdown of romantic attraction – the end of the honeymoon – begins when the savior cannot deliver. Since both individuals in a romantic attraction view the other as a savior, this disillusionment is shared." We begin to see the other person as s/he really is, with qualities we had not noticed before, that we may not be so "over the moon" about. He says that our life continues as before, but now with the addition of a partner.

Gary Zukav described romantic love in an equally amusing way on a TV program, by speaking about "Earth school". For as long as we live on earth, we go to Earth School, the University of Life. Here we can, among other things, choose the class on Love. The first term (foundation level) is about romantic love. After that we are supposed to attend more advanced classes – and there are many – but most people choose the romantic class over and over again, only with different partners!

---

1 Dagens Nyheter (August-September 2001)

Romantic love is an illusion in that we fall in love with an image we have created of the other person and then are disappointed when the two do not match. I have projected certain qualities on the other person which I need to develop in myself.

When the fog of love lifts, we return to our own personal basic mood with anger, sorrow and the like, and need to start working on our development once again. Gary Zukav says that the day we are as equally attentive to what is going on inside us as in the outside world we will become our own salvation.

The illusion ends but when the magic glow fades we can begin to consciously bring love into the relationship. The romantic attraction brings our old, unresolved problems to the surface and gives us the opportunity to heal them in the present moment. It helps us to see through the unconscious love, the ego's conditional love: I love you as long as you love me, as long as you behave in a certain way and do what I want – the part of us that comes from the fragmented state and has a need to control.

When we start to take responsibility for our immature sides, we can also appreciate the opportunity for development and increased inner security and maturity with which we have been presented. The conditional love is really not love because it is affected by fear. But in most cases, superficial love is likely to exist side by side with unconditional love, as we develop.

Romantic love/passion takes us – with its high vibrations – beyond duality, and passion can also, as we will see later on, be a path to a higher form of love – to a spiritual breakthrough. (From passion to compassion.)

Conscious love

If romantic love is a short term relief from the fragmented state with the help of another person, then true love is about being whole within yourself.

Of all the illusions I had to free myself from, the illusion of passion as being the greatest love, was the hardest to let go of when I started working with myself. All the beautiful love histories, all the romantic "you complete me's" – could they be just a precursor to a more authentic love?

In *Freedom from the Known*, Krishnamurti wrote that if you really love your man or woman, you would love him/her just as much even if s/he were to leave you for another person. Otherwise it would be just possessiveness, power struggle and similar feelings, and not true love that you felt – a hard message to digest maybe. But finding lasting happiness through another person is a somewhat deceptive solution because the long-awaited state would be gone if the person in question disappeared from your life.

We probably have to realize that we can only find authentic love within. The feeling of love that we experience does not actually come from other people, it is rather certain people and situations that make us open our heart chakra. A resonance happens between our vibrations so that love is released *within us*.

Love never ends. We have to block it – close our heart center. Love is a state of consciousness that we can choose and which requires constant practice. Every single day brings events and situations that challenge our ability. If we want to free ourselves, to grow and become whole, all the lessons we need come with the situations and people we meet. We can use what each day offers – to either grow or fall back.

The problems are not in the relationships as such, they are within us – and as the psychiatrist and author Elisabeth Kübler-Ross writes in *Life Lessons*, all too often we get rid of our partners instead of our problems.

Other people reflect what we need to address in ourselves. It is easy to forget that we only see the world from our personal, narrow perspective, our own interpretation program.

All arguments – regardless of what they seem to be about on the surface – are really about the same thing: the emotion that arises within me; I do not feel sufficiently loved, appreciated, respected. I feel rejected, abandoned, insufficient – and I consider it to be the other person's fault.

But if we take a step back instead, breathe and notice what is going on within us: this is how I feel, this is what I do – and allow ourselves to explore the emotion, we can see that it is *not* about the other person. *It is about what is triggered within me.* Which of my ideas trigger these emotions?

Feel free to use the exercise in Chapter 7 "To breathe with our feelings" and/or "The emotional layers", Chapter 8. You can also use "Solving problems through heart focus" in Chapter 15.

By moving to my heart/the whole I can see through my old habits, see my ideas, thoughts and emotions. See what is my own rubbish and what belongs to the other person. For as long as I am unaware, I will create the same situations over and over again.

Even if I change partner, the same lessons will apply but in a new setting, until I stop projecting my emotions and take care of them myself. How I feel is related to my own physical sensations – and everything I am able to sense in my body, I can also take responsibility for.

Through ignorance/lack of awareness, we can take a relationship to the edge of no return, but not actually *beyond* the edge – if both parties understand the reasons for their behavior, realize that the injustices have come from the ego's fear and if both are 100 percent committed to taking responsibility for the relationship. Then there is the potential to continue with a conscious development perspective, a willingness to help each other evolve. But it places great demands on total honesty, both individually and jointly.

Acceptance is the beginning of conscious love. Acceptance of each other's differences and needs, otherwise we are trying to change the other person.

Love is not demanding – rather it shares its wisdom. It is fear that is demanding, something which is easy to see when we are in a coherent state; hence, we can help each other to a greater maturity.

We also do not need to rule out a relationship just because it no longer gives us the vibes it once did. They do not come from the other person, they come from within me, because I opened my center and we both lived from heart to heart. If we do not feel these vibes anymore, then we have closed our heart center and need to open it again.

By paying attention to, and focusing upon the beauty in each other, these are the qualities we are nourishing. Attention is energy and –

as we saw earlier – what we pay attention to, grows. We can focus on strengthening, instead of undermining each other, through a lack of feedback and so on. We all want love and appreciation, and it is therefore important that we have a loving tone in the relationship so that we do not unnecessarily hurt each other and block our love. We can deliberately nurture what puts us into a coherent state, see the feeling of alliance in the relationship as the most important – and when conflict does arise, visualize that our partner *really* is on our side, which he/she is in the deepest sense, if we all are each other.

If you want to improve a relationship, try the following exercise:

Sit or lie comfortably and start relaxing your body. Focus on your heart and imagine that you are breathing through your heart (Chapter 15) and put yourself in a heart-focused state.

Bring forth an inner picture/emotion of the person with whom you want to improve your relationship. Visualize that you are building a bridge of light and love from your heart center to the other person's heart center.

By repeating this exercise when deeply relaxed, you can move the energy from the power struggle of the third chakra, up to your heart center. Sense how your feelings and choice of words change.

When you are in a heart-focused state, nothing and no one can upset your inner balance.

If needed, repeat this exercise before you meet the person in question, and if you notice that the meeting becomes strained, refocus your attention on your heart center.

In a conscious relationship we can – if we really want to – argue consciously, and air our views and emotions, and bring our fears into the light knowing that the other person will see that this belongs to me, and will realize that he is talking to a "three-year-old". Arguing from this perspective does not "impress" the other person or start any defenses, and we can take a closer look at the way we react – really be able to use conflicts and fears for our growth (which can spice up life and the relationship – it is an incredible privilege to be able to clear ourselves from all sorts of internal hang ups).

I once saw a metaphor of a good relationship in the form of a set of gear wheels connecting to each other and driving each other onwards. An image that illustrates the actual flow of energy in a relationship and how we can act as each other's "propelling principle".

In order to create a lasting relationship, both parties must be prepared to take full responsibility for their own thoughts and feelings. The awareness that we create our own reality leaves no room for accusation or victim roles. The more we realize that feelings arise within us, dependent on how we manage the energy flow, the easier it will be to free ourselves from the belief that they come from those around us. As long as I walk around with unprocessed pain within me, there will be something to "attach to" for everything that happens to me. But I can take personal responsibility for my inner balance and see that I am free to reinterpret my ideas. I set the limits.

As long as we live with the abyss inside, we cannot stay *permanently* in a coherent state. We run the risk of our relationships falling apart again and again, until we see and take responsibility for our unhealed wounds. By using our relationships as the true mirror for our healed and unhealed sides, we can move from the third chakra's life of struggle to the heart's level, allowing a whole new perspective and opportunity to develop in a dynamic *interplay*, instead of a "power play".

What if we attract the people we need to take us further in our development – people who have a complementary pattern, which forces us to deal with our problems (which I think we can often see in the rear-view mirror).

What if relationships are not primarily intended to make us happy, but to give us the opportunity to grow and mature. Joy and happiness arise naturally as we come into contact with the essence.

Even if we are in a great relationship, each of us needs time for ourselves in order to develop, to find our own driving force and be able to retain contact with our center. Being able to enjoy my own company is an indication that I am in contact with the whole – and therefore a sign of health.

Reality is always subjective and I can take responsibility for creating a reality that makes me and those around me live and feel as well as possible. Allowing ourselves and each other to develop our higher potential and realizing that love is not about being overprotective, overly "caring" or worrying about others, which actually comes from a lack of confidence and trust. We can learn to see love as a strong, positive force – the highest working energy, the true life force.

Humor and playfulness

What we humans are said to regret the most as we approach death is that we did not take life more lightly. We realize with sudden clarity that it probably did not have to be so serious and wish that we had dared to take a more playful attitude (that instead of struggling, we could have developed through joy).

Humor and laughter is a great "lubricant" in our relationships and there has been much recent writing and research about the relieving and healing effects of humor and laughter.

During the past 40 years the time we laugh each day is said to have reduced from 18 to 6 minutes. A child laughs on average 400 times a day, an adult just 15 times. Humor and playfulness are the first to abandon us when we are stressed, afraid, when we enter a fragmented state, but humor is also what instantly raises our vibrations and takes us to a coherent state, for instance, through a real burst of laughter.

Real humor puts us in contact with the whole, enabling us to see life from a higher perspective.

Fear also has its laughter, for example scornful or malicious laughter; having "fun" at someone else's expense. But this kind of laughter does not have the liberating and healing effect. We can easily imagine how it would feel in our body after this kind of laugh, compared with the good vibrations we experience when we laugh really "heartily". The highest form of humor is commonly regarded as being able to laugh at yourself!

Note that it can sometimes be tempting to laugh-off important issues instead of addressing them.

A reliable measurement of a good relationship is to look each other deep in the eyes and be able to laugh together. We can also practice this mentally.

Think of some people around you and sense who you could look deep in the eyes and laugh heartily with. There you have a pure energy flow between you. If it is difficult to smile at some people, there are maybe some things you need to address.

Conversely: do people turn their gaze when you look them deep in the eyes? If this happens repeatedly, you can be certain that they carry old grudges that they have not processed.

Relaxation promotes a humorous approach and we can practice finding the joy within us. In a heart-focused state, our lips are easily drawn into a smile.

If we smile at another person, that person cannot resist the impulse to smile back. We are obviously made to automatically answer with a smile. Try it yourself!

Genuine meetings

When we are in contact with our own authenticity, we bring forth the authenticity in others, and vice versa.

Only when we are in contact with our center, can we experience genuine meetings, where we meet in oneness, beyond duality, beyond views and opinions – where we can have a real dialogue. Such meetings often stay with us for the rest of our life as they leave an imprint within us on a deeper level of reality. They are infused with a strong feeling of togetherness, where you feel like twin souls, as if you had always known each other and can feel a totally magnetic attraction. What really happens is that we meet ourselves in the other person – at a higher level.

Passion for life

In her book *Intuition*, Anna Bornstein gives an excellent depiction of a higher meaning with passions, how restrained passion and attraction can lead us deeper inside ourselves and help us to heal the inner separation gap. She speaks about the pain we often suffer when our heart "is prised open" and how an unexpressed passion "burned away" the more superficial ideas and emotions that hindered and distorted the deeper wisdom from her inner being.

She describes the consuming passion as not primarily physical but as a higher form of togetherness, where words and touch "seemed to disturb the intimacy, rather than deepen it". She writes that normally, when we are hit by strong passion, we live it out which makes a large part of the potential remain unconscious. But if this is not possible, she writes "you get to experience the passion in a different way. It flares up within you, and you experience it as heat and fire. By burning in this way you begin to understand something about the fire that is inherent in life. You recognize it in other people's actions. This is not something you think consciously, it is intuitive knowledge, a new perspective that opens up."[2]

A friend of Anna Bornstein's explains in the same book: "We felt no desire when we were closest. It flared up when we felt far away and could not reach each other. Therefore I believe that passions have more to do with a feeling of isolation and confinement within oneself than they have with true love ... ." She says that her strong emotional experience remained long after the man had disappeared out of her life and that the passion transformed to a healing process. She describes it as "a kind of fusion" in her inner being, "often accompanied by an inner ecstasy" ... "I felt free in the true sense of the word, because I was whole in myself." The passion also started a transformation of her state of consciousness, which she says gave her life "the most profound meaning".

Even though it may be tempting to raise our frequency level through a new partner and although it may be difficult to resist this due to the "feeling of going under" which characterizes passion – the belief that we cannot live without this person – we can often just as

2 Author's translation.

well practice where we are. If we cannot fully express our feelings, they have nowhere else to go other than deeper within us, which – if we are open to it – will take us closer to the essence.

Both love and sorrow raise our vibrations. Grief is a form of love. We only grieve what we love. Sorrow opens our heart center and what we take to heart is transformed. In grief, we can reach depths (which transform into love), that will stay with us for the rest of our lives.

The restrained passion is also – if we so wish – a great opportunity to learn not to relate to an object (Chapter 13). To see through the energy pattern – the trap in taking our energy from the other person and placing our well-being in the hands of someone else. If we can resist the fear of going under, being wiped out and instead explore the pain and the void, we can slowly but surely reach the wholeness where we can draw our energies direct from the source. In this way, we can maintain the heightened level of energy which will gradually transform into a passion for life itself.

Meetings of this nature are among the most overwhelming that we can encounter and it may be helpful to understand that passion can also have a higher purpose, that we need not feel threatened if it suddenly engulfs us, but instead welcome it. See it as part of the maturing process. Growing and developing involves many trials and challenges which give us the chance to see through our illusions.

All too often, love and sex are seen as the same, often portrayed this way in the press where celebrities profess their addictions to sex in their constant search for momentary contact with the whole. In the passions described above, the physical element is not the strongest; the meeting is on the spiritual plane which can therefore be very confusing. We meet in oneness, at energy levels we perhaps not previously encountered, and therefore do not understand how to handle. Here, it is not enough/does not help to live out the passion on the physical level; the transformation takes place on a higher plane and takes us to a higher state of consciousness.

What if "Mr/Miss Right" is the one who makes us develop.

Giving in to your attachments/fears gives temporary relief, while overcoming them provides permanent freedom. When we are in contact with our center, free and belonging is the same thing. Real freedom comes from love and is no longer divided. Freedom is "in" life. We cannot experience true freedom "from" something because then we are in duality.

Love is eternal and indivisible. It stands above duality. We make it difficult with our dualistic thinking where we divide things up and compare one with another.

Sit or lie comfortably, take a few deep breaths and focus your attention on your heart.

Recall an experience that filled your heart with love, something that made your heart melt. It could be a person, a newborn baby, beautiful scenery or similar. Relive this event in your imagination, as if it was happening right now. Experience all the details again – sights, sounds, feelings, insights.

Stay with this experience until you can sense the love in your heart and your body. Then focus your attention on the actual feeling of love.

Now, be aware that the very quality of love which gave life to this event is timeless. You can evoke this feeling within you whenever you want, simply by focusing your attention on this feeling of love. The more you are able to engage your senses, the more intense your experience will be.

By repeating this exercise often, it will become easier and easier to reconnect to this state of love, and the more love you will radiate and experience in your life.

Take the time you need, then slightly move your hands and feet, take a few deep breaths, open your eyes slowly and come back to the room. Feel that you can take a part of this feeling into your everyday life.

Developing our ability to love means an inner expansion. It is the state of love itself that gives the satisfaction, enables us to live in inner harmony, in a coherent state. What we give out and take in is ultimately about which frequencies we are at, how we manage the energy within. Love is giving in its nature and is its own reward.

We are related to everything and everyone and our meetings can either put us in a loving state, or in fear – in a separate state. The more we can stay in the connected state, the more we also begin to love everything; duality becomes more diffuse, more blurred in its outlines.

Chapter 20 – Beauty

What the brain does when it transforms energy from non-form to form is outside of my field. But I can accept that it does so and I am sincerely thankful that we have been given the privilege to experience the world in such a fantastic way, with sound, light, color, nature – this never-ending miracle. Just imagine that our brain has the ability to transform these vibrations and frequencies to all this beauty!

So far, we have mostly talked about how to create a heightened feeling of life, balance and harmony within by working with our thoughts and feelings. But we can also take advantage of the outside world to move to higher frequencies – deliberately choose places, people and music that awaken this heightened feeling within us. Personally, my exploration of the formless world has made me more fascinated by the world of form, than ever before.

We all know how stimulating and uplifting it can be to take in beautiful scenery, a piece of artwork or to listen to music that touches us. The beauty resonates within, puts us in tune with higher frequencies, with the whole, and takes us into a loving state. Just like a loving state also allows us to see and embrace the beauty that is woven into everything, to see qualities other than those perceived by our intellect.

When, for instance, we look at a piece of art that moves us we first take it in as a whole. It affects our whole being. Only later does our intellect take a closer look at the parts, at single details, at the actual composition and starts to reflect about it all.

Beauty is crucial for our well-being and health. When we see something beautiful, dopamine is secreted in the body, which strengthens our immune system, among other things. More recent research has suggested that there might exist networks of nerves in our brain that can be susceptible to harmonious proportions and rhythms.

Beauty is healing. Having a beautiful view outside the hospital window shortens the time needed to stay in hospital – something that anthroposophists, for instance, have been good at understanding and making use of.

But we can all increase our understanding of how body and mind is influenced by what we take in and intentionally make use of beautiful shapes, colors, light, sounds and nature to reach higher-frequency vibrations. Also raise our awareness of how our *interpretations* influence what we see, hear and feel and more easily become aware of the beauty beneath the surface. See the beauty in ourselves, in others, in relationships and consciously focus on this, in both the inner and outer sense.

Beauty is in the eye of the beholder. Even if we as individuals may have different opinions of what is beautiful, there seems to be an underlying harmonic order, from which beauty emerges.

The golden ratio

By making ourselves familiar with the principles behind the golden ratio we can gain an *intellectual* explanation for what we have often already perceived on the intuitive level.

The golden ratio can be found everywhere in nature. It is reflected in all physical forms of expression; in the construction of the pyramids, Notre Dame, in the musical scale, in mathematics, in DNA, in the solar system and the entire universe. It is found in our bodily proportions and during meditative states this relationship also appears in our brain.

The golden ratio is described as an underlying code of harmonic patterns which we intuitively perceive as beautiful. It is thought to provide the most harmonic proportions in the relationship of the parts to the whole and vice versa.

According to the principles of the golden ratio, the perfect harmony is in the number 1.618. It is also called the divine proportion and is usually illustrated as a line segment divided into two parts; so that the ratio between the shorter part and the longer part is equal to that between the longer part and the line segment itself – commonly referred to as the golden, or divine, section.

This ratio is also found in the rhythm of our heart and our breathing pattern. (For example, a breathing rhythm with the proportions: inhalation 5, exhalation 8 and rest 3, see Chapter 7).

As humans, we are built according to these proportions and we are in turn part of the bigger picture.

Here, I would like to give some, albeit obvious, reminders of all those things around us which are beautiful, healing and energy-raising. Mostly for free! All we need to do is pay attention and appreciate them.

Sound

Music is said to strike a chord within us, and this may be more true than we realize. According to the string theory, the world is made up of strings of energy – micro-strings that vibrate in many different ways and form everything that exists in nature. An immense cosmic symphony, where everything originates from vibrations of the same basic string.[1]

We can compare this with the explanation of OM (Chapter 16) where everything that exists is seen to eminate from the vibrations of the OM sound, and this sound is therefore seen to have such a beneficial and rejuvenating effect on our body.

Underlying codes also seem to exist in music, codes which we are able to receive and which help us reach higher levels of consciousness, a raised understanding of the larger context. Especially the music of Mozart, Bach and others has been noted for its harmonic proportions. More recently, music has intentionally been composed with the principles of the golden ratio in mind.

Even if music may be easiest to associate with vibrations, everything in the universe seems to vibrate and emit sound. We all partici-

1 From the TV program *Universum svänger* based on the book *The Elegant Universe* by Brian Greene, one of the leading stringtheorists. (Sweden's Television, Vetenskapens Värld, 2004).

pate in the "cosmic symphony". Our language is made up of vibrations, and different words give different vibrations. Silence is alive and we can learn to "hear" even the silence and sense its vibrations.

In the silence the world reveals itself. I associate these words with Franz Kafka, but I am not really sure where I heard them. How well we enjoy being in silence can be a yardstick of our inner centering. Do we feel comfortable in silence or do we become restless and long for activities, for sounds?

If we humans are ultimately only vibrations, it is not strange that we react so strongly to music, birdsong, waves and the like, and that we can enter into a harmonic "co-vibration" with these sounds.

Consciously listening to sound is usually very pleasant and also a very good way of rooting ourselves in the present. See the exercise in Chapter 18 or use this shortened version.

Sit comfortably and relax. Start to consciously listen to the sounds you become aware of – for example, the wind, waves, children's voices, the sound of a car in the distance. See how your consciousness follows the sounds as they arise. Feel how restful it is to be present in the sounds you hear.

We should be protective of the "endangered" sounds and the places where we can still enjoy nature's healing sounds without disruptive influences from civilization. Be careful with what we let our senses take in, where we fix our gaze, what we listen to, how we interpret our experiences. Also learn to listen inwards for our own tone, discover our own "soul tone" and be able to sense the presence of a deeper identity beyond form.

Harmonic rhythms tend to place less stress on the body and provide energies that give us vitality. We can see this in dancers, who often remain youthful into their later years. Moving in harmony with music seems to charge the body with good energies. This can be compared to an elite sportsman, who is said to age 20 years faster than a non-sportsman. Maybe something worth considering.

Light

Light plays a part in all living things and is the basis for all life. Our eye is a lens which directs light to the brain, which then interprets and transforms it into patterns, forms and colors. Even our body rhythms are influenced by the amount of light we receive – both outer and inner light.

The outer light enters through our eyes and up to the pineal gland which regulates melatonin – our sleep hormone – and determines our level of wakefulness. Melatonin is produced when it is dark and its production is inhibited when it is light. During the lighter times of the year we have melatonin in our bodies only at night, but during the darker times – especially during long grey spells – we have roughly the same levels of melatonin during day and night. This means that people with sleeping problems often sleep poorly during the winter season, as they do not receive enough sleep hormones during the night, and instead feel tired during the day due to high levels of melatonin.

During summer, we often get enough light without having to think about it. During winter – depending on where we live – we might need to actively make sure we get enough light. Take advantage of the light available by going out *at least* 30 minutes every day when it is at its brightest. Make sure we walk in open places where the sun is unobstructed, for instance near a lake where the water reflects the light or where the snow is bright and sparkling, all to maximize the effect. We can also see to it that we stay as near to windows as possible. Studies show that people are healthier, the closer to the window they sit in the office.

If we are able to capture the available light, we have, even in Sweden, sufficient light during the winter to escape depression due to lack of light.

The *inner* light is also of great importance for our health and we can deliberately bring more light into our lives by processing negative thoughts and emotions. Thoughts and emotions are energy on different frequencies and we often talk about light thoughts and dark thoughts. “A light is switched on” when we have an idea and so on.

Working with inner light means that we revitalize our cells and reach higher frequencies of vibration. When we change our level of consciousness, we are also changing our light frequency.

To gain an insight into how inner light is able to transform, we can practice bringing light into a difficult situation.

Sit comfortably and relaxed, close your eyes and think of a situation that you would like to see in a new "light". Visualize the image as you see it now. Then pour light onto the picture and see with your inner eye how the situation appears when you throw light on the matter.

Light rejuvenates body and mind and we can use it in many situations. Working with breathing and light has a quick transforming effect. We can simply imagine that we are breathing light into our whole body.

Light can also help us when we come to a crossroads in life and have to take a new path.

Sit comfortably and relax, observe your breathing and feel that your body and mind are at peace. Imagine yourself in the situation at hand and the decisions you need to take. Paint a picture in your mind's eye of some alternative paths you could choose. Then see yourself wandering down each of these paths and feel which one contains the most light.

Love and trust raise the frequency of our inner light.

What if love and light is ultimately the same thing.

Sunlight

The importance of the sun for us and all living things hardly needs to be discussed. One "fine" day we will probably come to understand more about the sun's energy and the intelligence in the light.

The sun's rays bring pleasant relaxation, make our bodily boundaries "float out", raise our vibrations and can, like few other things, quickly put us into a more coherent state.

A great Indian doctor and wise man recommended – as a remedy for *all* illnesses – early morning walks in the sunshine. Taking in the sun's first and last rays is valuable for our health and regenerates our life force.

Once, many years ago, my husband and I were in Southern Europe, wandering down a deserted beach. It was late in the afternoon and we sat down on a couple of abandoned café chairs to wait for the sunset. Just before the sun went down, people came from all directions out of the shadows and stood silently enjoying the scene. Nobody said a word! When the sun had gone down into the sea, the group dispersed, still in silence, and disappeared into the gloom. It was a special experience of togetherness and it says something about our devoutness for the sun, the light and the higher spheres.

Colors

For some years when the children were young, we lived near to a small garden market. The woman in the house was from Italy and mixed the most colorful buckets of flowers. On one occasion when I was there to buy tulips, I asked: "do you not have any bucket of a single color?" She looked at me with raised brow and said with indignation in her somewhat broken Swedish: "Marianne, nature does not look like that". A little episode that had a deep meaning for me. I still think about it and it was an eye-opener for me to see the unity in the diversity.

Colors are light vibrating at different frequencies. They influence our cells, and bright colors raise the cells' vibration level. Colors can be healing and are often used for this purpose.

We spoke in Chapter 14 about how our energy centers are considered to vibrate in different colors and at different speeds and we can use colors to give us strength and dissolve blockages. We can practice sensing which color or colors speak to us on different days. This tells us which parts of us need more energy and we can consciously use colors to raise our vibration. Note that the color black contains no light.

There are many meditation techniques that make use of colors and here is one that I find very pleasant.

Imagine that you are walking along a beautiful beach. Feel the sand between your toes, the smell of the sea and hear the waves lapping on the shore. In the distance you see a rainbow of brilliant colors reaching down to the waterside.

When you get to the rainbow, you walk first into the red color and let it enclose you. Breathe the red color in and breathe it out into your body.

Then move to the orange color. Here everything is orange. Breathe the orange color in and breathe it out to every cell in your body.

Now proceed to the yellow color. Feel how the vibrations from the yellow light affect your body. Breathe it in and let it pour through your body; take in as much as you need of the yellow light.

Continue to the bright green light and let it flow through you. Everywhere it is green. You can feel how vitalizing the green light is. Breathe the light in and breathe it out to your whole body.

Then move on to the clear blue light. Enter into it and sense how healing the blue color is. Feel how you become immersed in the blue color. Breathe it in and spread it out to your whole body.

Now go over to the dark blue lilac, the indigo-colored light, and let in wash through your body. Feel how soothing it is. Give your body a refreshing shower in the blue-lilac color. Breathe in the indigo-colored light and breathe it out into your body.

Finally, enter the white light and feel the brightness in your whole body. Let the light surround you and allow yourself to be filled by it. Breathe the light in and spread it out on the exhalation. Feel how the white light permeates all parts of your body.

Sense whether some part of your body needs more light and if so, fill up a little more there.

Then emerge from the rainbow and back onto the beach, to the place where you began your walk.

Finish the exercise and come slowly back into the room. Open your eyes, stretch and feel calm, happy and in balance.

You can also balance your energy centers by simply sitting down and focusing in turn on your different energy points, and imagine that you spin color into them, until they feel vibrant and alive. Start from the bottom with the base center, with the color red and continue in the same order as above.

Water

Many of us have certainly heard of the Japanese author and researcher Masaru Emoto and his water experiments. I have not read his books myself, but have seen examples of his and others' water experiments here in Sweden.

Some experiments involved taking water from different streams and, after freezing it, they studied the ice crystals and found significant differences in the harmony and beauty in, for example, water taken from a mountain stream compared to tap water.

Water was also taken from one and the same source, classical music was played to one part of the water and rock music to another part; one part was talked lovingly to, while another was exposed to swear words – with more or less the same result as above. The water that got to hear the beautiful music or beautiful language had some brilliant patterns in its crystallization, while rock music and negative language caused chaotic patterns in the crystals.

What conclusions can we draw from that? Well, as far as tap water is concerned, it seems that "dirty information" remains, even when purified. Water seems to be affected by its surroundings, for example by the vibrations of our language.

Water carries information. We humans are, in the main part, made of water, our cells contain water and we know that information spreads throughout our whole body. Every thought we think is communicated to each and every cell and quite possibly they are also spread through our bodily water. Could it be then, that we are able to create health and harmony via the water in our cells? An interesting thought indeed.

Personally, I love water and over the years have reflected a great deal on it. What is it that makes people willing to pay fantastic amounts of money for a sea view? It is true that we once came from water, we were submerged in amniotic fluid for the first nine months of our lives and we are made up of about 70 percent water, but what is it about water that makes us feel so good, what does it get going within us?

In our country house we have an outdoor shower that I – to the amused bewilderment of people around us – insist on using from early spring to late autumn, even though we now have an indoor shower. But it gives two completely different experiences. To stand in the greenery, with the birdsong and the sun shining on me, creating a prism of colors in the water stream has a strong, revitalizing effect, and the essence in this experience is the *water*. It would not be the same thing to just stand there in the greenery. No, it is the water that makes the experience.

A few years ago, a good friend of ours became ill with cancer. She loved to swim, but the last two summers when visiting us, she was too tired and did not want to go in the water. With some gentle persuasion, she eventually crawled in and exclaimed half an hour later "this is a miracle, I haven't felt so good for a year". The following year she had the same experience, the resistance was even stronger then, but she experienced the effect as magic. Of course, taking a dip improves our circulation, but I think there is more to it than that. The energy of fresh water has an incredibly rejuvenating effect on us – especially outdoors in nature.

The sound of powerful waves is almost like a drug. Even the ripple of a brook or a little "waterfall" in the room has an invigorating effect and gives a sense of timelessness. Can perhaps the sight itself and even the sound of water increase the alpha waves in our brain? Can water "speak" to us?

Nature

Being in nature helps us to tune our instrument and puts us in harmony with the greater energy flows in the universe, makes us experience timelessness and eternity.

According to research, sick people become healthier when spending time outdoors. The cosmic radiation of energy, which is experienced stronger outdoors, is good for us, and walking barefoot outside provides an extra influence of earth energy. Being outdoors strengthens our spiritual energy and is important if we want to raise our vibrations.

We can consciously look for places to which our own energies respond, where we experience beauty, harmony and enhanced vitality.

The more we open ourselves to these higher energies, the fewer "diversions" we need. Nature offers all of the beauty and drama that culture is able to stage and convey – the most beautiful works of art, the greatest concerts – and brings healing for the whole of our being.

As we humans are part of nature, we might even call it self-healing. In the serenity and the silence, we can hear the forest talking to us, feel the power of the mountains and hear the ocean's tale of eternity. We can become "high" on these energies, but without negative side effects or a hangover.

In Sweden it is easy to be a nature lover, even if you live in a big city. Our unique legal right of access to open country means we can easily go out in the forest, feel the scent of soil and plants. A few hours in nature vitalizes our cells, making us feel reborn.

Charisma

Charisma is usually associated with beauty, both internal and external. Our radiance is a consequence of how centered we are, how well our parts are in harmony. During periods of chaos in our inner, we often look like a pale imitation of ourself or a shadow of our former self, and these periods interchange with periods of radiance and energy.

The magnetism, with which charismatic persons can take a public with their presence, is a presence that is contagious so that we also reach a higher level of presence and harmony with the essence.

People with a strong conviction in their mission can have very strong charisma. It is an advantage to learn to interpret this energy so we can even see through the deception. (The devil most certainly also has his attraction.) We can ask ourselves what effect this energy has on our inner, which parts of me does this energy speak to. Do I feel in harmony with my higher Self or am I drawn to a lower level?

"Recreation"

Beauty, in both its outer and inner forms, starts the creative flow within us. It contains a rejuvenating power, makes our energy system feel reborn, truly "re-creates" us after periods of hard work and constantly refills us, if we learn to use it in the right way.

Beauty in this form does not carry a price-tag, is not about expensive equipment or facelifts. It is about reaching a deeper level of reality, where, through contact with our core, we see other connections and get the chance to see beyond the form and surface. A delayering towards the simple, the genuine, the more lasting.

Beauty speaks directly to our heart, to the life force within us and to our creative power. We only need to open ourselves to this beauty, to actively seek it and be careful with what we take in. Be aware of what we fill ourselves with, what we identify with and from what we create our self-image – everything from TV programs to more spiritual nourishment. It is not about judging or devaluing, just about making sure we get enough high-frequency energy to keep us in a connected state.

Opening our minds to beauty rejuvenates us. We see the world differently depending on the frequencies we are tuned in to. To change the frequency of our vibrations is to change our life. The greater the coherence, the less wear I am subjected to; and therefore the greater the happiness and the vitality. Thoughts of beauty are thoughts of love.

Chapter 21 – Vision, goals and meaning

Living a meaningful life, feeling that we fulfill a function, that our life "matters", makes our life force bloom.

In quantum physics and Eastern teachings, we gain the insight that we live in a conscious and intelligent universe – a meaningful universe. And because we are all part of this meaningful universe, there is quite likely also a meaning to our own, individual life. If I am part of everything – I am also part of the *meaning* of everything.

If we are all co-creators of everything that takes form, and together we create the world now, it is also important to understand the purpose of my own life, to find my own individual meaning. What is *my role*, what is my unique contribution to shaping this world? What can I give and what do I *want* to give? What I do with my talent is my gift to life?

We spoke earlier about the importance of having a balance between non-formed and formed energy; between "being" and "doing". We Westerners are often more adept at managing formed energy, used to having activities and always being "on the move". But maybe the non-formed energy is the basis for the formed energy. The more I have my identity in Being – the more I know who I *am* – the easier it is to see what I need to do (and not do). I can start to direct my energy towards that which is essential for my development and let my talent and my work become a creative expression of who I am.

Presumably, we are free to create what we want all the time, but with our current perspective of reality this can be hard to understand. We need to experience it ourselves, gain *first-hand* experience that we are able to influence our life and our health. When we consciously start working with goals and visions, it will be confirmed – time and again – how our intention and expectations trigger events, and things start to happen in our life.

Imagination is greater than knowledge.
Albert Einstein

Creativity

Matti Bergström, M.D., Professor emeritus, neuroscientist and author, had a dialogue[1] with Kjell A Nordström, Ph. D. in economics and author, on creativity, innovation and the brain's struggle between chaos and order. They were both convinced that there is – apart from the IQ and EQ – a third intelligence, a creative innovative intelligence which they named virtual intelligence (VQ), but that this intelligence can also intimidate people. They implied that in our society, we have become good at imitating, but that few are capable of creating something new. In this context, they also spoke about the important role playing has for creativity and maturity, and referred to a study from the USA, which showed that criminals often had not played as children; and that the Self therefore never got the chance to mature.

Creativity is a sign of good health. Studies show that creativity is associated with happiness and love, not with fear and depression. It has also been shown that cooperation is more conducive to creativity than competition, and that people whose primary motivation is money rarely accomplish innovative things. Our creativity vanishes with too much routine work and we are also less creative when under time pressure. A hectic, stressful pace of life inhibits our creative flair, while peace and joy release it. We are most creative when our thoughts are not too controlled, and we can find many examples of the connection between creativity and relaxation.

Newton lay under the apple tree when he discovered gravity. Archimedes was in the bath when he exclaimed his famous Eureka. It has been said of Einstein that he only worked for half of the day and sailed for the remainder. True or not, this sounds like a great way of stimulating our creativity. We have probably all experienced

1 Radio Sweden: Stafetten (Summer 2006).

that our best ideas pop up when we are occupied with other things; often things that do not require too much thinking, such as working in the garden or taking a walk in nature.

Innovation occurs through interaction between our visionary, creative intelligence and the intellect. Creative ideas do not tolerate order; too much structure has a restraining influence on the creative process. Scientists experience first, before they formulate their theories. Einstein said that thinking is just a small part of the creative process and comes in towards the end.

I often have my best ideas in the early morning, before I am fully awake, and for this reason, always have pen and paper by the bed. I can then "download" information which the intellect can later sort out and structure on the computer.

Studies show that being slightly careless can be fruitful, that a moderately careless person is more flexible, better at improvising and more creative than a thorough person. It is obviously an advantage if we can cope with having a slight mess around us.

Our brain needs challenges to work well and develop – learning something new stimulates the convolutions of the brain. Our brain is set up to ask why and search for relationships. We are naturally focused on goals and meaning, which supports evolution. Asking questions opens the door to new levels of consciousness.

If everything is basically just energy – a primary reality from which everything emerges – and if everything we create comes from this void, the sea of energy, it is important that we lead our lives so that we are in continuous contact with this energy, with the source. We can practice putting ourselves in a state of consciousness that allows the universal intelligence to flow through us, to create a good climate for break-through experiences and help our creativity, for instance through moments of stillness, meditation and being in nature. To make sure that we have harmony and balance inside to give our consciousness the chance to receive the creative impulses which want to express themselves, that we are open to what wants to take form.

Our common future is influenced by the extent to which we as individuals develop our creative intelligence. What each one of us creates has significance in the larger flow of ideas; it will have an impact upon our society's development and the world we create.

We talked earlier about the creative agony, the confusion when something new wants to find its way from non-form to form, from chaos to order. Creativity often requires solitude. As our ideas are taking form, the "connection" needs to be strong and often we can only have one single person near us.

Inner success does not provide
so much money,
neither can it be bought for money.

True needs

I Could Do Anything, If I Only Knew What It Was ... is the name of a book by Barbara Sher, author and career consultant, and this title well illustrates our dilemma and our restlessness, when we wonder what we should do with our lives.

The type of activity-focused society we currently see, with its "quick experiences", will probably soon be followed by a society where we will look to deepen our experiences, instead of chasing on the surface. A longing to live following our genuine needs and be part of something bigger than ourselves. Genuine *self*-esteem and *self*-knowledge is rooted in the *Self* (and has nothing to do with either ego or performance) and in contact with the Self, we can begin to see what wants to be expressed through us – let our "doing" spring out of "being".

We can begin to discern our true needs – the needs that come from the essence – and examine how our heartfelt wishes and core values look, make contact with the deeper driving force that is with us our whole life, which carries us through difficulties and gives the fundamental meaning to our life. For as long as we are stuck in the ego, we will not come into contact with our higher purpose and have to grope in the intellect and the outside world for "guiding principles".

We can also make use of role models in the search for our deeper values. People we admire reflect our own values and we can start to ask ourselves what these people represent to us.

Write down the names of some people you admire. These could be living people, historical figures, a character from a book, movie and the like. What qualities do you value in these people? What exactly is it that you regard so highly? Write down the insights you have. These qualities are important for you – you have them already – but think about how you could develop them further in yourself.

Conscious choices

Conscious choices lead to conscious development. Our choices become our reality, our identity and together they form our life. Every choice I make is also a valuation of myself. What I am today is the sum of all my choices to this point, and I would do well to ask myself which of my choices correspond to my fundamental values.

A good way of achieving this is to – in everything we do – ask ourselves the question: *What is the purpose? What do I want to achieve with this?* Everything we do has a positive aim, and by asking these questions, I can clarify my motives on a deeper level. Which of the things I do play a part in my higher purpose, and which are just "busyness"? This makes it easier to sort and prioritize, to say no to things that no longer feel stimulating, and thereby create room for the new to take shape.

By consciously using the word "choose" instead of "must" we gain a clearer understanding of our way of doing things. When we *choose*, the power comes from within; when we "must", we are steered by our surroundings. Sense the difference in energy between the lines "today I choose ..." compared to "today I must ..."

All choices have a consequence and lead to new choices. Certain choices open certain doors, other choices open other doors. We all have to live with the consequences of our choices, but in every moment we have the chance to take new decisions and we can try to make the "highest" choice in every situation; choices that lead us to authentic power.

Practice seeing the potential for development/growth or stagnation/ shrinkage in the choices you make and focus on the growth potential – that which takes you to a new level of development.

Keep in mind – if you think you have made a bad decision – that we always get a second chance. Life asks and invites us all the time. Try to see the lesson in every situation.

Finding our purpose

If we live in a world of infinite possibilities, how do we discover our purpose among them all? We probably do not need to search for it, our mission will find us. Life asks questions of us and we could use everything that happens as a guide; we get clues all the time. The difficulty in seeing this is because we are not shown the whole picture in advance. *There is no ready-made path to follow.* You create it as you walk. We have to accept that we can only see to the next bend. Once there, new perspectives open up. Looking in the rear-view mirror, we can often see that we have been heading for our purpose for a long time.

Relaxation and meditation help to keep us in a receptive state, where we are more responsive to our inner guidance and can more easily find the path that is closest to our heart. Our talents are usually found in what we love doing and our mission is about expressing our talents in our own unique way. We can begin to put questions to our inner being to break-down our mental barriers and put ourselves on the right track.

Here are some questions to consider. Sit comfortably, relax and listen to your heart!

What are you interested in? What is exciting? What are you touched by? What gives you joy? Remember – what we like doing the most is not always what we are already good at. Dare to move outside the box!

What do you love doing? What do you do when you can decide for yourself? What makes you lose track of time and space? What did you love doing when you were a child?

What do you dream about that you don't tell anyone? Even daydreams can point out unfulfilled needs.

In which situations and with which people do you feel alive, does your voice becomes strong and devoted?

What would you do if you were not afraid of other people's opinions, if no one had views on what you did?

What would you do if you were financially independent and had a 100 percent guarantee that you would succeed? That question usually takes away our blockages.

What would you regret not having done, if you had only a short time left?

How do you define success? What is success for you? What do you need to achieve in order to accept and appreciate yourself?

If you feel that you do not have the energy for these questions right now, ask yourself: *if you had the energy, what would you do then? If you knew, what would it be?*

We often stop ourselves too quickly. "Too old, wrong education, too expensive, I can't support myself by doing that" and so on, instead of just letting it emerge, giving it time to take shape. The path is the adventure! We can develop our talents through love, start at the hobby level and let them give us joy. When we do things we love doing and when we find our purpose, work feels more and more like a much-loved hobby.

If you have many interests and wishes and find it hard to choose, consider what you can do now, in 5 years, in 10 years. We do not need to do everything straight away. Also remember that our purpose does not need to be anything out of the ordinary or remarkable. It could quite simply be doing something we already do – but in another way.

Being a bus driver in Stockholm city may not be everyone's first choice of a dream job. A good friend told me a few years ago that when she took the bus home as usual, the passengers were given a fantastic guided-tour of the beautiful old mansions along the street by the female driver. As she was getting off, my friend went over to the woman to thank her, and asked her how she knew so much about the history of the houses. The woman answered that she had driven that route every day for a long time and started to become so curious about the houses that she had gone to the library to read about them. She thought it gave an extra dimension to her work and wanted to share the fascinating history. My friend felt very elated and excited after this trip. We can all probably make our work more interesting in different ways, and as usual, it is very much about being present in what we do. *How* we do it, rather than what we do.

How do you know when you have found your purpose?

You no longer search for it and you do not question the meaning of your life.

When we find our purpose, it is easy to prioritize. Time becomes available because we do what we want to do the most and thus there is not much else to tempt and distract us. When we truly decide to fulfill our mission we are also given the power to carry it out.

Play for a while with the thought that we could all work with what we dream about. How would it look if we left our jobs and went away to do what we love the most. Yes, how *would* it look? Let your thoughts loose for a moment? What a boost in creativity for society. What an energy flow. What happy faces we would see. What an increase in health. Would that be the solution to sick leave? And who would do the "crap" jobs? We are all different, with different wishes. Crap jobs, if there are such things, would naturally be paid better. What does a crap job look like? One time, when we did a group exercise on our dream job compared to the worst imaginable, it became apparent that the "worst imaginable" was someone else's dream job. We laughed at that many times.

> *We would not worry so much for what people say about us, if we knew how seldom they think of us.*
>
> Unknown

The worst scenario

Following our intuition often means doing things that we really not dare to do and when we set out on new paths, our inner usually protests. We need to take care of this feeling as well. Find out how our inner protestor looks – observe, let through, welcome – so that we get a picture of what is stopping us. Our motivation can often be double-edged – there can be an inner conflict between the different parts of me. Ask yourself: *exactly what* is stopping me, *exactly what* am I feeling...?

You can use the exercise "my optimist and my pessimist" (a connected state versus a separate state) to more clearly see what your inner resistance looks like.

Divide a piece of paper in two columns, and write "my optimist" as a title on one half and "my pessimist" on the other. Write down honestly how your optimistic and pessimistic sides view the question at hand.

When I had decided that I would write this book, but was still running courses and had difficulty starting (I had never dreamed about writing a book and put it off as long as I could), I explained to a client who had difficulty in starting what he wanted to do that I had discovered a voice within me that said: "It will be a *mammoth job*, it will take all of my time for at least a couple of years. I will not be able to do *anything* else, and then it won't come to anything anyway!" My client exclaimed cheerfully: "Damn, you are worse than me!" We had a good laugh. But it is important to know how your inner resistance looks.

What is stimulation and what is negative stress? Both positive stimulation and fear can be felt as tension in the body. An unusually clear example of this is the widespread fear of standing in front of a large group of people – by far the most common phobia – where we are forced to separate from the group, get everyone's focus, risk condemnation, rejection, being seen as useless, which easily puts us in the fragmented state. (See Chapter 8, *The emotional layers.*)

Personally, I have placed most of my fears there. A few years after my crisis – with all the anxiety and disorientation involved – I was asked to start giving courses, but had taken on a real phobia of talking and a strong fear of taking on anxiety. My spontaneous answer was that I did not want to, but I could also see, during relaxation, that I actually did want to – if I only dared to – and I understood that I would be restricting myself if I said no. My fear was so strong though, that in all seriousness, I calculated that I could have a heart attack and die in carrying it out; but I also saw that on one level, I would die anyway – from disappointment because I had not dared to – from never knowing if I would have managed. It was with much training and self-persuasion that I said yes. I decided that I would rather die from fear than from disappointment. There was also the chance that I would make it, even if I could not see it at the time.

One way of moving ourselves from fear to love, if we are nervous before a performance, is to think "give". What can I give? What can I contribute? This helps us calm down. We do not need to master everything, we give of what we know.

Moreover, it is perhaps not the most important to be successful at all times, but rather see what we are doing, see our patterns and thereby over the long term be able to release ourselves and rise above these limitations (where we see even ourselves from a very limited perspective).

In order to evolve we have to step out of our comfort zone, expand our framework, which often means doing things that I currently do not dare to. Growth occurs when I am on the limit of what I believe I am capable of right now, and moving beyond that limit takes me to a higher level of development. After all, it is easier to puncture our fears than to live our lives in too narrow a cage – and the path is *action*.

The path to action is being.
Lao Tse

The Vision

Even if our life's mission may change over time and take new directions, we can make it part of a comprehensive, preferably life-long vision – such as working for a better world. Developing a life-plan with an underlying meaning in what we do, a basic motivation to live by.

Vision generates stimulation and motivation. Vision is based on feeling – passion – for what we want to create. I would like to quote Rolf Österberg from *Corporate Renaissance*, whose description of a vision is the best I have seen. He writes: "A vision has no specific form. It is abstract, not measurable in terms of time and quantity, and it gives a direction. It has life, is constantly moving and growing during the course of the journey. There is no prescribed method of realizing a vision; a vision realizes itself. It attracts to itself the means of its own realization, thereby causing our actions to become focused in a certain direction. To a large extent it is an unconscious process experienced as 'things just come to me'."

Vision emanates from a longing, a desire. It emerges from my higher Self, my heart. Vision anchors itself deep inside. The strong feeling and conviction creates a state of expectation within us, we send out signals that trigger forces into action for realizing our vision. We can compare this with expectations of recovery, for example, that start our body's self-healing process.

What if there is an intelligence in the universe which responds to our heart-based expectations.

When vision comes from our core, we do not need much of a helping hand from the outside world. We are drawn to it and cannot escape. We trust our intuition without always understanding why or being able to see the outcome in advance. The result presents itself when the time is right.

We dare to surrender to the process and enjoy it. We give in to something bigger. We simply cannot resist.

Intention/will

A deep vision brings with it a strong *intent*, a true desire to turn our vision into reality. This intention cannot be "pretended", if we really do want to put forces into action. It does not matter what we say or do on the surface, it has to come from deep within us; then vision, intention and goals are unified.

Decisions and choices taken from the heart do not stress. They are experienced as freedom and feel rather more like a privilege even though we can sometimes work day and night for what we believe in. We *want* to, the will comes from our core and requires no *extra effort* – compared to the willpower that we are forced to muster when we are not anchored in our center and do not follow our inner desire.

Vision and intention will have certain consequences. We may have to make some changes, maybe change our lifestyle. To succeed in implementing these changes, our intention needs to have a strong emotional foundation. Our feelings give momentum; the true desire withstands the impulses of the ego and carries us through difficulties as it sees the long-term advantages.

Sit comfortably and relax, take a few deep breaths and explore your underlying intention in what you do. Observe one or more situations in your life, see how you act in these situations/relationships and sense the true purpose behind them. What is the essence in what you want to achieve?

Our intention can often be different to what we thought, and our actions do not always agree with our deepest desire and what we want to achieve. Do not be surprised if you discover hidden wishes and intentions that have not yet reached your everyday consciousness.

If everything is basically possibilities and if nothing can manifest without first taking form in a consciousness, our vision, intention and state of mind are crucial for what we create. We are the tools that can transform "the energy waves of possibility to the particles of reality". Then I can start to understand why we attract different situations, how we create our individual realities.

Intention is decisive – it is what creates the result. Due to our intention we bring about/create certain events. Strictly speaking, we should not start anything at all until we are clear about the underlying intention.

Goals

Goal images are a more tangible version of our vision and intention, more everyday pictures of our vision. What do I have to do to live and act in line with my vision?

What we focus upon is given the highest priority in our brain and we need to be clear about our intention in order to create an inner picture/feeling that expresses it. Like vision, a vivid goal image is rooted in the heart, it is a *goal based on desire*. It should be tempting to spend time with our goal images, to "play with the thought", to visualize our life when the goal has been reached. *How does my success scenario look?*

It is not necessary to believe, right from the start, that we can reach our goals. By repeating our goal images, our doubts are gradually broken down and dispelled. But a goal image is more than just a daydream; it expresses my intention to realize my goal.

Personally, the importance of goal-setting was strongest in the beginning, when I started to explore my life – to put myself "on track" and experience the feeling that I could influence my life – see that I *am* not a victim of circumstance, that I *can* change my views, that I *can* improve my relationships, my career and so on. It was important to set goals even though I was not quite sure where I was heading – but to begin moving towards something worth striving for and gain confirmation of my ability. As I came into contact with a deeper intuition, the goals often became redundant. The vision and intention was sufficiently strong to take me in the right direction.

To want to, and succeed in changing behavior, we need to feel that we are heading towards something better. It is important that we first add the right feeling, and let that feeling influence the future. Our state of mind is all-important in being able to use our thoughts as tools for achieving what we wish, and being able to charge them with a strong feeling of certainty. It is "the heart" that creates. The goal should be magnetic – giving us energy and drive in our day-to-day living.

Images of our goals have to be positively designed and express what we want to attain – see the result as if it has already happened!

Even if the vision is often lifelong, we can mix short term and long term goals – to ensure we are on the right track – but let time and the route to the goal be secondary to the outcome. Often life takes us on different journeys than we had expected.

Are you clear about the consequences of your desire? What does your desire mean for you and those around you? We can ask ourselves: does my desire lead to growth for myself and others. Identify the growth potential! What qualities do you have to develop to reach your goal, and what qualities does your new life require? If you were to reach your goal tomorrow, would you then be willing to receive what you wished for?

Get a feeling for whether your goals are expansive and stimulating, or whether they are tiring and wear you down. If the latter is the case, you have probably set a goal which does not come from your heart or is maybe a "must" goal? I "must" be better at this or that. A need that probably comes more from those around you, rather than from your own true needs.

If our inner image and our will diverge, the inner image usually wins. When we are totally convinced, all of our energy moves in the same direction.

The power of thought coupled with a deep desire from our heart, is enormous. Anchor your goals in your inner during deep relaxation. As we saw in Chapter 5, the theta brainwave state is regarded as being the most favorable level for the programming of goal images. In this state, the integration happens more quickly, we go beyond duality, beyond doubts and fears.

Sit or lie comfortably and relax. Focus on your breathing and allow it to become deep and slow.

Evoke a picture/symbol of your desire. See yourself when your goal has been reached. How do you look? How do you move? How does your life look? What are you doing? Use all of your senses to paint a vivid picture of your goal! Charge the picture with a strong feeling. How does it feel in your body to have reached all this?

Repeat your goal images until they feel natural, until they are integrated in your self-image.

Spend plenty of time with your goal images. Give them room, grow with them. Play with them! This way, you will expand your boundaries. Remember that you are only "competing" with yourself. *You* set the limits for what you want to reach.

Setting goals does not mean that you need to plan a long way in advance. Through goal programming, we chart the course, can more easily live in the present and then adjust the course as and when needed.

Goals coming from our heart are easy to attain because we really desire them. Decisions taken from our intellect without being rooted in our heart, on the other hand, require willpower.

If, for some reason, you cannot accomplish your goal (you dream of being a pilot, but have poor sight) look at the *essence* of your desire and see how you can obtain it in another way. For example, if being a pilot stands for freedom, maybe travelling, see how you can fulfill this with another career.

If we are too much "in the head" and are too focused on our goals, it is easy that the feeling/passion, which gave rise to the vision, becomes diluted; that we start to struggle and miss the ongoing guidance from our inner.

We need to have a clear vision and intention, have trust and be observant for the signs that guide us to our goal, which can sometimes look different to the image we have created.

When I was going to write this book, I set – to be ambitious (and to make work more structured) – milestones, which delayed me on several occasions. Instead of going with the flow and writing what wanted to be written, I had intellectually decided what I should write at different points of time. It took a while before I was able to let go of the milestones and put my trust in vision and intention.

When our mission comes from the heart, we often do not need milestones to get things done. It is more that we cannot resist moving forward. Nor is it laborious, it just comes to us – if we can resist being meddlesome and interfering with the process.

Instead, we can train ourselves to be more sensitive to what resonates within us, what wants to emerge through us, the "random" events that take us further. Let the whole thing develop or "unfold" at its own pace.

Nothing that evolves
follows its original plan.
Freely translated from
Edmund Burke

Synchronicity

Many of us have probably experienced that when we start to follow our inner voice and yearning, strange things start to happen. We are helped by seemingly random events. We meet the person who can answer a certain question; books are put in our hands and so on.

The term synchronicity was coined by C. G. Jung, who dedicated a large part of his life to researching the connections between people and events that are not apparent in the physical world, but which seem to exist on a deeper level. Jung defines synchronicity as "a meaningful coincidence of two or more events, where something other than the probability of chance is involved".

Joseph Jaworski, lawyer and founder of The American Leadership Forum writes in his book *Synchronicity*: "At the very moment when we are struggling to attain a sense of personal autonomy, we are also caught up in vital forces that are larger than ourselves, ..."

Peter Senge, Ph.D., scientist and author, writes in the foreword to the same book, that "a flow of meaning" arises in our life, that we suddenly seem to attract things in a strange way "as if we were surrounded by a magnetic field with magnets being aligned spontaneously ....”; but that this does not occur spontaneously at all, that these magnets ”are responding to a more subtle level of causality”. He says that synchronicity is a *result* and nothing mystical. It happens when we reach a deeper commitment, participate in a larger context.

Nothing really happens by coincidence, it just looks that way on the surface. For me, synchronicity is about attentiveness, being observant and interpreting the signals we receive, understanding what wants to take form through us; and in order to succeed, our state of mind is crucial. To gain access to this flow of information, I have to be anchored in my center, connected to the higher intelligence. The relational, more wavelike state of consciousness is a prerequisite.

Synchronicity often occurs when we are at different crossroads, when we honestly ask ourselves where we are going. Suddenly events and encounters start to happen, and life takes us in a completely different direction than we had thought.

This reminds me of the “whirlwind carousel” which was very common when I was growing up. It was a carousel with wagons that partly went round a circular track and partly rotated on its own axis. Several people could sit in the same wagon, and at a given point the wagon started to spin at a dizzying speed. We were taken away with the whirls until we were completely exhausted with laughter, and then a period followed where the wagon only moved slightly back- and forwards, while we jealously watched other wagons in full spin. We tried to influence our wagon: ”if everyone moves this way or that way, if everyone does this or that” – but to no avail, until suddenly, at a certain point, it speeded up again and took us away for new spins. This is how I see synchronicity. At certain times it is calm, you could almost believe that you had been imagining all of your experiences, until it suddenly takes off again.

This timing seems to arise from underlying patterns and often brings about big changes when the time is right. A heightened insight into these underlying symmetries can help us to have more patience, to dare to let go, trust the process, and also be able to enjoy the calmer periods. It is calm because nothing needs to happen right now. When the time is right, it will take off again.

Once, when I was thinking about these things, I saw an image of myself sitting on an elephant in a beautiful saddle, carried through life at the pace it develops. I do not need to force anything or take detours. The elephant (my higher Self) knows which path I shall follow, where I am going and what experiences I need in order to develop – and all at a pace depending on how fast I am able to understand the teachings in every experience. I wish that I always had the patience to live like this. Reluctantly, I realize that of course, my development would go much faster then!

When we start to actively follow our inner voice, when our intention is honest, it seems we gain a helping hand in life.

If the basic force in the universe is love, could it then be that when we begin to follow our inner voice and longing, we come into "synch" with the development of the universe?

What if the universe strives to express its highest potential and that we – when we start to develop – come into a sort of co-vibration with the bigger picture.

Meaningful encounters happen in a meaningful universe and we can aim to live in a way to retain the contact with this flow. Be observant for what wants to emerge and sometimes dare to let things be, in the sense that they are for some time allowed to exist only in Being. Have the patience to let things unfold the way they are meant to.

An interconnected world

”Thought creates the world and then says ‘I didn’t do it’.” The words are David Bohm’s and they certainly make me smile. They describe a reality that is far from the one I believed in when I was growing up. Who would have thought that reality lies in our brain! Surely, we thought that it was in the outside world.

What is happening in society today is a (r)evolution *inside* humanity. The new thought is growing of its own accord and not through outside pressure. It grows through desire and needs and cannot be stopped. It is self-generating and a natural evolutionary leap.

We live in a world of possibilities where the future is not predetermined. An intelligent universe, one consciousness, from which the world can take shape – a base energy that appears to be able to express itself in an infinite number of forms. What immediately springs to my mind here is Barbapapa and his lovely family, who are all able to swiftly transform their own energy, as and when required, and create what they need!

Consciousness and matter seem to be a question of vibrational speed and density, in constant transition between build up and breakdown. Even our “self” seems to be part of consciousness – “a temporary condensation of vacuum energy” as one of my students put it. For my own part when looking back, I can see that it was not “my *self*” who cracked up in 1980 – but my perception of reality. The healing process was about development, learning to understand life in another way, expanding my consciousness.

We find ourselves in the midst of a universal raising of consciousness, which gives us the chance to see reality in a way that we have previously not been able to, because our mind was not adapted to it. A consciousness-raising that allows us to be co-creators of the world that is emerging.

Just like the cells in our body can interpret the information we give them and send it to all parts of the body, maybe our consciousness can interpret signals from our larger "body", interpret the information that exists in the universe.

What will it mean to be humans in a world, where everything is considered to be basically energy? Where we have our deepest identity in Being, inside us, where we understand that we are responsible for what is expressed in the world. Where the main purpose in life is to develop to higher levels of consciousness.

To give some everyday examples: How would journalism look if it was focused on human growth and development? How would the business world look if money was not the primary focus, and it was recognized that people could be driven by completely different forces, where money came as a consequence of us being clever and devoted to what we do? How would success be defined if money was just one energy among others? What would it mean for our relationships if we accepted that we are all each other?

The questions are infinite. I will not be tempted to predict the future, the questions are interesting enough. But I think we can draw some conclusions.

The end of the road

Our old model of reality has reached the end of the road. It is simply no longer useful in the light of recent research findings. We are moving on to a new level, characterized by associative thinking and a holistic view, where we unite logic and feeling, brain and heart. Where the holistic model will complement the logical, analytical model.

This transformation will have an influence on all facets- and aspects of life – our view of knowledge, of work and so on. We will be less result-oriented and more process-oriented.

An overriding requirement will be meaningfulness, and questions of meaning will demand a different kind of knowledge. The search for the underlying entity will increase the need to integrate diverse research disciplines. The quantitative research methods of today will be complemented by qualitative methods to increase our knowledge of the inner reality; knowledge that cannot be obtained from the outside world.

Our challenge will be to balance outer prosperity with inner well-being. In order to be able to manage our inner development, we also need the outer security. Food, shelter and a peaceful world. Inner development requires time for reflection and processing.

This raised consciousness will help us to deal with problems and difficulties in society from a higher level. As long as we only see the parts and not the whole, our efforts are doomed to failure. At the level of opinion we will find it difficult to unite.

We can only create a better world through free will. Everything involving coercion is transient in nature. The way to accomplish it is to raise our level of consciousness; to consciously choose another lifestyle because it *gives* more.

Many people now seem to be tired of the superficiality in our society – the constant rush and over-consumption. The threats to the environment are accumulating and we are starting to realize that our lifestyle and our actions are beginning to come back on us.

Perhaps, environment- and climate change will be the outside threat, which (according to the old, well-known pattern) can make people come together and take a joint responsibility for our planet – to cooperate instead of competing and thereby create a more viable society.

Two scenarios of the future

In *Synchronicity*, Joseph Jaworski describes two future scenarios – one positive and one negative.

In the negative scenario, fear takes over. Globalization feels threatening, people are afraid of losing their national-, religious- and cultural identities. Countries close their borders and struggle with each other, with isolation and increased division as a result. We witness a downward spiral, a more fragmented world with increased environmental disruption and reduced prosperity. A world that will not be able to take care of the bigger questions like climate and the environment, or be able to feed its inhabitants.

In the positive scenario, people unite over borders, we dare to be mutually dependent on each other, can share our discoveries and inventions, meet challenges together and take common responsibility for the important issues. Globalization gives rise to a faster liberalization, which in turn accelerates globalization. We get a rising prosperity spiral.

What if we were able to unite our consciousness and our creative gifts, be fellow humans in a rising spiral of well-*being*.

For this to come about, it is important that as many of us as possible create these positive images inside, that we consciously form the image of our future, of a boundless world with a mutual exchange of knowledge, goods and services. A peaceful world with a genuine prosperity, with political and economic freedom.

The energy in such joint images becomes incredibly powerful and has a big impact. For example, it has been shown that if a few hundred people sit and meditate in one place, crime sinks markedly there for some time. These types of experiment have been carried out many times and such effects can be used for many purposes.

Thus, in this book, I will describe only a positive future scenario.

Back to the individual

Personal development will be highly valued in the holistic society. How well we are able to solve the problems of the world and ensure our own survival depends on how we, as *individuals*, are able to raise our awareness. We are the society.

Even if our own responsibility can seem daunting in the beginning – that we are participating in what is being created – I believe that this will be a real turn on for most of us. To take responsibility, in the sense of *responding* to life – that what I do with my life, what I contribute, really does matter. That all our lives and actions contribute to the unity that is now emerging.

There is enormous power and dynamic in this view of the world (compared to the belief that we are victims of an objective, predetermined reality). The insight, that my ideas, talents and actions are important, paves the way for an incredible curiosity and urge for discovery: "What is the meaning in this? How can I solve this?" We live in a constantly ongoing existential adventure.

Could it be more exciting?

I think that the insight of all our influencing possibilities will release enormous creativity and an urge to contribute. The SQ in our society is still so low that it is hard to get collective solutions to work; they do not give growth, but often have a restrictive influence. We need more mature people to gain a better society. Working collective solutions come through free will, because we see the common good. The more I develop myself, the more I also contribute to a common raising of human consciousness. We develop the world through our inner work.

Modern technology, globalization and increased travel will make it easier for us to understand that we participate in everything. Today, we meet and become interested in other cultures, countries and people in a way that was previously not possible. We do not need to look too far back to see a time when people only knew what was happening in their own village, and were only loyal to their own group, family and so on. Today we go outside our own group and feel empathy for, and solidarity with, what happens all over the world.

We need not be especially altruistically-minded to want to create a better world. Unlike ego-realization, realization of the Self will be of the same benefit to the individual as it is to the whole. What is good for me is good for the world. Such a perspective of life creates enormous possibilities. What I do to others, I do to myself. The pieces start to fall into place. It is a win-win situation for me as an individual, for those around me, for society and the planet. *Bingo*!

Poor is not the one who has little,
but the one who never gets enough.
Jean Guéhenno

Consumer power

More people will take part in deciding in the future society. We can already see today how individuals are taking matters into their own hands, starting debates and influencing public and governmental opinion via blogs and the like. We have a lot more channels through which to make ourselves seen and heard than we had in the past.

As consumers, we have the power to choose which company, program, newspaper we allow to grow and which brand and product we want to see on the market. As a result of rising awareness, products that take a toll on the environment will be harder to sell, and companies that do not take responsibility for human questions will not survive.

At the same time as we see our relationship with everything, each person is also unique. We will see an increased demand for products that are tailored to our unique needs.

Diversity will be seen as enrichment and an asset to society. The more we understand the underlying unity, we will also embrace differences. We will be fascinated by the many variations and forms which are expressions of the universal intelligence. When fear subsides, difference will be richness.

We are expected to be less sensitive to trends, create our own fashion and build personal "brands". We wish to express who we are through clothes, lifestyle and so on. As I write this, I see an article[1] about a number of clothes designers who have put their foot down to oppose the increasingly high tempo in the fashion industry. They say that the creative process is not being given enough space and have launched the concept of Slow Fashion – "a sustainable fashion that lives for more than one season".

Today's over-consumption as seen in the Western world will lose its attraction and most likely move towards a more sustainable consumption, where we, through what we wear can clearly declare our level of consciousness, where we are in our development. We will maybe come to a point where brand names signal our level of maturity, and it will not be so cool if our belongings signal "consciousness level 1".

1 The Swedish newspaper Svenska Dagbladet (August 17, 2008)

With every choice, we have the opportunity to select between what affirms life and what is life-hostile. The insight that everything we do has repercussions on everything else will make us extremely conscious consumers, and increasingly more people will live in "voluntary simplicity", where we buy only what we really need – what comes from our true needs. The new energy-labeling of products will make it far easier for us to choose sustainable products.

Journalism for a better world

What would it mean for our world if journalism too directed its energies to nourish what leads to development. If in their investigation and probing, journalists focused on solutions and human growth.

How would it look if when writing a story, they always asked themselves: what is the underlying intent, and took responsibility for having an intention that takes things forward. That is, an honest, investigative journalism with a higher purpose than just angles and scoops. For instance, investigative TV without scapegoat-thinking, with a focus just on solutions and betterment instead of people being pilloried in public, who are often made scapegoats only because they are part of the current system.

What kind of investigative journalism takes us to a higher level, what is only "digging" and take us to a lower level?

What if there were "Journalists for Development" (in the style of Médecins Sans Frontières).

The business world

The business world will play a vital role in the transition we are currently undergoing. A new economic thinking is emerging which will show consideration for our planet, nature and the genuine needs of people. As people in the developed world gain other values and no longer identify themselves so strongly with their belongings, patterns of consumption will change. In its place, much of the material consumption will be taken over by the developing countries, where demand is expected to explode.

Globalization has helped our companies to grow. Of the one hundred largest economic units in the world today, 51 are companies and 49 are countries, and in the future, multinational companies are predicted to have more influence than countries. Large multinational companies can only operate in an open and free world and it is essential for them to support democratization and stability.

Our altered way of looking at life will also change our view of work, which will be seen more as a development process, where meaningfulness and growth is valued more than pay and job titles. Growth will increasingly be seen to mean human growth and we will see more products and services that promote this growth. Successful businesses will work for sustainable development.

In order to meet these needs, companies will have to go through their own maturity process, be driven by a vision beyond generating profit – go from seeing profitability as the primary goal to seeing personal and human development as the most important.

Rolf Österberg writes that in the future, we will see work as a process for human growth, where the highest priority of a company will be to serve as a platform for the personal development of its employees. He says that in this new company, we will go to work to "get energy" and describes a business life that focuses on giving "nourishment to life". Where people work with products and services that add something to society and fellow humans.

Companies will be started up for the chance of development, challenge and growth they give and small businesses will increase. Small, flexible, agile businesses where the owner/owners work in the company and give it content. Where cooperation with other small businesses takes place in networks and is driven by a joint vision.

Today, there are already "goal-less" but vision-loving teams, that are driven only by their vision and later follow their feeling of what they should do. It has been found that people sometimes – if they stare too much at the goals and despite having achieved them – have not noticed that markets have developed in another way.

We are going to see a working life with less distinction between work and leisure. We will work longer but take pauses now and then, to study, take care of children, travel and develop in ways other than through work.

In a publication[2] from the Royal Swedish Academy of Engineering Sciences (IVA) we can read about the altered working- and business life of tomorrow and that many of the terms we now use have lost their meaning; that words like ”working hours, permanent jobs, unemployed, golden handshake, leisure time, holidays, retirement, income tax, time studies, collective agreements et cetera, are only used in crosswords.”

As it probably will become more common that people are “out of work” for periods, it will be more important than ever that our identity is rooted in who we *are*. Today, becoming unemployed can often be devastating, because too large a part of our identity is placed in what we do, and because we *value* it that way. But with a different view of work, where we combine work with time for growth in other areas, we will broaden our view of development and realize that we can grow in every situation that life gives us.

What if the biggest potential for growth in society is to set free people's inner resources, our dormant creative powers.

Serving leaders

Good leadership requires high SQ, or a holistic view, visionary thinking, creativity and intuition. That we have developed a relationship-awareness and are clear about the purpose in what we do. As long as we are driven by the ego, power, fame and money, we are unable to be good leaders. We need to have reached a level of maturity where we want to see others grow as well.

As we ordinary people develop, we also place greater demands on our leaders. We need to raise our level of consciousness to be able to choose leaders who have insight, the desire to serve their organization, company, and humanity as a whole; who can exert a leadership that enriches and strengthens the people who are involved.

---

2 10 bilder från framtiden (1997).

Joseph Jaworski, in *Synchronicity*, describes a leadership that emanates from Being and from the understanding of reality; he writes: ”A true leader thus sets the stage on which predictable miracles, synchronistic in nature, can – and do – occur”. Peter Senge writes in the foreword of the same book that: “Ultimately, leadership is about creating new realities.” To be open to what wants to emerge.

We need to create a climate where developed people with access to their feelings and intuition can devote themselves, and be *willing* to take on assignments. This is hardly the situation today where people, for example politicians, often need a suit of armor in order to survive. These kind of leaders are of little use to society. On the contrary, they can destroy humanity.

Realizing that the majority of our leaders today see the world from a fragmented perspective can horrify me. How would our world change if we had leaders who saw the world from a perspective of oneness?

It is worth remembering that politicians do not have any power of their own, they receive their authority from us voters. If we take away our support, they have no power as such.

Oren Lyons, Professor and Indian chief from Onondaga County, New York, who regularly visits Sweden talks about “the seventh generation”, that their leaders in every decision have to consider seven future generations. Somewhat different than the politics of today where the overriding perspective is often the next election.

It is essential that we on the grass-roots level learn to select and elect those people who are driven by a desire to serve humankind and that we also *support* these leaders, so that they can live in contact with their center and act from a higher state of consciousness.

Above all, we need to develop our *own* leader, maintain contact with our inner guidance and be sensitive to what wants to develop and take shape through just me. When reaching a certain level of maturity, serving the good will be the only meaningful, that which provides real satisfaction and joy of living.

School – learning for life

Modern technology, a changing business life, together with the desire to develop and work with what we really want to do, makes an impression even in school, which will be more modeled to support individual talents and needs of students.

The constantly-improving technology is taking over many of today's working tasks and releasing time and energy for other activities. Society will need creative individuals with ideas of their own, "*enterpris*ing" individuals who are able to create diversity. Students will increasingly pick their own subjects according to their interests. We will get a learning society with the focus on learning throughout life.

We now know that we learn more effectively if we are happy and balanced, and consequently more energy will be directed towards creating an environment conducive to learning. Children have high SQ, they question constantly and really want to understand, to put things into a context, and we will support our children's natural curiosity and reflection even more.

Teachers will be seen more as mentors and coaches, who help their students to find their own strengths and talents. Mature teachers, who besides being able to convey the subject knowledge, will also have developed their own inner leader.

The computerization of our society makes it easier to find knowledge direct from the internet and be able to study from home. But the increasing amount of available knowledge requires a developed ability to be able to sift through, evaluate and combine the available information. The amount of information produced in the last 30 years is said to be as large as that from the previous 5000 years!

Knowledge will become increasingly valuable. Knowledge is easy to take with you both in your own country and abroad, and an open world offers the opportunity to move to places with favorable work- and life conditions. We will also see more of free and creative professions, where people are driven by their own passion and talents and will in many cases create their own occupations and assignments.

We will be training throughout our lives and because more people are working with what they truly wish to they will also want to work into later years.

It will be especially important, as we become older, to have positive visions of the future and that we continue to develop. We know today that we are directed by expectations and that the brain's capacity to build new neurons is much bigger than previously thought. Factors such as a stimulating environment, attractive and interesting activities, exercise and learning new things means that more neurons are formed in essential parts of the brain. Curiosity and challenges keep us young and vital!

Male/female

A society characterized by a holistic approach will also include an altered view of "feminine" and "masculine". At the moment, the masculine, analytical, fragmented approach is valued more than relationships, care and coherence, for example; natural science is valued more highly than the softer issues.

Still, in our society, the debate on equality between the sexes is mostly on the job and pay level. But we will only get real equality when we learn to balance the male and female energy within us and realize that both are equally valuable.

From the nature and evolutionary perspective, the "male" and "female" are two complementary principles in the universe. Perfect from nature's point of view; where we have developed different qualities to ensure the survival of the species – two aspects, equally strong, equally valuable.

On the spiritual level, there is no division into male and female. This belongs to the dualistic, physical world. Traditionally, male is usually associated with energy and drive and female with relations and care. But both sexes carry both of these qualities and we can reach a synthesis – develop *a caring, relational drive/energy.*

The world needs more female thinking – the associative, intuitive. But female thinking can also be thought by men. The key is to enhance the feminine *aspect* (in both men and women) as we now have a bias towards the male – to see the *balance* between the principles as the important issue. Especially by women themselves as they have a tendency to devalue the female qualities. For example, when it comes to the differences in our brains where women often believe that if male and female brains have differences, it means that their brains are inferior. But the brains of men and women have developed differently in order to deal with different tasks and women are, in many situations, better equipped.

The balancing of the male and female principle is not necessarily helped by the fact that women are entering into politics and working life – if women enter the male structures and adopt male behavior, that is, further reinforce the "yang-world".

What I would like to call for is the female wisdom; the relational, caring talent which is needed to create a viable society. We all need to express that part within us – even men. There is no contradiction there.

From a universal perspective, it is all about development – i.e. which insights I have on my journey through life. Here, work can just as well be a hindrance to development as it is a springboard – depending on how I can use work for my growth. In this respect it is not important whether I choose a so-called male profession or female profession. That we think like this, is due to the prevailing values in society, that we are stuck in a perspective that is too narrow.

Women and men need to join forces to bring these issues to a higher plane; we do not have time for the pendulum to swing first in the female direction, before we reach a balance. Forced equality is still based on fear and mostly provides changes on the surface, which can be shattered by the slightest strain on society.

The key is for us all to follow our passion and yearning, devote ourselves to what we are interested in and put our efforts into equalizing the different categories of professions. Our human values are not in what we do. We will only reach true equality when we have our identity in Being. If we truly value the two aspects equally, this will also have an impact on the paycheck.

In the future we will see more androgynous people with a balance between the female and male energies and more rooted in the Self.

We do not describe the world we see,
but we see the world we describe.
Joseph Jaworski in *Synchronicity*

Everything to gain

We have everything to gain from understanding our interconnectedness with everything in the universe, how we constantly affect, and are affected by, everything around us and how we contribute to everything that takes shape. How important it is that we take individual responsibility for our thoughts and feelings so that we can change them on the *energy level* before – due to our immaturity – we manifest them in a negative, *fear-based* development of the world.

We are in the middle of a paradigm shift, a shift in our life values. As I write this we are in a serious world "financial crisis" which gives a clear example of the importance of cooperation across the world and which will probably give this value shift a real boost.

More and more of us are now taking the step towards a new level of consciousness. The time is right and this is probably humanity's biggest chance for survival. We are living beyond our means, *nature's* means. In addition to taking care of the outer environment, we need to make a real environmental improvement in our *inner* being.

What if we are currently going through a collective identity shift – from the ego to the Self, from "doing" to "being", from the intellect to universal consciousness.

We now have tremendous opportunities to find new solutions and create a better world. We, in the developed world have the greatest responsibility here; we have sufficient education to understand and are also responsible for the greatest over-exploitation.

Globalization will require broader solutions and within a few years we will probably get to see a World council or similar to take care of the bigger decisions, climate-, environmental- and economic questions. I am personally less worried about the energy issues. Joint creativity will open up new good solutions. I see it more as a question of maturity than a purely technical matter. As I understand it, with current technology, we are already able to warm up the whole of Europe through solar energy, if we so choose. Not to mention wind-, tidal/wave-energy and hydroelectric power.

We should of course continue to travel and meet other cultures, share experiences and promote openness, but in a way which offers sustainable development for our planet.

It is my belief that one day we will grow out of war and violence. Just as the personality is now in the process of unifying its parts, the earth is also bringing together its parts towards a greater unity. Power struggle, no matter where it occurs, will be seen as an outdated custom, not associated with a conscious, mature person. Power in this sense will be seen as an "earlier" form – the ego's need of superiority – compared to the more developed person's genuine power which comes from inside and which has no need of defending a position, but just acts because it is natural and gives meaning. External power requires resources – forcible means – in the *outside* world to remain afloat. The authentic power is enough in itself.

We humans must simply raise ourselves to a level where we do not destroy ourselves. Peace requires much more from us than war and violence, and the change starts with us. Secure men (or women, for that matter) in contact with their center, do not use violence and do not start wars.

Our current, fragmented world view creates pain. We have to offer a lifestyle that is more attractive. We can see this in our young people, where depression and questioning is on the increase. They do not find sufficient motivation and purpose in the present, outgrown conception of reality.

To succeed with this we need a policy which aims to facilitate personal growth, coexistence and co-creation. Along with modern technology, this will make it harder for authoritarian regimes to suppress information and knowledge. In an interconnected world, with joint, life-promoting visions, it will become more difficult to make people go to war. As individuals, we can increase and coordinate our thinking to more and more harmonic vibrations. A raising of awareness coming up from the "grass-roots" and spreading to our leaders.

In conclusion, some words from psychoanalyst and philosopher Erich Fromm in *The Art of Loving*: "If it is true, as I have tried to show, that love is the only sane and satisfactory answer to the problem of human existence, then any society which excludes, relatively, the development of love, must in the long run perish of its own contradiction with the basic necessities of human nature."

We should dare to believe that love is the strongest force in the universe; if it was not, we would have been wiped out long ago.

What if we could place the word love in the middle of the circle model!

With this book, I have wanted to show how, through our development and by adopting a new perspective of reality, we can make a quantum leap to a new level of existence – to a more coherent state. I have woven together personal development with societal development; the everyday simple things, with the harder to understand – in the belief that we need to see through the parts to view the underlying whole. To see how everything in existence is an expression of one and the same basic energy. See how we are born out of non-form into the dualistic world and eventually return to non-form. See our human connectedness and our connectedness to nature, the planet and the whole universe. Maybe not even stop there; scientists are now talking about parallel universes and the multiverse. If we fail here on earth, maybe we will reemerge as a "possibility" in another universe. But why not take the chance to use our gift here and now?

We humans need challenges and problems to solve in order to feel good and develop. Those who work for a better world feel better than those who do nothing and see themselves as victims. Our energy will be used for something, so why not for what is the most important for us. We can ask ourselves the question: what do we want to remember that we did with our lives, once we are old?

Where should we start our development you may be asking. Start where you are, with what interests you. If you are interested in the power of thought, start there. If you are curious about yoga, meditation, start there. They are just different approaches to the same unity. Actually, they are all the same course – the course towards wholeness.

With a positive development, we will, in the future, be able to live in greater harmony, with a balance between logic and feeling, between the male and the female aspects, with a synthesis between the brain and the heart. We will be able to live in a lighter and more loving world, in contact with our inner guidance – the only sustainable development. We are living in the middle of a miracle, but rarely have the time to see it.

Yes, dear reader, this tale has now come to an end – but hopefully our world has not. Wouldn't it be exciting to see what sort of world we could create – if we accept that everything is connected in one inseparable whole, that we are all parts of each other, if we take the responsibility to be conscious thinkers and feelers, take responsibility for the world we create.

The world changes only if we change and it changes *as* we change. We need to be clear on the intent of what we do – for our own sake and for the world.

It is up to each and everyone of us if we are going to succeed.

What if this really is paradise. But in a Do-It-Yourself structure!

Bibliography

Arntz, William & Chasse, Betsy & Vicente, Mark: *What the Bleep Do We Know!? Discovering the Endless Possibilities for Altering your Everyday Reality.* HCI 2005

Assagioli, Roberto: *Symbols of Transpersonal Experiences.* Course compendium

Bryan, Mark & Cameron, Julia & Allen, Catherine: *The Artist's Way at Work.* William Morrow and Company 1998

Buscaglia, Leo: *Born for Love.* Ballantine Books 1994

Calleman, Carl Johan: *The Mayan Calendar and the Transformation of Consciousness.* Bear & Company 2004

Campbell, Don: *The Mozart Effect.* Avon Books 1999

Capra, Fritiof: *The Tao of Physics.* Fontana 1979

Carse, James P: *Finite and Infinite Games.* Free Press 1986

Chopra, Deepak: *Quantum Healing.* Bantam Books 1989

Chopra, Deepak: *Unconditional Life.* Harmony Books 1992

Chopra, Deepak: *Ageless Body, Timeless Mind.* Three Rivers Press 1994

Chopra, Deepak: *The Seven Spiritual Laws of Success.* Amber-Allen Publishing/New World Library 1994

Chopra, Deepak: *The Path to Love: Renewing the Power of Spirit in Your Life.* Harmony Books 1997

Chopra, Deepak: *The Spontaneous Fulfillment of Desire.* Harmony Books 2003

Csíkszentmihályi, Mihály: *Flow. The Psychology of Optimal Experience.* Harper Perennial 1991

Dychtwald, Ken: *Bodymind*. Jeremy. P Tarcher 1986

Dyer, Wayne W: *Manifest your Destiny. The Nine Spiritual Principles for Getting Everything You Want*. HarperCollins 1997

Dyer, Wayne W: *Your Sacred Self. Making the Decision to Be Free*. HarperCollins 1991

Fast, Julius: *Body Language*. M Evans 1970

Ferrucci, Piero: *What We May Be. Techniques for Psychological and Spiritual Growth Through Psychosynthesis*. Jeremy P. Tarcher/Penguin

Fontana, David: *The Elements of Meditation*. Element Books Ltd. 1991

Forward, Susan: *Emotional Blackmail: When the People in Your Life Use Fear, Obligation and Guilt to Manipulate You*. Harper Collins Publishers 1997

Frankl, Viktor: *Man's Search for Meaning*. Simon & Schuster 1970

Frankl, Viktor E: *The Doctor and the Soul: From Psychoterapy to Logotherapy*. Vintage 1986

Frankl, Viktor E: *The Will to Meaning: Foundations and Applications of Logotherapy*. Penguin 1988

Fromm, Erich: *The Art of Loving*. Continuum 2000

Garfield, Charles A: *Peak Performance. Mental Training Techniques of the World's Greatest Athletes* Tarcher 1984

Gawain, Shakti: *Creative Visualization*. New World Library 1985

Gawain, Shakti & King, Laurel: *Living in the Light*. New World Library 1986

Goleman, Daniel: *Emotional Intelligence*. Bantam Books 1995

Goswami, Amit: *The Self-Aware Universe: How Consciousness Creates the Material World*. Putnam's Sons 1993

Greene, Brian: *The Elegant Universe: Superstrings, Hidden Dimensions, and the Quest for the Ultimate Theory*. Vintage Books 2000

Haich, Elisabeth: *Initiation*. Unwin Paperbacks 1965

Harmann, Willis & Rheingold, Howard: *Higher Creativity.* Jeremy P. Tarcher 1984

Harrison, Steven: *Doing Nothing – Coming to the End of the Spiritual Search*. Jeremy P. Tarcher 1997

Hartland, John: *Medical and Dental Hypnosis and its Clinical Applications*. Bailliere Tindall 1977

Hay, Louise L: *You Can Heal Your Life*. Hay House 1987

Hendricks, Gay & Hendricks Kathlyn: *Conscious Loving – The Journey to Co-commitment*. Bantam Books 1990

Hendricks, Gay & Hendricks Kathlyn: *At the Speed of Life*. Bantam Books 1993

Hendricks, Gay: *Conscious Breathing: Breathwork for Health, Stress Relelease and Personal Mastery*. Bantam Books 1995

Hendricks, Gay: *Achieving Vibrance*. Three Rivers Press 2001

Hesse, Hermann: *Siddhartha*. New Directions 1951

Hopcke, Robert H: *There Are no Accidents. Synchronicity and the Stories of Our Lives*. Riverhead Books/Putnam 1996

Houston, Jean: *A Passion for the Possible.* Harper San Fransisco 1997

Huffines, LaUna: *Healing Yourself With Light, How to Connect With the Angelic Healers*. HJ Kramer 1994

Jampolsky, Gerald G.: *Out of Darkness into the Light: A Journey of Inner Healing*. Bantam Books 1989

Jampolsky, Gerald G: *Teach only Love*. Bantam Books 1986

Jampolsky, Gerald G & Cirincione, Diane Victoria: *Love is the Answer*. Bantam Books 1991

Jaworski, Joseph: *Synchronicity: The Inner Path to Leadership*. Berrett-Koehler Publishers 1996

Jeffers, Susan: *Feel the Fear and Do It Anyway.* Arrow Books 1991

Jeffers, Susan: *End the Struggle and Dance with Life.* St. Martin's Griffin 1997

Kabat-Zinn, John: *Wherever You Go There You Are.* Hyperion 1994

Khalsa, Dharma Singh & Stauth, Cameron: *Brain Longevity.* Warner Books 1997

Koestenbaum, Peter: *Is There an Answer to Death.* Prentice Hall 1976

Krishnamurti, J: *Freedom from the Known.* Harper and Row, Publishers 1969

Krishnamurti, J (Editor Mary Lutyens): *The Penguin Krishnamurti Reader.* Penguin Books Ltd 1970

Kübler-Ross, Elisabeth & Kessler, David: *Life Lessons.* Scribner 2000

Lama, H H Dalai: *Ethics for the New Millenium.* Little, Brown & Company 1999

Lama, H H Dalai & Cutler, Howard C: *The Art of Happiness.* Riverhead Books 1998

Langer, Ellen J: *Mindfulness* Perseus Books 1989

Laszlo, Ervin: *You Can Change the World. An Action Handbook for the 21st Century.* Green Books Ltd 2002

MacLaine, Shirley: *Going Within.* Bantam Books 1990

Millman, Dan: *Way of the Peaceful Warriour – A Book that Changes Life.* H J Kramer 1984

Moody, Raymond A: *Life after Life. The Investigation of a Phenomenon – Survival of Bodily Death.* Bantam Books 1976

Moody, Harry R & Carroll, David: *The Five Stages of the Soul.* Anchor Books, Doubleday 1997

Myss, Caroline: *Anatomy of the Spirit – The Seven Stages of Power and Healing.* Harmony Books 1996

O'Connor, Joseph & McDermott, Ian: *Principles of NLP.* Thorsons 1996

O'Connor, Joseph & Lages, Andrea: *Coaching with NLP*. HarperCollins Publisher 2003

Olsen, Scott: *The Golden Section, Nature's Greatest Secret*. Walker and Company 2006

Ornstein, Robert: *Multimind*. Houghton Mifflin Co. 1986

Ornstein, Robert & Sobel, David: *The Healing Brain – Breakthrough Discoveries about how the Brain Keeps Us Healthy*. Simon and Schuster 1987

Ornstein, Robert & Sobel, David: *Healthy Pleasures*. Addison Wesley Publishing Company 1989

Ornstein, Robert: *The Evolution of Consciousness. Of Darwin, Freud, and Cranial Fire. The Origins of the Way We Think..* San Val 1992

Redfield, James: *The Celestine Prophecy. An adventure*. Warner Books 1993

Redfield, James & Adrienne, Carol: *The Celestine Prophecy. An Experiental Guide*. Bantam Books 1996

Redfield, James: *The Celestine Vision. Living the New Spiritual Awareness*. Warner Books 1997

Robbins, Anthony: *Unlimited Power*. Simon and Schuster 1986

Robbins, Anthony: *Notes from a Friend*. Simon and Schuster 1995

Roman, Sanaya: *Soul Love*. HJ Kramer 1997

Russell, Peter: *The Awakening Earth. Our Next Evolutionary Leap*. Routledge & Kegan Paul 1982

Satir, Virginia: *Making Contact*. Celestial Arts 1976

Segal, Jeanne: *Feeling Great. A Personal Program to Speed Healing and Enhanced Wellness*. Newcastle Publishing Co, Inc 1983

Segal, Jeanne: *Raising your Emotional Intelligence. A Practical Guide*. Henry Holt and Company 1997

Sher, Barbara & Smith, Barbara: *I Could Do Anything If I Only Knew What It Was: How to Discover What You Really Want and How to Get It*. Dell 1995

Shone, Ronald: *Autohypnosis: A Step-By-Step Guide to Self-hypnosis.* Thorsons 1987

Siegel, Bernie S: *Peace, Love and Healing.* Harper & Row 1989

Tolle, Eckhart: *The Power of Now – A Guide to Spiritual Enlightenment.* Namaste Publishing 1997

Tolle, Eckhart: *The Power of Now. Essential Teachings, Meditations, and Exercises from The Power of Now.* New World Library 2001

Weil, Andrew: *Spontaneous Healing.* Alfred A Knopf 1995

Wilber, Ken (Editor): *The Holographic Paradigm and other Paradoxes.* Shambhala 1982

Wolinsky, Stephen H: *Hearts on Fire – The Tao of Meditation.* Quantum Institute 1996

Wolinsky, Stephen H: *Quantum Consciousness. The Guide to Experiencing Quantum Psychology.* Bramble Books 1993

Wolinsky, Stephen H: *The Beginners Guide to Quantum Psychology.* Quantum Institute 2000

Yesudian, Selvarajan & Haich, Elisabeth: *Self Healing, Yoga & Destiny.* Aurora Press, New York 1966

Yesudian, Selvarajan & Haich, Elisabeth: *Yoga and Health.* Unwin Paperbacks 1988

Yutang, Lin: *The Importance of Living.* Harper Paperbacks 1998

Zohar, Danah: *The Quantum Self.* Quill/William Morrow 1990

Zohar, Danah: *ReWiring the Corporate Brain.* Berrett-Koehler Publishers 1997

Zohar, Danah & Marshall, Ian: *SQ Connecting with our Spiritual Intelligence.* Bloomsbury Publishing 2001

Zukav, Gary: *The Dancing Wu Li Masters – An Overview of the New Physics.* Rider/Hutchinson 1979

Zukav, Gary: *Soul Stories.* Free Press 2000

Zukav, Gary & Francis, Linda: *The Heart of the Soul: Emotional Awareness.* Free Press 2002

Österberg, Rolf: *Corporate Renaissance. Business as an Adventure in Human Development.* Paraview Special Editions 2003

Books in Swedish

Bornstein, Anna: *Tankar om Buddhismen som Psykologi.* Svenska Dagbladets Förlag 1994

Bornstein, Anna: *Kroppskänning. Att vara en kropp med själ.* Svenska Förlaget 1999

Bornstein, Anna: *Intuition – att förena huvud och hjärna.* Svenska Förlaget 2000

Calleman, Carl Johan: *Mayahypotesen* 1994

Coué, Emile: *Hur man vinner herravälde över sig själv genom medveten autosuggestion.* Biblioteksförlaget 1923

Dahlbeck, Eva: *På kärlekens villkor En vandring i laglöst land.* SELLIN 1996

Dropsy, Jacques: *Leva i sin kropp. Kroppsuttryck och mänsklig kontakt.* Natur och Kultur 1991

Ehdin, Susanna: *Den självläkande människan.* Forum 1999

Eriksen, Thomas Hylland: Ögonblickets tyranni. *Snabb och långsam tid i informationssamhället.* Bokförlaget Nya Doxa 2001

Granqvist, Hans: *Lilla meditationsboken.* Svenska Dagbladets Förlag 1992

Granqvist, Hans: *Andas rätt och må bättre.* Svenska Dagbladets Förlag 1993

Ingvar, David H : *Rapport från hjärnan. Om medvetande, minne, sömn och drömmar.* Bonniers 1971

Ingvar, David H (Editor): *Hjärnkunskap och vitterhet.* Svenska Dagbladets Förlag 1994

Jönsson, Bodil: *Tio tankar om tid.* Brombergs 1999

Jönsson, Bodil: *I tid och otid hemma och på jobbet.* Brombergs 2002

Kierkegaard, Sören: *Antingen - eller och Begreppet ångest.* Wahlström & Widstrand 1986

Langlé, Annika: *Ljus och färg som helande kraft.* Energica Förlag 1991

Lundmark, Lennart: *Tiden är bara ett ord. Om klockornas makt och hur man bryter den.* Rabén Prisma 1993

Martinus: *De levande väsendenas odödlighet.* Hälsans Förlag 1981

Martinus: *Världsfredens skapelse Jaget och evigheten.* Världsbild Förlag 1999

Minett, Gunnel: *Andningen som helande kraft.* Energica Förlag 1990

Paijkull, Maria & Uneståhl, Lars-Eric: *Jo, du kan! Hur du tränar dina mentala förmågor och får ett rikare liv.* Veje International 2002

Pollak, Kay: *Att välja glädje. En bok om att få ett bättre liv.* Hansson & Pollak Förlag 2001

Pollak, Kay: *Att växa genom möten.* Hansson & Pollak Förlag

Pullar, Anne Cecilia: *Från tanke till handling. Avslappning och mental träning i ett helhetsperspektiv.* ICA Bokförlag 1996

Stinissen, Wilfrid: *Vandring till sanningen.* Libris 1987

Stinissen, Wilfrid: *Evigheten mitt i tiden.* Libris 2002

Uneståhl, Lars-Eric: *Integrerad mental träning.* SISU idrottsböcker

Uneståhl, Lars-Eric (Editor): *Hypnos i teori och praktik.* Veje Förlag 1990

Uneståhl, Lars-Eric: *Självkontroll genom mental träning.* Mind Trainer AB 1991

Uneståhl, Lars-Eric: *Den nya livsstilen.* Veje International 2001

Vrethammar, Annastina: *Tänk dig ett bättre liv. Om affirmationer och positivt tänkande.* Trevi 1993

making messages from

loving hearts

available to a global audience

cocreators @lightspira.com
www.lightspira.com

www.ingramcontent.com/pod-product-compliance
Ingram Content Group UK Ltd.
Pitfield, Milton Keynes, MK11 3LW, UK
UKHW041857190726
13854UKWH00002B/950